KITSON'S IRISH WAR

MASTERMIND OF THE DIRTY WAR IN IRELAND

GW00659992

DAVID BURKE

MERCIER PRESS

Dedicated
To all victims of state violence

MERCIER PRESS
Cork
www.mercierpress.ie

Cover design: Sarah O'Flaherty

© David Burke, 2021
ISBN: 978 1 78117 798 3

A CIP record for this title is available from the British Library.

Printed and bound in the EU.

Contents

Dramatis Personae

BAKER, Albert: a soldier in the Royal Irish Rangers who deserted while in Belfast in 1972 and joined the UDA. He became a British military intelligence asset.

CARVER, Lord Michael: Chief of the General Staff (CGS) of the British army on Bloody Sunday. He worked with Frank Kitson in Kenya and Cyprus.

CHICHESTER-CLARK, James: prime minister of Northern Ireland, 1969–1971.

DUNNET, Sir James: Permanent Under-secretary at the Ministry of Defence, 1966–1974.

EASTWOOD, David: MI5 officer who was Director of Intelligence Northern Ireland on Bloody Sunday.

FARRAR-HOCKLEY, Maj.-Gen. Anthony: Commander Land Forces (CLF) Northern Ireland August 1970–August 1971. The CLF was the second most senior rank in Northern Ireland in the early 1970s. Gen. Robert Ford succeeded him.

FAULKNER, Brian: prime minister of Northern Ireland, 1971–1972.

FORD, Gen. Robert: Commander Land Forces in Northern Ireland on Bloody Sunday. A former paratrooper with counter-insurgency experience in Palestine and Aden, he succeeded Farrar-Hockley as internment was introduced.

HEATH, Edward: Conservative party prime minister of the UK, 1970–74.

HERRON, Tommy: Vice-chairman of the UDA who ran that organisation's assassination programme. He had a relationship with British military intelligence through an officer who went by the *nom de guerre* 'Capt. Bunty'.

JACKSON, Michael: a captain in 1 Para and adjutant to its commander Lt Col Wilford in 1971–2. He later rose to become Chief of the General Staff of the British army.

KITSON, Frank: British army counter-insurgency expert who served in Malaya, Kenya, Cyprus, Oman and Northern Ireland. He was the brigadier in charge of the 39 Brigade area which included Belfast, 1970–72.

LAGAN, Frank: Chief Superintendent with the RUC in Derry on Bloody Sunday.

LEWIS, Byron: radio operator with the Support Company of 1 Para on Bloody Sunday. His testimony was crucial in forcing the British government to set up a new tribunal which became known as the Saville Inquiry. He revealed that he saw his colleagues fire at unarmed civilians in Derry on Bloody Sunday.

LODEN, Edward Charles: the major who commanded 1 Para's Support Company on Bloody Sunday.

MacLELLAN, Patrick: brigadier of 8 Brigade which oversaw military operations in Derry. He later rose to the rank of general.

McMULLEN, Peter: corporal with 1 Para based at Palace Barracks who deserted the British army and joined the Provisional IRA.

MOONEY, Hugh: Foreign Office official who worked for the Information Research Department (IRD), a propaganda organisation attached to the Foreign Office.

OBSERVER B: an agent of both British military intelligence and MI5 who had access to the 'no-go' area of Derry in 1972.

SAVILLE, Lord Mark: chairman of the Saville Tribunal into Bloody Sunday. While he vindicated the reputation of the victims vilified by Lord Widgery in his report on Bloody Sunday, he offered no plausible explanation for the behaviour of the paratroopers who perpetrated the massacre.

SMITH, Howard: Foreign Office official appointed by Edward Heath as the UK Representative (UKREP) to the Stormont government of Northern Ireland. He later became the director-general of MI5, 1978–1981.

TUGWELL, Col Maurice: British army officer who ran psychological operations in Northern Ireland.

TUZO, Maj.-Gen. Harold: General Officer Commanding Northern Ireland (GOC, NI) on Bloody Sunday.

WIDGERY, John Passmore: Lord Chief Justice of England and Wales, 1970–1980. He chaired the Widgery tribunal into Bloody Sunday in 1972. He vilified the murdered civilians on Bloody Sunday in his report into the atrocity.

WILFORD, Lt Col Derek: Commander of 1 Para, 1971–2.

ORGANISATIONS, TERMS, LOCATIONS AND ACRONYMS

8 Brigade: British troops stationed in Derry and its environs were assigned to 8 Brigade. Its HQ was located at Ebrington Barracks in Derry.

39 Brigade: British troops stationed in Belfast and the eastern side of Northern Ireland (excluding the South Armagh border region) made up 39 Brigade. Its HQ was located at Thiepval Barracks, Lisburn, on the outskirts of Belfast.

APC: armoured personnel carrier such as a Saracen, sometimes referred to as a 'pig'.

Ballymurphy: a predominantly Catholic/Nationalist area of Belfast. The Ballymurphy massacre took place here in August of 1971.

BIS: British Information Service.

B-Specials: members of the Ulster Special Constabulary, a part-time force disbanded in 1970.

Bogside: an estate below the Derry Walls. It is predominantly Nationalist/Catholic. The name derives from the fact it was built on an area of peat bog.

CDCs: Citizen Defence Committees.

CLF: Commander of Land Forces, the second most senior rank in the British army in Northern Ireland in the early 1970s.

CO: Commanding officer.

Creggan: a predominantly Nationalist/Catholic housing estate in Derry built on a hillside above the Bogside.

DYH: Derry Young Hooligans.

Ebrington Barrack: the HQ of 8 Brigade in Derry.

Fianna Fáil: the Irish political party in power in the Republic of Ireland during the Kitson era. Led by Taoiseach Jack Lynch.

Fine Gael: the Irish political party in the Republic of Ireland which led the opposition during the Kitson era.

Fort George: British army base located on the banks of the River Foyle on the northern outskirts of Derry adjacent to the Strand Road.

FCO: Foreign and Commonwealth Office.

Free Derry: first 'no-go' area in Northern Ireland.

Garda Síochána: the police force of the Republic of Ireland.

Glenfada Park: a small estate of low-rise flats adjacent to the Rossville flat complex in Derry.

HQNI: Headquarters NI, based in Thiepval Barracks in Lisburn.

HMG: Her Majesty's Government.

Internment: imprisonment without trial.

IRD: Information Research Department: it was part of the Foreign Office. It ran propaganda campaigns for the British government.

JSIW: The Joint Service Interrogation Wing of the British army which trained RUC Special Branch officers in interrogation techniques in April 1971.

Kitson's Private Army: see the entry regarding Support Company below.

Knights of Malta: a voluntary paramedic organisation.

Low-intensity operations: a low intensity operation is any military operation other than those in a conventional, high-intensity war. They may include counter-insurgency, counter-guerrilla warfare, counter-terrorism, unconventional warfare, intelligence, peacekeeping, peace enforcement, security force assistance, nation-building, civil affairs, and information operations.

Mau-Mau: Kenyan rebel movement which opposed British rule in Kenya.

MI5: Britain's internal security service, active inside the United Kingdom and her overseas colonies. It is attached to the Home Office.

MI6: Britain's overseas intelligence service. It is attached to the Foreign Office.

MoD: Ministry of Defence. It is responsible for the British army.

MRF: Military Reaction Force (sometimes referred to as the Mobile Reaction Force), an undercover unit of the British army set up by Brigadier Frank Kitson in Belfast in the early 1970s. It was the forerunner of many similar units active in Northern Ireland during the 'Troubles'.

NICRA: Northern Ireland Civil Rights Association: organisers of the anti-internment march through Derry on the day of Bloody Sunday.

OC: Officer in Command.

Official IRA: the Marxist wing of the Republican Movement which emerged after the split in December 1969. Its Chief of Staff in the 1970s was Cathal Goulding.

Operation Banner: the operational name for the deployment of British troops in Northern Ireland from 1969 to 2007.

Operation Calabra: the designation given to the interrogation programme of the prisoners who were swept up during internment by the British army in 1971.

Operation Demetrius: the codename provided to the internment swoops which took place in August 1971.

Operation Forecast: the plan by 8 Brigade of the British army to monitor and control the NICRA march in the city on 30 January 1972

Operation Hailstone: an action launched in July 1971 to lure the so-called 'Derry Young Hooligans' and the Derry IRA into the open so that soldiers from 1 Para could confront and arrest them.

Operation Linklater: an arrest operation launched shortly before internment in 1971. It was designed to collect information from those arrested – about IRA targets in their localities and elsewhere. It was hoped the information collected would enhance the prospect of capturing IRA leaders during the then forthcoming internment swoops.

Operation Motorman: the British army operation which ended 'Free Derry' on 31 July 1972.

Orange Order: an organisation formed in 1795 named after King William of Orange. Catholics. Its purpose is to defend Protestant interests, including the union with Britain.

Order 2/72: the order issued by Brigadier Patrick MacLellan of 8 Brigade in Derry to deal with the NICRA march that took place on Bloody Sunday.

Palace Barracks: HQ of 1 Para on the outskirts of Belfast.

Provisional IRA: the wing of the IRA which emerged after the IRA split in December 1969 with the intention of ending British rule in Northern Ireland. Its chief of staff from 1970–72 was Seán MacStíofáin.

PSYOPs: Psychological Operations.

RHC: Red Hand Commando: Loyalist paramilitary organisation led by John McKeague.

RUC: Royal Ulster Constabulary, the police force of Northern Ireland.

RUCSB: RUC special branch.

Saracen: an armoured personnel carrier used by the British army and sometimes referred to as a 'pig'.

SDLP: Social Democratic and Labour Party – a nationalist

political party supporting a United Ireland achieved through non-violence.

Sinn Féin: Republican political party. It is the political wing of the IRA.

Sticky: a nickname given to a member of the Official Republican movement.

Stormont: the home of the government of Northern Ireland.

Support Company 1 Para: elite section of the 1st Battalion of the Parachute Regiment. The title 'Support Company' derived from the fact that the troops originally assigned to it had carried anti-tank guns, mortars and other weapons in support of their comrades. In Northern Ireland there was no need for these types of weapons. It became the cutting edge of 1 Para and was known and feared throughout Belfast as 'Kitson's Private Army'. The soldiers attached to it were responsible for the shooting of civilians in Derry on Bloody Sunday.

Tánaiste: Deputy Prime Minister of the Republic of Ireland.

Taoiseach: Prime Minister of the Republic of Ireland.

Thiepval Barracks: A large military complex at Lisburn on the outskirts of Belfast. It was home to HQNI which oversaw all military operations in Northern Ireland and 39 Brigade which was responsible for Belfast and its environs.

UKREP: the United Kingdom Representative to the Stormont government of Northern Ireland.

UDA: Ulster Defence Association, established in 1970. Declared illegal in 1992.

UFF: Ulster Freedom Fighters, a cover name used by the UDA when it carried out assassinations.

UVF: Ulster Volunteer Force, a Loyalist paramilitary organisation.

INTRODUCTION

THE DIRTY WAR IN IRELAND

Just after 5 p.m. on 14 August 1969, two companies of the Prince of Wales' Own Regiment drove into Derry's Guildhall Square. As the troops descended from their jeeps to the growing excitement of gathering Bogsiders, they had little inkling that this was the opening moment in a thirty-year British army operation that would become known as *Operation Banner*, its longest ever in peacetime; nor that almost 1,500 soldiers would be killed and over 6,000 wounded in Northern Ireland in the years to come. Nor indeed that within just years, this same army (now being welcomed by cheering Bogsiders as their unlikely protectors while an exhausted RUC withdrew, tails between its legs) would be interning hundreds of Nationalists without trial. Nor that it would ultimately end up facing the European Court accused of torture. The Bogsiders could not have suspected that within three years, just around the corner from Guildhall Square, the same army whom they welcomed would carry out Bloody Sunday, murdering their friends and relatives.

But surely the political establishments in London, Belfast and Dublin must have recognised, on that extraordinary afternoon, England's historic Irish problem, after a half century of partition, was back with its gaping wounds as raw as ever.

The British army came in to 'assist the civil power' as the official government hand-out politely put it. The political reality, however, was that they were there to keep matters in check while the politicians came up, once again, with a solution to the Irish problem. It was a military task that proved hugely complex to achieve within the legal and political strictures of the liberal democracy which was the United Kingdom of 1969.

Harold Wilson, the British prime minister 1964–70, had been busy implementing a policy of colonial withdrawal, 'East of Suez'. Under this, the British army had departed from places as far flung as Aden, Kenya and Malaya. But the act of soldiering in the old 'white man's burden' colonies was polar opposite in terms of strategic and military competence to that operating within the United Kingdom. While concentration camps and punishments like castration or the death penalty were liberally utilised in Mombasa and Kuala Lumpur, they were obviously not suitable for deployment in Northern Ireland.

By far the greatest crisis the government faced was how to lawfully deal with a raging insurgency, without resorting to their long-practised counter-insurgency methods. To put it quite simply how could you get away with fighting a 'dirty war' on your own doorstep? A soldier on a street in Northern Ireland, even in an armoured car and equipped with a self-loading NATO issue rifle, had no more legal power of arrest than any civilian had. When there was trouble, the troops were obliged to wait for the RUC to turn up before anyone could be taken into detention. The troops, who, in the main, had been equipped and trained to deal with invading Soviet Warsaw Pact forces, found themselves patrolling the back-streets of Derry's Creggan estate and Belfast's Ballymurphy.

Only a few now bother to deny that a 'dirty war' in Northern Ireland followed. It was fought behind elaborate official denials against a background of disinformation and duplicity. In the years since, the barest bones of information have been disinterring themselves from secret graveyards.

Hundreds of innocents were swept up in this dirty war, many died and still their relatives await the simple justice of being told the truth about what happened to them. But piece-by-piece this story is taking shape and I hope that in relaying as much as I can of the account of Brigadier Frank Kitson's War in Ireland, this will lay bare that hidden narrative.

The Kitson era spanned September 1970 to April 1972. It is apparent from an indiscreet book Kitson published in November 1971, entitled *Low Intensity Operations*, that he believed the Catholic-Nationalist community was the enemy he had to confront. He engaged in an experiment to adapt some of the techniques he and his colleagues had developed in the colonies for use in a part of the UK to defeat the IRA. Ultimately, the experiment backfired.

The low point of the Kitson debacle played out on a crisp winter's afternoon in Derry. On 30 January 1972, shots began to ring out in that city. The fingers curled around the triggers belonged to 'Kitson's Private Army', an elite group of paratroopers more properly known as Support Company of the 1st Battalion of the Parachute Regiment.

Information continues to trickle out about Kitson's Irish War. Yet, many questions remain unanswered, especially about Bloody Sunday:

* Why did the soldiers of Support Company murder a group of unarmed people who were predominantly young males?
* Was it simply a case of a handful of out-of-control mavericks going on a rampage?
* Did a selection of key operatives acting on orders from their superiors set out to 'teach' the Bogside a lesson for allowing the IRA build a stronghold in their midst?
*Or, in the most malign scenario, was it an attempt to provoke a battle with the IRA as part of a plan to smash Derry's no-go area?

The Saville Inquiry into Bloody Sunday, which was established in 1998 and reported in 2010, did not delve deeply into this abyss, but it did reveal a number of clues that point toward some very dark corners in which Kitson and Col Derek Wilford (the commander of 1 Para), are found lurking. So too is their former superior, the late Gen. Robert Ford, Commander Land Forces in Northern Ireland. Of this trio, Kitson is the one who has escaped real scrutiny. To fully appreciate his significance in the war in the early 1970s, and the road that led to the calamity of Bloody Sunday at the tail end of his time in Ireland, it is instructive to review the tactics that Kitson and his brothers in arms practised around the globe in the decades before they arrived in Ireland. Following on from the analysis, the narrative will return to Ireland where Kitson's relationships with Ford, Wilford and others will be considered in more depth.

1

'He was 120% soldier'

Frank Edward Kitson was a product of his class and time. Born on 15 December 1926, he was the eldest son of Sir Henry Kitson, a vice-admiral in the Royal Navy, and Marjorie de Pass, daughter of Sir Eliot Arthur de Pass. His uncle, Frank de Pass, was a recipient of a Victoria Cross medal. He was educated at Stowe, then second only to Eton in the ranks of Britain's most desirable boys' public schools. It had been established by J.F. Roxburgh to produce eager young men destined to rule over Britain's global empire. Kitson thrived in Stowe, becoming the head boy of his house. While a student, he developed a passion for blood sports. 'Ever since childhood I have spent long hours waiting in hides trying to shoot things', he once wrote.[1]

For over two centuries the Kitson family had supplied officers to the Royal Navy and his father fully expected him to join the ranks at the end of his schooling. This was not to be:

> Being asthmatic I was no use to the Navy so I had to join the Army instead. This caused some stir in the family, but as I was obviously unsuited to the Church there was no alternative short of breaking a father-to-son tradition which had lasted for over 200 years. In fact, there was little harm done as my only brother was in the Navy and there is something to be said for a family not having all its eggs in one basket. My housemaster at Stowe was actually pleased and said something about a 'narrow escape': he was biased, however, having been a regular soldier himself for twenty years.[2]

Kitson joined the Rifle Brigade in January 1945. He rose to become Gen. Sir Frank Kitson, GBE, KCB, MC & Bar, DL. He served as commander-in-chief UK land forces from 1982 to 1985 and as aide-de-camp to Elizabeth II from 1983 to 1985. Along the way, he fought the Mau-Mau in Kenya and was awarded the Military Cross. Thereafter, he confronted communist rebels in Malaya and subsequently helped suppress a revolt in Oman, while garnering some peacekeeping experience in Cyprus. He opposed the IRA in Northern Ireland in 1970–1972. A common thread in all of this was his devotion to intelligence gathering on a drift net scale. Rapt attention to detail was another of his hallmark traits as was the vigour he displayed during prolonged and intense interrogation of prisoners.

Physically, he was a small man with a sallow complexion, blue eyes and a 'high, nasal voice'. In terms of his personality, he was 'notorious for his dislike of small talk'.[3] Michael Jackson, who served as a captain in 1 Para in the early 1970s, described him as an officer with a 'very distinguished record of counter-insurgency operations in Kenya, Malaya, Oman and Cyprus'.[4] In terms of his personality, however, he was 'cold and remote'.[5]

Jackson recounts the story of a dinner party at which an 'ambitious young wife sat next to him. Her opening gambit was to say with a smile, "General, I have been bet I'll get at least half a dozen words out of you", to which he replied, "you've just lost" and didn't say another word to her for the remainder of the evening'.[6]

A man who worked with him in intelligence in Kenya

described him as 'a loner, utterly devoted to his work, who took little part in Kenya social life'.[7]

James Kinchin-White, a soldier who worked with him as his clerk in Cyprus 1967, recalls that he was:

an absolute stickler for SOPs [Standing Operational Procedures]. He re-wrote those for the British battalion UNFICYP [United Nations Forces Cyprus]. I was duty clerk one evening and, unfortunately, I got the job of typing them all up on Gestetner duplicator skins. As he handed the drafts to me, he said 'I'll sign these in the morning'. I laughed and he said, rather sheepishly I thought, 'I'm not joking' – exit stage left. I don't think I managed the task, but he never said anything. He was definitely a 'workaholic' – and expected the same from everyone.

He was cold, calculated and, I think he conveyed a sense of 'reliability', and ruthlessness in pursuit of objectives. But I have never seen or heard of him losing his temper. If you were a soldier heading for a fight, he was the kind of man you wanted to lead you. I am told that he did have a sense of humour, but that it was only revealed in appropriate company ... I met him and his wife, Elizabeth, by chance around 1998 – she was always the one who 'talked' while he focused on other things. 'Aloof' yes and 'curt' certainly, but never discourteous. One didn't 'cross' the man, he tended to come down harder on errant senior people rather than on junior ranks.[8]

Capt. Colin Wallace, a psychological operations officer, who knew Kitson from Thiepval Barracks in Northern Ireland furnished a statement to the Saville Inquiry into Bloody Sunday describing how Kitson had done 'much to enhance the army's [initial] intelligence gathering capabilities during the 1970s. He became something of a bogeyman to those in Left Wing politics because of some of the books he had written about internal security operations. A very bright, dynamic officer, his stern expression and tough, 'no-nonsense' style sometimes intimidated those who worked for him. Despite his stern exterior, he had a good sense of humour and a sharp awareness of political issues'.[9] When Wallace provided this succinct portrayal of his former colleague, he had not seen him for decades. During that time Wallace had become a high-profile whistle blower who shone a light on MI5 and military intelligence wrongdoing, hardly something of which Kitson would have approved. Wallace encountered Kitson at the Saville Tribunal hearings in London. 'I had not seen him since Lisburn. Our relationship then had been very good. I was the last witness before Lord Saville while he sat in Ireland and the first to give evidence in London. I knew he was on after me. As I was leaving, he was coming in with his legal team. We caught each other's eye, he smiled at me and we exchanged brief pleasantries but both of us were on the move and did not halt for a conversation. I am sure he recognised me, especially as he would have been aware of the witness list for the day.'[10]

Wallace also remembers Kitson as 'a classic no nonsense figure. When he was talking to you, he would focus his attention on you intently. His gaze was quite severe, quite penetrating. For junior officers this could be quite intimidating. His world was the army. He was 120% soldier.'

2

LEARNING TO KILL

Kitson's first overseas assignment was to Germany in 1946 with the rank of second lieutenant. He remained there for seven years. He found plenty of sport to occupy his spare time such as racing horses in Rhine Army competitions, trout fishing and 'many wonderful opportunities for shooting ... and by shooting I don't mean plugging holes in targets', he wrote.[1] Playing bridge and attending the opera also helped to pass the time. By 13 September 1949, he had found his vocation and was appointed as an intelligence officer at the HQ of the Armoured Brigade in Germany.

Half a world away, in October 1952, the Kenya Land and Freedom Army (KLFA) launched a rebellion against the white European colonist-settlers in their homeland. The British army and the local Kenya Regiment resisted them. The latter included British colonists, local auxiliary militia and some pro-British Kenyans. Later, MI5 was deployed to help suppress the rebellion. The KLFA, also known as the Mau-Mau, consisted of rebel tribesmen from the Kikuyu, Meru, Embu and other Kenyan communities.

In July 1953, Kitson was transferred to Kenya 'to do a job connected with Intelligence'.[2] After seven years, he was glad to be leaving Germany. He was twenty-six.

The Mau-Mau rebellion was inspired by a desire on the part of the Kikuyu and other Kenyans to reclaim by armed insurrection land taken from them by the British. Kitson, however, seemed to think that opposition to Britain was inspired in large part through the intercession of witchcraft. He had a rose-tinted view of Britain's presence in the country:

> During the half century in which the British had ruled Kenya they had dispelled the fears which had formerly come from raiders, slavers and disease, but the fear of magic was still a powerful force. As I sat at home reading about the witch-doctors and their ways, I too felt that fear, flickering faintly across the four thousand miles which separated me from the Kikuyu.[3]

He did not see the Kikuyu as civilised people. Instead, he described how they:

> relied mainly on magic and therein lay the greatest of all the horrors which beset them. Most witch-doctors were not malign in the sense of wishing harm to their clients. On the contrary, they doubtless did their best. On the other hand they sat in the middle of a web of superstition which bound the whole tribe in thrall to an unseen world of spirits, omens, curses and blood.[4]

At this time in his life, Kitson kept a Bible by his bedside.[5] A clue as to the type of Christian he was can be gauged by the fact that on his first Sunday in Nairobi he attended a service in the local Anglican cathedral and wrote later: 'I sat next to an African woman who had bad halitosis and I was surprised to find that there was no segregation of races into separate parts of the building'.[6]

The British campaign against the Mau-Mau was merciless. In 1953, Gen. George Erskine, commander-in-chief of British armed forces in Kenya reported to the secretary of state for war, Anthony Head, that in the early days there had been a 'great deal of indiscriminate shooting by the Army and Police' and he was 'quite certain' that prisoners had been:

beaten to extract information. It is a short step from beating to torture, and I am now sure, although it has taken me some time to realise it, that torture was a feature of many police posts. The method of deployment of the Army in the early days in small detachments working closely with the police ... had evil results.[7]

... I very much hope it will not be necessary for [Her Majesty's government] to send out any independent enquiry. If they did so they would have to investigate everything from the beginning of the Emergency and I think the revelation would be shattering.[8]

What were these 'evil results', the revelation of which would have been 'shattering'? In *Cruel Britannia, A Secret History of Torture*, Cobain summarises some of the atrocities in Kenya::

Men were whipped, clubbed, subjected to electric shocks, mauled by dogs and chained to vehicles before being dragged around. Some were castrated. The same instruments used to crush testicles were used to remove fingers. It was far from uncommon for men to be beaten to death. Women were sexually violated with bottles, rodents and hot eggs.[9]

This all took place against a background of curfews, internment and capital punishment. Over 1,200 Kenyans died dangling at the end of a noose.

One of the torture victims was Hussein Onyango Obama who had served with the British army during the Second World War in Burma. When released after six months in detention, he was emaciated, suffering from a lice infestation of his hair and had difficulty walking. He died in 1979. His wife informed journalists that he had told her that the British had 'sometimes squeezed [his] testicles with parallel metallic rods'. They had also 'pierced his nails and buttocks with a sharp pin, with his hands and legs tied together with his face facing down'. Hussein Onyango Obama was the grandfather of Barak Obama.[10]

One British officer quoted by David Anderson in *Histories of the Hanged* revealed just how brutal the campaign became. He described how a police officer was interviewing three suspects:

> … one of them, a tall coal-black bastard, kept grinning at me, real insolent. I slapped him hard, but he kept on grinning at me, so I kicked him in the balls as hard as I could … when he finally got up on his feet he grinned at me again and I snapped. I really did. I stuck my revolver right in his grinning mouth … and I pulled the trigger. His brains went all over the side of the police station. The other two [suspects] were standing there looking blank … so I shot them both … when the sub-inspector drove up, I told him the [suspects] tried to escape. He didn't believe me but all he said was 'bury them and see the wall is cleaned up'.[11]

Kitson recalled his initial thoughts upon arriving in Nairobi in August 1953 thus:

> Soon afterwards we went for a walk in Nairobi. By this time it was dark but there still seemed to be a lot of Africans wandering about. The main streets were well lit but not the smaller ones, and as we walked past the entrance to one of these I saw two or three men squatting round a watchman's fire some fifty yards away. I had been interested to see the Africans at close range in the street. I may even have been a bit excited. I had thought so much about the notorious Mau-Mau and their murders, mutilations and brutalities that I was naturally elated at last to be on the threshold of such things. But the sight of the three men round their fire had a different effect. This brought back to my mind stories of another sort. Stories of age-old magic rites, of bestiality, obscenity and the power of unseen forces. Again I felt the uneasiness which I had experienced in England but this time it was more than a faint flicker.[12]

Kitson's ingrained colonial attitude can be gleaned from another passage in his 1960 book, *Gangs and Counter-Gangs*. He was assigned to Narok in the Masai region. According to Kitson, the Masai:

> were not interested in the Mau-Mau. The Kikuyu were running the [Mau-Mau] movement and the Masai were their hereditary enemies. Unfortunately they had intermarried a lot with the Kikuyu as so many of their own women were barren due to congenital syphilis. From these mixed marriages there grew up a large colony of half-breeds who had forsaken the nomadic life of the proper Masai and who were working in shops and sawmills throughout the area. They proved to be enthusiastic supporters of the movement and by April several [Mau-Mau] gangs had formed and were doing quite a lot of damage.[13]

Kitson experienced no difficulty operating in the grotesque hell that Kenya had become. After dinner one night a colleague said he wanted to have a quick look in the Tigoni mortuary because he was missing an informer who might have found his way in there. 'The shambles inside was past all describing', he wrote.[14] There 'must have been eighteen bodies in a place the size of a small summer house ... Some of them had been there for five days and were partially decomposed. They were all lying around tangled up on the floor as there were no slabs in the Tigoni charnel house'. His colleague behaved as though nothing was wrong and 'continued talking about whatever it was we had been discussing before we got there, as he rummaged around in the human wreckage. After a few moments while I looked out through the door I forced myself to look back inside again. In a surprisingly short time I found that I was no longer bothered by the sight. But for the smell, I might even have been looking at a lot of old bicycles lying on the ground ... Now I had seen something more revolting than I could have imagined – even the cinema could not have produced such a spectacle – and I had found that I hardly minded at all. From that time on I felt more sure of myself.'[15]

***

Kitson would go on to work closely with MI5 in Kenya and used the experience to fine-tune a counter-insurgency technique that involved the use of 'counter-gangs' or 'pseudo gangs'. This was a practice of ancient pedigree. The Chinese military general and Taoist philosopher, Sun Tzu, had ordained centuries ago that 'to understand your enemy, you need to be your enemy'. That attitude underpinned the concept of the 'pseudo-gang' and, in more modern times, has become known as asymmetric warfare. The principle involves the use of 'friendly' or 'turned' insurrectionaries to attack other insurgents and their supporters. In reality, it is State terrorism by proxy.

Some argue the concept can be discerned in the Yeomanry of 1798 in Ireland (or further back when Elizabethan and earlier English conquerors used Irish against Irish). Certainly, the counter-gang idea was in full flow in Kansas and Missouri during the American Civil War, and the British used it in South Africa during the 1899–1902 Boer War. The Second World War had so many such units, space does not permit a review. The French deployed similar tactics in Algeria in the 1950s and 1960s.

Kitson described how rebels could be turned through 'carrot and stick' tactics to work for the British. With their native appearance and local knowledge, they could move about freely with the aim of infiltrating and deceiving the rebels. Adopting the appearance of the enemy and generating confusion behind enemy lines was a tactic which the British had exploited not long before this in Palestine. When one of Kitson's pseudo-gangs in Kenya met a band of rebels, they would either eliminate them or report their location to their headquarters. In his 1960 publication, Kitson gave a detailed account of how this was done with the help of one Mau-Mau fighter he called 'George'.

Kitson wrote about his experience in Kenya in two books, *Gangs and Countergangs* (1960) and *Bunch of Five* (1977). The foreword to his first publication described Britain's presence in Kenya as a 'benevolent autocracy of good Colonial administration'.[16] 'The Mau-Mau were associated in my mind with all that was foul and terrible in primitive savagery'.[17] He described the thrill of chasing one wounded and bleeding Mau-Mau quarry thus:

> This time there was a much bigger pool of blood. We started moving forward very slowly on hands and knees to see between the coffee bushes. Eric was in front as usual. Suddenly I caught sight of a bit of a rag just to Eric's right and shouted a warning. I even went so far as to draw my pistol, which I seldom did for fear of accidents, but it was unnecessary. Eric and Bill Henning launched themselves simultaneously on the wretched fellow, who was made prisoner with little fuss. The hunt was over but it had been fascinating while it lasted. There is no doubt at all that one cannot savour the full thrill of the chase until one hunts something which is capable of retaliation.[18]

In his 1977 offering, he revealed that most British soldiers in Kenya 'saw evidence of revolting Mau-Mau brutality from time to time, and probably regarded the finding and disposing of gang members in the same way as they would regard the hunting of a dangerous wild animal'.[19]

***

Kenya suffered its own Bloody Sunday, which took place in June 1953 shortly before Kitson's arrival. In his books, he ignored it and other British atrocities despite the fact that two of them contained purported histories of the conflict. The massacre was perpetrated when Major G. S. L. Griffiths of the King's African Rifles B Company descended upon the Chuka area of Kenya with his troops on 13 June. His intention was to flush out the Mau-Mau he believed were lurking in the nearby forest. Griffiths demanded of a prisoner they had captured that he assist them, but the captive refused. In response, he ordered his men to rip open a hole in his ear with a bayonet. After they complied, a piece of string was threaded through the wound and used as a leash for the next four days. A second prisoner had to watch what was happening. When he too refused to help, his ear was amputated. He continued to resist and was shot dead.

Over the next two days Griffiths' troops captured a number of Mau-Mau rebels on the boundary of the forest. On 17 June, a patrol of ten men led by an African warrant officer began to search farmland on the edge of the forest. They came across a group of men whom they ordered to lie face down, after which they set upon them. Two of them managed to escape later, when they were sent to fetch food. The other ten were shot on the ground at close range.

The following morning another nine men and a child were murdered in cold blood in a clearing near a small coffee farm at the edge of the forest. Some of the soldiers chopped off the hands of six of the corpses and brought them back to their camp.

The next day the man with the string leash looped through his ear was murdered.

News of what happened soon spread. Gen. Erskine told his troops that he would not 'tolerate breaches of discipline leading to unfair treatment of anybody', and ordered that all of his officers should 'stamp at once on any conduct which he would be ashamed to see used against his own people'.[20] Having spoken so laudably, Erskine then proceeded to orchestrate a cover-up of what had happened at Chuka.

All of the troops involved in the massacre were arrested and held at Nairobi's Buller Camp. A military inquiry was convened on 22 June but its findings were not made public. Erskine wrote letters to the local chiefs stating that 'investigations have satisfied me that whoever is to blame, it is not any of the persons killed'.

Files were not sent to the attorney general and hence prosecutions did not take place, allegedly due to lack of evidence. Instead, the families of those massacred were given compensation.

Griffiths was charged with the murder of two other Kenyans in a separate incident, one which had taken place a few weeks before the Chuka massacre. He was acquitted but then arraigned before a second court-martial, this time charged with the murder of the prisoner whose ear had been tethered to the lead. He was convicted, stripped of his rank and received a seven-year sentence. He eventually wound up in Wormwood Scrubs where Seán MacStíofáin of the IRA was serving a seven-year sentence for his botched attempt to steal guns from an armoury in Felstead with Cathal Goulding and Manus Canning. MacStíofáin later formed the Provisional IRA and became its first chief-of-staff. In his memoirs he wrote of how he had read about Griffiths, who had been involved in the torture of prisoners and decided that given the opportunity:

> we would give him a thumping. Unfortunately, when he and I came face-to-face I did not have the chance. It was in the library, where I was always accompanied by an officer who would take me from my cell, stand beside me while I selected my books and bring me back to be locked up again. Anyway, there was the cashiered torturer, looking a bit new and uncertain.
>
> 'I say, where does one pass these books out?' he asked me.
>
> I felt a strong temptation to let him have it there and then, but with that prison officer beside me I could see my few precious privileges going up in smoke if I did. Instead I ignored the question and deliberately turned my back. The warder said nothing.[21]

MacStíofáin and other prisoners felt that Griffiths seemed 'very bitter about his come down and was doing his time really hard'. He was moved to an 'open camp' a few months later.

In the same passage where MacStíofáin described his encounter with Griffiths, he added that:

> Little did I know it in Wormwood Scrubs, but at that very moment another British captain in Kenya was beginning to devise a new theory of counter-insurgency. His name was Frank Kitson. He was to become our deadliest enemy in the North.[22]

It took six decades for Britain to come to terms with what had happened in Kenya. In 2011, the Foreign and Commonwealth Office 'rediscovered' 1,500 previously classified files on the counter-insurgency campaign against the Mau-Mau at a secret facility at Hanslope Park. They detailed the way Kenyan prisoners were beaten to death, burned alive, castrated and kept in manacles for years. In 2013, the British government paid out £19.9 million in compensation to 5,228 survivors.

Kitson had provided the readers of his 1960 book with the impression that his nation had behaved honourably in Kenya: 'The Security Forces certainly had better weapons, better kit, better transport and better command arrangements than the Mau-Mau but they had firmly fastened one of their hands behind their back with the cord of legal difficulties.'[23]

While he acknowledged some wrongdoing, he blamed it on mavericks and extenuating circumstances. He alleged that 'once in a way, someone would take the law into his own hands and strike a blow where one seemed necessary, because the existing legal methods of dealing with the situation were not good enough. Looking back, I am sure that this was wrong. This conduct saved countless loyalist lives and shortened the Emergency. All the same it was wrong because the good name of Britain was being lost for the sake of saving a few thousand Africans and a few million pounds of the taxpayers' money. Regardless of their popularity, the leaders of the Government and Security Forces stood four square against such practices, which were anyhow very rare'.[24]

***

Kitson flourished in Kenya. He became Military Intelligence Officer for the Nairobi area and established a Special Methods Training Centre where courses were presented to field intelligence officers. Kitson caught the attention of Gen. Erskine who once donned civilian attire and drove to Kiambu to visit him and hear him read one of his papers on intelligence techniques. So impressed was Erskine, he provided the forward for Kitson's 1960 book.

Kitson also impressed the chief of staff of the British army stationed there, Gen. Michael Carver, a high flier who proved beneficial to his future career. Carver rose to the pinnacle of the British army in 1971, Chief of the General Staff. Carver's relationship with Kitson remained so close that Carver would wrote the introduction to his 1971 book.

The citation he received after Kenya pointed to a bright future:

> Since August 1953 Captain KITSON has been responsible for the production of Mau-Mau intelligence in the southern parts of the Emergency affected area in KENYA. He has had the task both of identifying the terrorist organisation and obtaining contact information.
>
> He has built up a military intelligence organisation which is the best in KENYA.
>
> He has made excellent progress in identifying the enemy organisation.
>
> His greatest success has been in developing methods for the procurement of contact information. His methods have set the pattern for the rest of the Colony. They involve small parties in the guise of Mau-Mau mingling by night with the Kikuyu in areas where the presence of terrorists is suspected. On numerous occasions the precise location of a gang has been established. Danger is inherent in such operations. Captain KITSON, accompanied by no more than one other European and two or

three Kikuyu, whose loyalty has often been in doubt, has on several occasions, come face to face with armed terrorists; he has invariably engaged them, often with success.

By the exercise of the highest qualities of personal leadership and example, he has achieved the adoption of his methods by his subordinates, mostly young and inexperienced members of the KENYA Regiment.

On two occasions in the last year Captain KITSON has been ordered on leave because of overwork.

Captain KITSON has consistently performed dangerous duties of an unusual nature, and calling for the highest degree of initiative, imagination and leadership. In doing so, he has achieved standards far above those to be found normally in an officer of his rank and experience.[25]

Officially, the Mau-Mau uprising lasted until 1960, although it had largely petered out by 1958. By then, Kitson was long gone, having left in 1955 for another trouble spot, Malaya, where he served as a company commander with the Rifle Brigade.

3

Genocide and Slavery

Malaya, Oman and Cyprus

According to a profile of Kitson published in a Rand Corporation booklet produced for a symposium on counter-insurgency in 1962, he 'developed and perfected a novel approach and technique for the collection and utilisation of the special kind of intelligence that is indispensable in guerrilla warfare.[1] He was able subsequently to apply this experience in the anti-terrorist campaign in Malaya, where he had command of an infantry company in 1957'.

Kitson never made any bones about the fact that he went to Malaya to kill. He appeared before a TV crew sent out from Britain while stationed in the country to describe in a matter-of-fact way certain ambush tactics in which he and his troops were engaged:

> **Interviewer**: Why do you set these ambushes?
> **Kitson:** We set them when we get information from the police that the terrorists are coming to a certain place. We can then go there, lie in wait for them and kill them.
> **Interviewer**: How often are they successful?
> **Kitson:** Well, not very often. Naturally there are a high proportion of failures but 'tis the best way of killing terrorists and that makes the failures worthwhile.[2]

By now – if not long before – he had become an advocate of

the Maoist dictum that the relationship between insurgents and the population supporting them was akin to that between a fish and water. He later propounded that if a 'fish has got to be destroyed it can be attacked directly by rod or net ... But if rod and net cannot succeed by themselves it may be necessary to do something to the water ...' This could even include 'polluting the water'.[3] In other words, non-combatant members of a community caught up in a conflict could become fair game for strong-arm tactics. A lot of water was polluted in this manner during the fight against the insurgents in Malaya.

Kitson's time in Kenya had not blunted his colonial attitudes. He described one individual he met in Malaya as 'brown rather than yellow and had a prominent jaw and teeth which made him look a bit like a monkey'.[4]

As in Kenya, he was prepared to point out the excesses of the rebels while ignoring those of his own side. He described how the communist rebels had staked a village leader to the ground so he could be eaten alive by ants for refusing to cooperate with them.[5] Kitson was not, however, bothered by the strict curfews imposed on Malayans while others were transported wholesale to the 'new villages' or concentration camps.

Malaya too suffered its own version of Bloody Sunday. It took place on Sunday 12 December 1948 when soldiers from the Scots Guards murdered twenty-four unarmed villagers during an atrocity that became known as the Batang Kali massacre. Although Kitson was not involved in it – he was in Germany – he never expressed any regret for what had taken place at Batang Kali, nor for any of the other war crimes, human rights abuses or excesses perpetrated by the British administration in the country

***

Kitson's experiences in Kenya and Malaya did not imbue him with a sense of compassion for his fellow man either. On the contrary, a blinkered and pitiless mind can be gauged from what he did between 3 July 1958 and 29 November 1960, when he worked at the War Office 'writing and planning [the] Jebel Akhtar expedition'. This involved formulating a plan to suppress a rebellion in Oman and Muscat which he compiled while war crimes were being perpetrated with the aid of Britain on an almost daily basis against the Bani Riyam tribe. Specifically, the Royal Air Force was involved in indiscriminate bombardments resulting in the annihilation of men, women and children in the interior of the country.

In the 1950s Oman and Muscat were ruled by the Sultan of Oman, Said bin Taimur, who had been educated by the British at Mayo College, 'the Eton of India'. He often spent his summers as a guest at London's best hotels, something he financed by diverting the country's oil revenues into his personal Swiss bank accounts. However, the Sultanate was little more than a British colony with the profligate Sultan in nominal charge, while his British advisers ensured the region was run in accordance with their wishes.

When Britain's interest in the region came under threat in 1958, Britain's prime minister, Harold Macmillan, dispatched Julian Amery, his son-in-law and an under-secretary at the war office, to Oman to reorganise the Sultan's army. Amery, a veteran of the Special Operations Executive (SOE) and MI6's intrigues in Albania, had remained close to his colleagues in the secret world. He became under-secretary for the colonies, 1958–1960.[6]

Amery asked his former SOE and MI6 colleague Col David Smiley to go to Oman to beef up the sultan's army. In *Bunch of Five*, Kitson described Smiley as 'a man of medium height and very fair hair' who had taken over 'the job somewhat reluctantly'.[7]

Slavery was still practised openly in the country with the Sultan owning 500 black captives. Britain had set a laudable example to the world by outlawing slavery in 1833, and her navy had done much to stop the trafficking of captives thereafter. Despite this proud history, Macmillan, Amery, Smiley and Kitson were prepared to support the Sultan's regime.

On the other hand, Ranulph Fiennes, who became a world-renowned explorer and had served in the Sultan's army, wrote that:

> ... the British were bolstering a corrupt regime where the Sultan and his chosen few lived sumptuously, enjoying the first fruits of oil wealth while the mass of Omanis lived out their narrow lives in squalor and illness benefiting not at all from the culling of their country's riches ... [the] Sultan seemed determined to perpetuate the mediaeval gloom of Oman. And here I was volunteering my services to the military machine that upheld the old man in denying eight hundred thousand Omanis their rightful inheritance; the benefits of human progress, hospitals and schools.[8]

One of the figures Kitson and Smiley both dealt with was

the half-brother of the Sultan, Sayid Tariq, whom Kitson described as a 'most impressive man: four-square, aquiline and vigorous'.[9] There was a ruthless side to Tariq. Smiley describes how he was sitting in his office one day when news came through to him that one of his soldiers, a sergeant, had been ambushed and killed while another three had been wounded. Their patrol was still under attack. He learned that help was on its way from Nizwa where Tariq was based. He sent out his medical officer in the only available aircraft, which had no room for him, and he stayed behind and waited all day for news about what was happening. That night the aircraft returned with the body of the sergeant and the wounded. In the morning, Smiley flew up in it in time to witness the closing stages of the battle which his troops were winning. By then the rebels had 'melted away' to the mountain. Smiley was informed the fighters who had set the ambush hailed from a place called Muti; moreover, that this was something which had taken 'place in full view of the village' at Muti. When he met the Sultan's half-brother, the latter's face 'was black with anger' and he growled at him: 'we will settle with Muti once and for all … It shall be burned to the ground. Prepare your men, David, and come with me.'[10] Smiley was prepared to participate and assembled 'a strong force of SAF and Tarik's askers' (sic). When they reached Muti, Smiley found 'there wasn't a living soul in the place … not even women and children':

> We went systematically from house to house, setting each one alight with paraffin until nothing remained but smouldering ruins. Muti would prepare no more ambushes and harbour no more minelayers; and to close this supply route to Talib we

stationed an outpost of SAF prominently on the hill commanding the ravine. Talib would receive no more supplies that way and perhaps that splendid sergeant would not have died in vain.[11]

Kitson omitted this atrocity in the chapters dealing with Oman in *Bunch of Five*.

The rebellion was eventually suppressed by troops from the Special Air Service (SAS).

***

In 1963, Kitson was sent to Cyprus which had recently achieved a degree of independence from Britain. He arrived as part of a UN peacekeeping force which stood between the Greek-Cypriots and Turkish-Cypriots.

In *Bunch of Five,* he explained that since the UN contingent did not have an intelligence organisation, he and his troops in Nicosia began to collect 'every scrap of information' which came their way. He described this as a 'chain reaction' process. Phase one of the procedure was to collect the names of anyone who was taking an active part in the affairs of the two Cypriot communities. No detail was too small. Nicknames were even collected. 'Using telephone directories and trade directories we discovered where some of them lived and where they worked, and then we examined the background of people living nearby, or working in the same business, in the hope that a connection in ordinary civil life would lead to a connection in one or other of the fighting organisations.'[12] Every detail his officers discovered was placed on file and index cards were opened. The work resulted in a plethora of names, addresses, telephone numbers and car registration details. Soon the information 'began to snowball' and by 'staring for hours at this conglomeration of facts and figures we began to discern the outline of the opposing organisations', he wrote.

The next phase involved distilling and presenting it to his commanders for examination and testing. Troops were put into observation posts to watch the activities of 'particular groups, or individuals' and to talk to locals. He also ordered patrols to follow new telephone cables, which he felt 'had perhaps been laid for the purpose of linking one group of fighters to another, and this could lead to more addresses and more names'. He described the whole process as a 'very interesting and enjoyable game which kept everyone usefully occupied and greatly increased our potential as peace-keepers'.[13]

The paths of Kitson and Lord Carver intertwined again in Cyprus. When Carver arrived to assume overall command of the UN force in Cyprus in 1963, he concluded it had been labouring under two handicaps: first, a lack of access to intelligence; and second, the limitation on what it could do. As he pointed out in his 1989 book, a UN force could not have an intelligence organisation.[14] Hence, any attempt to find out what the two factions on the island were up to, 'whether overt or covert, was regarded by them as spying, and produced strong, sometimes violent, reactions and protests'. Kitson solved the problem by linking his UN troops to MI5 and MI6's regional network. According to Carver, an excellent intelligence apparatus was developed under the control of Kitson.

***

After his UN tour of duty in Cyprus ended, Kitson returned to England where he was promoted again and sent to work in the MoD. He served as a General Service Officer (GSO) between 1 March 1965 and 31 July 1967. Then, in September 1967 he was appointed commander of the First Battalion the Royal Green Jackets, a post he held until September 1969. This enabled him to 'escape' from London.[15] One month later, the battalion went to Cyprus as part of the United Nations force. Although Kitson appreciated that by the end of 1964 the situation had improved, now in October 1967 there were further signs that trouble was about to erupt.[16] This materialised in the Battle of Kophinou where the UN had intervened to keep Greek-Cypriots and Turkish-Cypriots apart. When describing this episode, he made a telling remark about the need for British troops to be 'feared':

> Although soldiers operating under my command in a peace situation might not always be liked, I was determined that they should at least be respected and, if necessary, feared. For things to be otherwise is unfair on the soldiers and is inconsistent with the achievement of this aim.[17]

***

Kitson returned to London and, in October 1969, he was enrolled with the 'Defence Fellowship' at Oxford College where he set about writing a treatise that evolved into his controversial book, *Low Intensity Operations*. Prof. N. H. Gibbs, the Chichele Professor of the History of War at Oxford, oversaw the effort. When, in 1972, the author Sean Boyne contacted Gibbs, looking for information about the brigadier, he was told: 'Let me make one thing clear. I am not going to tell you anything about Brigadier Kitson as my pupil without his expressed permission.' Gibbs referred to the 'difficult situation' that prevailed as the reason for his caution but added: 'I like him. I admire him and he was a very good pupil.'

According to Colin Wallace: 'Prior to the deployment of the army in Northern Ireland, part of the training for soldiers about to undertake internal security commitment included watching two films: *Keeping the Peace*, parts 1 & 2. However, Northern Ireland quickly demonstrated that a completely new approach was needed and Brigadier Kitson was probably regarded as the person most likely to succeed at creating that approach.'[18]

Kitson left Oxford in August 1970 and was sent to Ireland on 18 September.[19]

4

'Suppression of the Irish'

Kitson strode into a political and paramilitary minefield in Ireland in September 1970.

The previous year the Ulster Volunteer Force (UVF), an underground Loyalist paramilitary organisation, had conducted a bomb campaign which had toppled Capt. Terence O'Neill, the prime minister of Northern Ireland. O'Neill, whose sins included meeting the Taoiseach, Seán Lemass, and suggesting that Northern Ireland be reformed to make the Catholic/Nationalist community feel more integrated and equal to the dominant Protestant-Unionist community, was forced out of office on 1 May 1969.

The following August, marauding gangs of Loyalists led by the RUC, B-Specials, the UVF and men who later joined the ranks of the UDA/UFF and Red Hand Commando, burned thousands of Catholics/Nationalists out of their homes, something that sparked the largest refugee crisis in Europe since the Second World War.

This prompted the deployment of the British army onto the streets of Northern Ireland. In the absence of a functioning IRA, the squaddies proved the only effective protection available from the Loyalist militants. The minority community hailed the soldiers as their saviours while extreme and militant Loyalists tilted against the forces of the crown. It was Loyalists who killed the first RUC officer of the 'Troubles', Victor Arbuckle, in October of that year during a riot. Their anger on that occasion was inflamed by the stripping of the RUC of its arms and the disbandment of the B Specials.

Groups of besieged Nationalists had formed citizens defence committees (CDCs) in 1969 before the arrival of the British army. As 1969 ended, the CDCs were still very much at the centre of events and offered an alternative to the IRA for those who wished to protect their communities. In contrast, those who would become members of the Provisional IRA, wanted to use the crisis as a springboard to mount a campaign to end partition. The CDCs consisted of businessmen, lawyers, priests, IRA volunteers and future members of the SDLP. In late 1969, and early 1970, they enjoyed excellent relations with the British army, Home Secretary James Callaghan and the new RUC Chief Constable, Sir Arthur Young. The CDCs negotiated arrangements with the army to allow them dismantle barricades.[1]

The honeymoon period was still evident that Christmas with some soldiers being invited to spend the holiday in local homes in the Bogside and Creggan in Derry. However, with nothing else to do while on duty, some soldiers began to halt civilians and ask them questions, even conducting random searches which generated ripples of annoyance. One of the tasks assigned to the troops in Belfast was to pull down the barricades that had been erected to keep Loyalist gangs out of Nationalist communities. Stormont saw this creation of 'no-go' areas and defiance of its authority and wanted the army to dismantle them. Some were removed with the co-operation of community leaders in return for the promise of more protection from the Loyalist gangs by the army.

Regrettably, some of the soldiers displayed contempt for the locals with whom they were rubbing shoulders and the disgruntled youths of the latter took umbrage. While the British government was pushing through more reforms, this failed to convince many that things were going to improve for the minority. As Eamonn McCann recounted:

> But in Rossville Street [in Derry] and the Falls Road [in Belfast] and a hundred other dusty streets in Derry and Belfast, things were different. Reforms had filtered through on to the statute book. An Ombudsman had been appointed. Derry Corporation had been abolished and replaced by a Development Commission. A points system for the allocation of houses was in operation. Moderate Unionists could, and often did, point proudly to this record of progress. None of it, however, made any difference to the clumps of unemployed teenagers who stood, fists dug deep into their pockets, around William Street in the evenings. Briefly elevated into folk-hero status in the heady days of August, praised and patronised by local leaders for their expertise with the stone and petrol bomb, they had now been dragged back down into the anonymous depression which had hitherto been their constant condition. For them at least, nothing had changed and they were bitterly cynical about the talk of a reformed future. 'We'll get nothing out of it. The Orangemen are still in power.' Occasionally they would stone the soldiers. It was small-scale stuff.[2]

Riots took place in March 1970 after commemorations for the 1916 Easter Rising. They were roundly condemned in most Nationalist quarters. There was further trouble in Ballymurphy in Belfast shortly after this in response to the start of the Orange marching season (April to August), which led to confrontations in the Bogside with the army deploying CS gas. Rioting went on for three days. Again, it was condemned on all sides.

While the IRA had been largely dormant before the arrival of the British army, it was now reorganising and determined to gain the support of Nationalists. The following it began to attract had little to do with the presence of the British army – at least not initially – but more to do with the strong-arm tactics of Stormont and the violence of street agitators. The latter included men such as Ian Paisley, John McKeague, William McGrath and their followers in the Shankill Defence Association and the Ulster Volunteer Force. This was aided and abetted by the now defunct B-Specials and the still extant RUC.

As 1969 passed into 1970, the Unionist government at Stormont strove to regain control of security policy for Northern Ireland and the machinery necessary to enforce it. The Unionists, led by Prime Minister James Chichester-Clark, could not achieve this while they and the British army were pulling in opposite directions. The increasing friction between Nationalist communities and the army, along with the appearance of the first green shoots of a reinvigorated IRA, provided the Unionists with a platform to promote their agenda.

They received a boost to their campaign when the Conservative and Unionist Party won the British general election in June 1970. Whereas the Labour government of Harold Wilson had been sympathetic to the Nationalist community, the new prime minister, Edward Heath, was more inclined to listen to his Unionist allies, especially as he wanted their support for his ambition to join the European Economic Community, or EEC, the forerunner to the EU.

The Tory-Unionist alliance meant that the Conservatives did not run candidates in Northern Ireland. In return, Unionist MPs supported the Conservatives in Westminster. One of the more prominent of their number, Knox Cunningham MP, had served as private secretary to Harold Macmillan.

When the Nationalist enclave of the Short Strand in Belfast was threatened by a hoard of militant Loyalists in June 1970, the British army, which should have been there to protect them, was nowhere to be seen. The enclave consisted of 6,000 Nationalists surrounded by 60,000 Loyalists. The Provisional IRA stepped forward as the last line of defence with some assistance from CDC members. They fought off the Loyalists in what became known as the Battle of St Matthew's. This garnered the Provisionals a lot of support in Nationalist communities.

In July what remained of the good relations between the military and the Nationalist community dropped off a cliff due to the Falls Road curfew. British troops conducted a search for arms belonging to the Official IRA in Belfast. They carried out this task in a violent manner with Scottish soldiers assailing residents, smashing their belongings and stealing from their houses. Intensifying this terror, the area was drenched in CS gas. Adding insult to injury, when the army had achieved domination of the streets, they escorted Unionist politicians on a tour of the area.

The Provisional IRA took the life of its first police victim in August 1970, the month before Kitson's arrival. The first British soldier did not fall until the following February.

***

Kitson assumed command of 39 Airportable Brigade from Brig. Peter Hudson on 18 September 1970.[3] This placed him in charge of all British army operations in Belfast.[4] The week before the hand-over, he visited Lisburn to arrange his and his wife's personal accommodation. During the visit he spoke to Lt-Gen. Sir Ian Freeland, to whom he would report, and Sir Arthur Young, the new RUC chief constable. Optimistically, both of them expressed their hope that the army would be withdrawn by the end of the year.

Freeland and Young had developed good relations with the Nationalist community, during the 'honeymoon period'. Kitson, however, was not cut from the same cloth. It is apparent from his 1971 book, *Low Intensity Operations* that he felt the enemy in Ireland was to be found among the Catholic/Nationalist community. He wrote that 'in the historical context it may be of interest to recall that when the regular army was first raised in the 17th century, "Suppression of the Irish" was coupled with "Defence of the Protestant Religion" as one of the two main reasons for its existence'. Kitson's bias was not swayed by any of the following factors:

* that the Loyalist UVF had instigated the bombing campaign which had unseated the Stormont prime minister, Terence O'Neill, in 1969;
* that the British army had been called in to protect Catholic-Nationalists from marauding Loyalist gangs in August 1969;
* that it was rioting Loyalist mobs who had killed the first RUC officer the following October;
* that it was the Loyalist-dominated B Specials which had had to be disbanded and the RUC disarmed that same year to quell violence, and that;

* it was militant Loyalists who had opposed and continued to oppose the reforms the British government had urged upon Stormont in the late 1960s and early 1970s.

Colin Wallace believes that Kitson was assigned to Belfast at the behest of Michael Carver with the support of the MoD. 'He was sent,' Wallace says, 'with the task of coming up with a strategy to suppress the disorder. This was a poisoned chalice. Part of the problem for him was that there was a lot of pressure to get results quickly. His reputation and background were a burden. He had written his book and was really the only person in Northern Ireland with counter-insurgency experience. Broadly speaking, in Aden, Cyprus and Malaya there had been one force challenging Britain, trying to gain independence. The army counter-insurgents went there to confront and suppress a rebellion. In Northern Ireland it was meant to be different: there were two warring factions and the army was meant to act as peacemaker and umpire, but that was not Kitson's speciality. Certainly, he had peacekeeping experience from his time in Cyprus, but his value to the MoD was in counter-insurgency. In the final analysis, the North required a different approach to what he could bring to the table.'[5]

Despite his views about the 'Defence of the Protestant Religion', Kitson had a stab at trying to win the 'hearts and minds' of the Catholic/Nationalist population. This was an increasingly ambitious task as it was being undertaken in the wake of the army's failure to protect Nationalists during the Battle of St Matthew's (June 1970) and the Falls Road curfew (July 1970). Despite these setbacks, the lines of communication between the two sides were still open. Lt-Gen. Freeland, who had been in Northern Ireland since 1969, had established and maintained contact with local leaders such as Jim Sullivan of the Central Citizen Defence Committee. The fact he was a senior Official IRA leader was not a secret. In his early days in Belfast, Kitson met with Sullivan and other prominent figures and encouraged his subordinates to follow his lead. The purpose of the contact was to exchange views and lessen tensions on the ground where stone-throwing rioting was taking place. Unquestionably, there was also an intelligence-gathering dimension to these interactions.

Kitson established a good working relationship with Sam Bradley, the RUC's assistant chief constable for Belfast. Together they established 'divisional action committees' consisting of soldiers and policemen who endeavoured to interact with community activists on a more formal basis. While some leaders were receptive to the committees, the Provisional IRA was set against them. The committees ultimately came to nought. Meanwhile, the stone-throwing, rioting and petrol bombing gathered in pace and intensity.

Slowly but surely, the hunter in Kitson – ever eager to tear his prey apart – came to the fore. The wolf in him had been lurking the background all along. After he had settled in to his new command, Kitson had informed Robert Ramsay, a senior Stormont civil servant, of 'his disappointment at the glaring inadequacies' of RUC and Army Intelligence.[6] According to him, 'movements such as the IRA' had three main components:

self-sacrificial ideologues, violent psychopaths and criminals with a vaguely political 'cover'. The way into such organisations was through the criminals. 'There will always be enough greed, jealousy and spite coursing around among that gang for us to exploit by bribery, bullying and misinformation.'[7]

As the weeks dragged on, the friction between the Nationalist community and the British army was becoming more intense. Paddy Devlin MP, who was also Secretary to the Central CDC of Belfast (and later an SDLP MP and minister in the short lived 1974 Power-Sharing Executive), blamed the Provisionals for provoking a lot of this trouble. He described in his memoirs how, since the spring of 1970, 'Provisional IRA-inspired rioting spread through Flax Street, Tiger's Bay, Lower North Street and Clonard areas like an epidemic. The trouble usually started with stone-throwing and ended up with petrol bombs being brought into play. The army threatened to shoot the petrol-bombers on sight but, although they killed one young man, the unrest did not abate. Several other factors made matters worse.' According to Devlin, 'Brig. Frank Kitson appeared on the scene to replace Brig. Peter Hudson. Kitson, famous for his efforts to suppress the Mau-Mau in Kenya, was an expert on combating terrorism and was brought to Belfast purely because of his expertise and skill. In my view his appointment was clear evidence that the military were going on the attack'.[8] The passage of time validated Devlin's prediction of a gathering storm.

It is clear from a paper Kitson wrote on 4 December 1971 that he did not perceive the Loyalist groups as targets, although he was wary of the trouble they might cause if provoked.[9] In this document he stated: 'If however the Protestants decided to oppose the enemy with an underground organisation using proper force like the IRA as opposed to mere street disorders, we would have a new campaign to fight which would involve as a start the setting up of an intelligence organisation capable of discovering how the new [Protestant] subversive group operated.'[10]

Kitson's 1971 paper contained a final paragraph which underlines the point that he perceived his mission as one directed against the Republican movement alone. In it, he stated that it was:

> no part of our business to recommend one solution rather than another but it is necessary for us to receive some direction beyond our immediate mission of destroying the IRA.[11]

While Kitson had been involved in a series of counter-insurgency campaigns, the tactics he and his ilk had deployed in the colonies were hardly suited to a modern, urban western European setting such as Northern Ireland. So, how was Kitson, with his anti-Nationalist bias, going to adapt to the situation that confronted him? The following questions legitimately arise:

* How could he deal with communities which frequently barricaded themselves away from the rest of society in 'no-go' areas?
* How might he eliminate the IRA, a secret army whose volunteers would soon be sniping at soldiers from dark corners before melting back into the community?
* Would it be possible to extract information from IRA suspects and supporters in his brigade area without resorting to brutal methods? Alternatively, might it be possible to deploy such means?

* Would it be possible to establish and train clandestine army murder gangs to eliminate the IRA?
* Would he collude with the array of Loyalist paramilitary organisations that were the enemy of his designated enemy, the IRA? These were men who were ready, willing and able to murder Nationalists as proxy assassins for him if he so chose.
* How could he present himself as a peacekeeper in his brigade area, when his real role was that of counter-insurgency expert?
* If he did not already have authority from the MoD, Home Office and wider British government to conduct a dirty war, even one with the handbrake applied partially, would they support him if he proposed and implemented extreme measures?
* If he was to resort to brutality, assassination and collusion with Loyalist terror gangs, would his colleagues in the covert world of intelligence be able to hoodwink the editors of the Northern Irish newspapers, the British press and the rest of the world's media?
* Did it matter to him that there was still support for the British army inside minority communities and that his actions might erode what was left of it?

Once ensconced at Thiepval Barracks at Lisburn on the outskirts of Belfast, Kitson began to build a secretive under-cover unit which drew on his experiences with counter-gangs in the colonies. The Belfast version became known as the Military Reaction Force or MRF.[12]

5

DRAWING A FIST

AND PULLING NO PUNCHES

Kitson's 39 Brigade occupied a large building at Thiepval Barracks, the Lisburn military complex on the outskirts of Belfast. A football field separated it from the structure where HQNI was based. The latter oversaw all British military activity in Northern Ireland. The field was sometimes used for football and cricket matches which were occasionally interrupted by the arrival of helicopters. From time to time, parachute training took place on it as well.

It was at Lisburn that Kitson tried to implement in Northern Ireland one of the successful techniques he had absorbed in Kenya and Malaya, the drawing together of all the fingers of the state into one fist to pound the enemy. In Belfast, this meant getting the RUC to work in tandem with the army.

Kitson had mixed results. On the positive side, he had developed a good working relationship with the assistant RUC chief constable in Belfast, Sam Bradley. Rather more unfavourably, however, the Unionist politicians at Stormont still managed to exert control over the flow of intelligence gathered by the RUC, particularly the Special Branch.

While Kitson's ostensible task was to maintain the peace in Belfast and its environs, he set about creating a clandestine counter-insurgency apparatus with assistance from the RUC. Initially, it was called the 'Bomb Squad' but soon morphed into the Military Reaction Force (MRF). The role of the Bomb Squad, was 'to collect, collate, develop and act upon intelligence relating to terrorist bombing activities'.

Although details are still unclear, the 'Bomb Squad' had become the MRF by late 1971, if not earlier. Based at Palace Barracks, MRF operatives sallied forth and prowled around Belfast in unmarked cars dressed in plain clothes.[1] The MRF pursued the surveillance operations of the Bomb Squad but carried out plain clothed assassination missions as well. One of the models for the MRF was the 'Q squad' which had been deployed by the British in Palestine. A declassified MoD document from October 1971, entitled: *Tougher Military Measures and Their Implication*, proposed: 'More aggressive tactics against gunmen such as the formation of Q squads in special areas, to mystify, mislead and destroy the terrorists.'[2]

The creation of the MRF as an assassination squad was in keeping with another MoD document. On 29 August 1969, the Ministry had published Volume III of its *Land Operations*. Under the heading, 'Counter-revolutionary Operations, 1st Part, Principles and General Aspects' one of the tasks assigned to the Special Air Service (SAS) was '(c.) The infiltration of assassination and demolition parties into insurgent held areas'.[3]

***

The MRF's mission was to suppress the IRA, not Loyalist paramilitaries. Like the counter-gangs in Kenya, a number of local insurgents were cajoled or 'turned' into working for it. They were called 'Freds' and lived in Palace Barracks near

Holywood with the MRF. They were conveyed around the back streets of Belfast in concealed vehicles to point out IRA targets to their handlers. Another technique Kitson deployed in Belfast came right out of his colonial play book: in Kenya, the army had draped white cloaks over informers with peep holes cut out for their eyes. In a slight variation on this, blankets were used in Belfast to enable the informers and 'Freds' to identify Republicans in line-ups.[4]

One former RUC CID detective who was involved in the establishment of the MRF recalled how Kitson was 'very hands-on' and believed that the 'only way to beat the terrorist was to terrorise them'.[5]

In an astonishing recording made in 1971, Kitson commented:

> In order to put an insurgency campaign down, one must use a mix of measures and it is sometimes necessary to do unpleasant things which lose a certain amount of allegiance for a moment in order to produce your overall result.

***

The MRF launched a series of attacks on unarmed civilians with no links to the IRA in 1972. Kitson had left by then, but no doubt monitored what was afoot with great interest from England where he was now commandant of the School of Infantry at Warminster. At best, the MRF killings were cases of mistaken identity; at worst they were provocations to get the IRA to come out of the shadows and take them on in street battles.

On 15 April 1972, two brothers, John and Gerry Conway,

were wounded at Whiterock Road in Belfast by an MRF unit as they went to their stall in the centre of the city.

On 12 May, 1972 Patrick McVeigh, a family man was fatally wounded in a shooting at the junction of Riverdale Park South and Finaghy Road North. Forensic tests on McVeigh and those who had been in his company proved negative. None were paramilitaries. McVeigh, a father-of-six, had been conversing with some of his neighbours at a Nationalist barricade. A vehicle approached them, stopped, and then reversed for a moment before its occupants opened fire. The MRF soldiers in the car later told an inquest that they had been fired upon by six men armed with rifles and revolvers. This was a lie. McVeigh was struck by submachine-gun fire, while four others were wounded. The army press office initially described the shooting as 'an apparently motiveless crime'. The McVeigh case was reopened in 1993. The following year detectives flew to Australia and England to re-interview former soldiers. However, the review did not lead to prosecutions.

On the same night, Eugene Devlin was shot while his friend Aidan McAloon was lucky to escape without injury at nearby Slieve Gallion. They were trying to get home in a taxi from a disco.

On 22 June 1972, four civilians were shot at Glen Road in West Belfast with a Thompson machine gun. A favourite tactic of the MRF was to make their assaults appear as if they had been perpetrated by paramilitaries. At the time the IRA was using Thompsons. The Tommy gun involved in this incident was privately owned by Capt. Hamish McGregor, one of the MRF's commanders. Another Thompson, which had been seized by the RUC from the IRA, was lent to the MRF by the Special Branch together with ammunition. McGregor had joined 1 Para in 1964 and went on to serve with the UN force in Cyprus. As part of 1 Para, he carried out operational tours in the Radfan in 1965, and was also attached to the Sultan's Armed Forces in Oman. He was awarded the Military Cross for his actions while serving with 1 Para in Aden in 1967.

Sgt Clive Graham Williams of the MRF unit, was on attachment from the Royal Military Police. A volley from his weapon struck three young men at a bus terminus on the Glen Road, and a fourth man whose bedroom was in the line of fire. Williams and McGregor were charged with illegal possession of a firearm and ammunition. Williams was also charged with three counts of attempted murder. Their trial was called in June of 1973 and will be described shortly.

On 27 September 1972, Daniel Rooney and his friend Brendan Brennan were shot at St James' Crescent, close to Rooney's home in Rodney Parade in West Belfast. Rooney died shortly afterwards in hospital. He was just eighteen. Brennan was wounded but survived. A statement from the army claimed five shots had been fired at a security force surveillance patrol in the St James' Park area and that fire had been returned. This was untrue. The army press officer claimed Rooney was a known gunman, but tellingly the IRA never claimed him as a member and he is listed on a memorial as a civilian.

A group of MRF soldiers, some RUC Special Branch

and MI5 set up at least two brothels in Belfast, both of which were fitted with hidden microphones and 35mm Olympus cameras. One of them was known as the *Gemini*. They opened in July 1970 with small advertisements offering 'relief massage' in Belfast newspapers. One was located on the Antrim Road in Belfast, the other on the Malone Road. The operation was directed by MI5 from offices in Churchill House, Government Building in Belfast. Bernie Silver, the notorious vice king from London, spent ten days in Belfast helping select the premises and advising MI5 on management techniques. He then returned to London where he recruited prostitutes for the brothels. Apparently, the employees were selected for their intelligence as much as their physical attributes. All were made to sign the Official Secrets Act and warned they would be jailed if they talked about their experiences. The Antrim Road brothel was the more expensive of the two establishments. At least one girl from Dublin was employed in the operation.

The IRA discovered the existence of the brothels and launched an attack on one of them on Monday 2 October 1972. The IRA then claimed they had killed two employees, a man codenamed 'Bossman Jim' and one of the girls during their assault.

That same day the IRA attacked the MRF's Four Square Laundry operation in Belfast. The MRF had used it to collect laundry from Nationalist communities which were tested for gunfire and explosive residue. The business also gave them the opportunity to drive around Nationalist areas. The laundry van had an observation post in its roof. An MRF soldier called Sapper Ted Stuart was killed during the attack.

Of all the outrages, the Glen Road shooting proved to be the nadir of the MRF's existence. Attorney-general, Sir Peter Rawlinson, QC, told the Secretary of State for NI, William Whitelaw, in 1973 that 'the whole case was extremely embarrassing and might become more so' because the 'blue Cortina car alleged to have been used' by the MRF in the shooting had featured in other alleged crimes.[6]

In November 1972, a review of the MRF ordered by the MoD found there was 'no provision for detailed command and control' and said a better-trained unit should replace it. In 1972, the operations of the MRF were brought under more centralised control and a higher standard of training achieved by establishing a Special Reconnaissance Unit (SRU) with all ranks under direct command of HQNI. It eventually mutated into 14 Intelligence Company.

'One of the problems with it', Colin Wallace contends, 'was that there was no formal structure behind it. There were no bureaucrats who could have found reliable people for it. Instead, a call went out to the commanding officers in Belfast to supply volunteers. Some of them used the opportunity to get rid of troublemakers. On top of this, the recruits weren't given proper training. They ended up living in a world of their own in Palace Barracks. Yet, somehow, this proved to be one part of the Kitson experiment that endured. The military and intelligence services kept refining the concept and produced new units based on it throughout the Troubles'.[7]

In June 1973, Sgt Williams went on trial for the Glen Road attacks. The possession of illegal firearms charges against him and his co-accused McGregor were dropped. Williams alone now faced trial charged on three counts of attempted murder. At his trial, Williams admitted to the MRF's existence, but the damage to the army was significantly limited because the firearms charges were not proceeded with. Because of that, whatever explanation there might have been as to why Williams had a Thompson submachine-gun on patrol never emerged in court.

After a brief trial, Williams was acquitted on all counts by a majority verdict.

Declassified documents from the National Archives show how concerned Whitehall was to prevent details of the unit being made public. One document read: 'There can be no useful purpose in admitting the existence of any such organisation' and 'There seems to be considerable advantage in maintaining as much confusion as possible.'

In his book, *Ghost Force*, Ken Connor, a former SAS Warrant Officer, who was involved in the creation of what later became known as '14 Int', disclosed:

> I was one of a three-man IRA assessment team sent to Northern Ireland to evaluate the Military Reconnaissance Force and the Four Square Laundry organisation. It soon became apparent that its cover was blown and the group of people running it were so out of control that it had to be disbanded at once.
>
> Without reference to each other, we all produced the same recommendation: it's been a useful tool, but it's well past its sell-by date. Get rid of it, acquire the needed skills, then reform it in a different guise. The result was 14 Int – the Fourteenth Intelligence Company. The SAS developed a selection procedure, ran the induction course and training and staffed the upper echelons of the company with SAS officers.

That gave the Regiment a means of maintaining its influence over an area that should technically have been controlled by the Intelligence Corps. The SAS could have its cake and eat it too, maintaining an involvement in Northern Ireland without using manpower that was needed in the Middle East.[8]

General Sir Mike Jackson, the former head of the British army, who served as a captain in 1 Para in the early 1970s, told the BBC in 2013 that although he had known little of the MRF's activities at the time, he admired the bravery of soldiers who had been involved in undercover work. 'That takes a lot of courage and it's a cold courage. It's not the courage of hot blood [used by] soldiers in a firefight. You know if you are discovered, a pretty gruesome fate may well await you – torture followed by murder.'[9]

6

KITSON'S TOP BRASS FAN CLUB

Lord Michael Carver had great confidence in Kitson whom he knew 'very well from Kenya' where they had fought against the Mau-Mau. In Cyprus, he disclosed, Kitson had 'worked with MI5 and MI6 as part of their intelligence gathering' apparatus while on UN duties under his command.[1] When Carver became the Director of Army Staff Duties, Kitson was offered to him as a lieutenant colonel. 'He was extremely good and I had a very high regard for him and so did people in Belfast. He is highly intelligent, well-educated and absolutely determined to do his best. He penetrates to the core of any problem. He is one of the army experts in low intensity operations. No one was better at this job in Northern Ireland than Frank Kitson'.[2]

So highly did he view Kitson, Carver wrote a glowing introduction to his 1971 book, *Low Intensity Operations*. Nobody, Carver stated, was better qualified than Kitson to write on the subject of counter-insurgency and the book was 'for the soldier of today to help him prepare for the operations of tomorrow. It will be the greatest possible help to him and I hope it will be read by all those concerned with training the Army.'[3]

Carver became Chief of the General Staff (CGS) of the British army on 1 April 1971. Insofar as the military command structure in Northern Ireland was concerned, the highest-ranking officer was the General Officer Commanding

Northern Ireland (GOC NI) who reported to Carver. Next in line was his deputy, the Commander Land Forces (CLF).

Kitson served under three GOCs NI: Lt-Gen. Sir Ian Freeland; Lt-Gen. Vernon Erskine Crum, who suffered a heart attack and was replaced by Sir Harold Tuzo on 2 March 1971. Born in Bangalore on 26 August 1917, Tuzo's appointment to Ireland was accompanied by a promotion to the rank of lieutenant-general. He, a graduate of Oxford, had commanded the 51st Infantry Brigade in Borneo from 1963 to 1965 where he had engaged in counter-insurgency operations.[4] Tuzo kept Carver, who was based in London, abreast of developments in Ireland. Carver paid visits to Northern Ireland 'about once a month' where he had discussions with Tuzo and went 'out on the ground to visit and keep in touch with the situation'.[5]

The role of the CLF had been created in the peculiar circumstances of the early 'Troubles'. Carver explained to the Saville Inquiry that in Northern Ireland in the 'early days', Gen. Freeland GOC NI had 'found it very difficult to deal with both the RUC and politicians and also keep hold of what the army was doing'.[6] A decision was taken to appoint a deputy and the CLF came into existence. Kitson served under two CLFs: first, Maj.-Gen. Farrar-Hockley who took up his post in August of 1970 and then Gen. Robert Ford who was installed a year later. Like Carver, all of these men were admirers of Kitson.

Tuzo and Farrar-Hockley were also stationed at Thiepval Barracks in Lisburn within the same complex as Kitson's 39 Brigade HQ. Carver and Farrar-Hockley were enthusiastic supporters of the MRF.[7] Undoubtedly, Tuzo was too.

Farrar-Hockley had accrued considerable counter-insurgency experience in places like Palestine, Borneo and Aden. With Kitson at his side, he proposed applying some of the techniques that had been developed in the colonies in Northern Ireland. This, he felt, could be achieved through 'the close integration of intelligence and operations; the use of the techniques, described by Kitson, aimed at separating insurgents from the people; embracing new technologies, techniques, tactics and procedures; and above all, changing the mindset'.[8] He and Kitson got on very well together. According to Farrar-Hockley's biographer:

> Developing a modern approach to complex counter-insurgency was not going to happen overnight, and it was as well for the army and the campaign in Northern Ireland that both Kitson and [Farrar-Hockley] began the process at an early date.[9]

Maj.-Gen. Robert Ford replaced Farrar-Hockley on 29 July 1971 just before internment was introduced. He attended the Royal Armoured Corps' officer cadet training unity at Sandhurst and was commissioned into the 4th/7th Royal Dragoon Guards (4/7 RDG) in June 1943. He took part in the D-Day landings in June 1944 and in operations throughout the North West Europe Campaign and was mentioned in despatches. He subsequently served with his regiment in Egypt, Palestine and Trans-Jordan. Attendance at Staff College, Camberley, was followed by a staff job at the War Office and then a return to 4/7 RDG. In 1960, he was posted to 20th Armoured Brigade as brigade major and, in 1964, he moved to the MoD on the staff of Admiral of the Fleet, Earl Mountbatten, Chief of the Defence Staff. Ford took command of 4/7 RDG in 1966 and commanded 7th Armoured Brigade two years later.[10]

According to Carver, Ford was 'very different' to his predecessor, Gen. Farrar-Hockley who, according to Carver, was the 'sort you needed to restrain; Gen. Ford was not. Tuzo was happy with the appointment of Gen. Ford'.[11] When one considers that Ford later recommended the use of live ammunition to quell riots in Derry, one must wonder what Carver's definition of 'restraint' might have encompassed.[12]

According to Gen. Mike Jackson, Kitson also commanded enormous respect among those who served under him and that 'within his area of responsibility he was the sun around which the planets revolved, and he very much set the tone for the operational style'.

***

The key politicians in London such as Heath and Carrington also knew about, and were supportive of, the MRF. Kitson produced a paper on 4 December 1971 that demonstrates that the MRF operated with the knowledge of the British government.[13]

Carver kept the politicians up to speed about the army's activities in Northern Ireland at meetings of the 'GEN 42' committee at 10 Downing Street. Heath's government made decisions about what to do in Northern Ireland at these meetings.[14]

Carver provided the Saville Inquiry with some insight into the relationship the army enjoyed with their political masters. Heath, he felt, had been 'very good to deal with' because he would listen to what he had to say without much comment before he would 'ask questions and make-up his own mind. He was influenced by his military background and wanted to solve problems by the use of military means'.[15] Heath's home secretary, Reggie Maudling 'was very laid back but with a sharp brain'.[16]

Carver disclosed that he had given the go-ahead for the creation of the MRF having received 'ministerial' permission, undoubtedly from Peter Carrington, the then Secretary of State for Defence:

> In fact, for some time various surveillance operations by soldiers in plain clothes have been in training, initiated by Frank Kitson when he commanded the brigade in Belfast, some of them exploiting ex-members or supporters of the IRA,[17] of which I was aware and for which I had obtained ministerial approval.[18]

Heath, a former soldier, was no shrinking violet. Carver told the writer Martin Dillon that, during a GEN 42 meeting in May 1972, Heath pronounced that it was legal for soldiers to shoot rioters if they 'obstructed the Armed Forces of the Queen' because this type of behaviour rendered them 'the Queen's enemy'. In such circumstances, the troops did not have to be fired on first before opening fire themselves.[19] Dillon reveals that the author of the advice was Heath's lord chancellor, Lord Hailsham.

In Northern Ireland, the army liaised with the Unionist government at the powerful Joint Security Committee which had been formed by Faulkner, Tuzo, the RUC, and two of Faulkner's ministers.

When Kitson furnished a statement to the Saville Inquiry in 2000, he played down his status as a counter-insurgency expert, instead describing his role in the most mundane of terms such as 'working with the police within my area of responsibility to ensure that law and order was preserved'.[20] There was no mention of the MRF's intelligence gathering operations, of the IRA volunteers it had 'turned', of operatives inside Loyalist paramilitary groups, or of the brothels set up to gather information in Nationalist areas. Instead, he deflected attention by stating that:

> At this time the Army relied on the RUC for intelligence; it was disseminated initially from Special Branch of the RUC to HQ Northern Ireland who would pass it on to the relevant Brigade HQ who would then pass it on to relevant units as necessary. Most intelligence was passed in writing or by word of mouth because the telephone was insufficiently secure.[21]

But the working relationship with the RUC had been nowhere near as productive as Kitson told the Saville Inquiry. He was more forthcoming about the difficulties he had encountered when he spoke to the military historian Jonathon Riley in September 2014. The problem, he explained, was that the Unionist government controlled the army's access to RUCSB intelligence. As things stood, it was passed to RUC headquarters at Knock, Belfast, and then, 'depending on the agenda of the Stormont government, passed back selectively to HQNI and so on down the line'.[22] Kitson's colonial experience had taught him that police-army co-operation was best 'fused at the lowest practicable level if timely action was to be taken and results achieved'.[23] In other words, he wanted intelligence gathered by the RUCSB on the ground to be passed to his local battalion officers without delay. 'Unofficially, moves were made in this direction, but it was not until the end of the year [1971] that any real progress was made at higher levels'.[24]

When Kitson appeared at the Saville Inquiry in person on 24 September 2002, he presented a sanitised version of his career. There was no mention of exploiting 'bribery, bullying and misinformation' to defeat the IRA let alone a hint of the MRF.[25] Instead, the picture he presented was that of a dutiful, if somewhat unimaginative, officer who kept his head down and followed the routine orders of his superiors:

> I was never asked for my views on security policy outside my own Brigade area. I knew nothing about political decisions which governed security policy and very little about the situation elsewhere in the Province [*sic*].[26]

This was misleading for he had often shared his views on security policy with his superiors. He had, for example, supported Farrar-Hockley's proposal to extend the duration of the tours undertaken by the battalions that visited Northern Ireland, so they could better get to grips with the challenges they faced. Indeed, he may have originated this policy. He had advocated just this type of approach in *Low Intensity Operations*.

He had also learned a lesson from the Falls Road Curfew fiasco and had exerted his influence with his superiors to prevent a repeat occurrence. When an operation was suggested for a large-scale search of Ardoyne, he opposed it. His opposition was noted in London and prompted a response 'that although small-scale, routine searches should continue; no major, large-scale operation was to be mounted without approval from Whitehall'.[27]

He also played down any interest, let alone involvement,

in Derry claiming he was only aware of it in 'very general terms':[28]

> I was not particularly aware of it that I can remember. I mean, if you had asked me on 5th January 1972 what was going on in Londonderry, I might have known a bit more than I can remember.[29]

Why did Kitson try to write himself out of the history of the counter-insurgency campaign in Northern Ireland? When compared to his writings on Kenya, Malaya and Oman, it was most uncharacteristic. No such bashfulness is to be found in his books *Gangs and Countergangs* and *A Bunch of Five* which addressed his earlier career. Clearly, he had a compelling motive for downplaying his true role in Ireland.

Another issue he distorted was the nature and behaviour of the troops he trained in Northern Ireland. The most ferocious of these were the troops of 1 Para who were stationed at Palace Barracks.[30] Kitson used 1 Para as a reserve unit in his brigade area, sending it out to support the other battalions when the going for them got tough. Kitson would have us believe that they behaved faultlessly. Accounts provided by them, however, paint quite the opposite picture, and a disturbing one at that.

7

COLLECTIVE PUNISHMENT

In his book, *Low Intensity Operations*, Kitson wrote:

> however great the restrictions imposed on the use of force by soldiers, every effort should be made to retain the respect and awe of the civilian community for the ultimate in terms of force which they might use. If an impression can be built up that although the troops have used little force so far, they might at any moment use a great deal more, the people will be wary and relatively fewer men will be needed. Admittedly an element of bluff is involved and one of the most difficult tasks facing a military commander is to get the maximum value out of it without having the bluff called. But risks have to be taken when countering non-violent subversion in the same way as they do in other forms of warfare, and it is up to the officers of the army to study carefully how best to take them.[1]

Low Intensity Operations was written before he arrived in Ireland. Ominously, his tour of duty did not alter his perspective on this issue. In his 1977 book he described how the starting point in the army's relationship with the civilian community should be that the troops were to be respected, and if necessary 'feared'.[2] In Belfast, 1 Para became a violent instrument of utter dread.

As noted earlier regarding Malaya, Kitson had embraced the collective punishment of a community where its members were deemed to be affording assistance to insurgents.[3] He expanded upon this in his 1977 book revealing his view that conditions could be made 'reasonably uncomfortable for the population as a whole, in order to provide an incentive for a return to normal life and to act as a deterrent towards a resumption of the campaign'.[4]

In an Irish context Kitson may have viewed the MRF as his 'rod or net', whereas 1 Para was the poison that he could pour into the water to punish the wider Nationalist community and thereby discourage support for the IRA. It is hard to conjure up another explanation for 1 Para's behaviour while Kitson was in command.

1 Para was a reserve regiment without a particular territory to call its own. When it turned up, its members all too frequently began to mete out violence with fists, boots and rifle butts. Vandalising Nationalists' homes was commonplace, as was fracturing teeth and stealing wallets during searches.

The behaviour of 1 Para was too much for some of Kitson's colleagues. During the summer of 1971, two commanding officers in Belfast asked Kitson's HQ to keep 1 Para away from their patches.[5] Yet, when asked about this at the Saville Inquiry, Kitson replied:

> So far as I can remember none of the deployed battalions that took companies of 1 Para under command complained to me of the way in which they carried out their duties. I felt that I was lucky to have 1 Para.[6]

Kitson described 1 Para as 'an experienced and professional battalion in which' he had 'great confidence' and how, in his experience, 'they were entirely even handed as between the two religious communities'.[7] This statement does not stand up to scrutiny. Col Wilford, the man who commanded 1 Para, believed that virtually all Catholics were IRA supporters.[8]

According to Gen. Ford, while all three parachute

battalions were present in Northern Ireland at different times, the other two did not have the same reputation as the first battalion:

> 1 Para had been deliberately trained by Frank Kitson to develop this reputation – as a stabiliser – in his brigade area. So that when things went wrong they came and were tough. But they didn't break the rules.[9]

Kitson and Ford's favourable assessment was not shared by a number of former paratroopers in 1 Para who have put pen to paper. One of them, Byron Lewis, described how they sometimes treated soldiers from other regiments – 'crap hats'– with extreme violence and disdain:

> I was in the Anti-tank Platoon and can remember on several occasions groups of my friends waiting in ambush to jump on some helpless 'crap hat', be he a Fusiliers or whatever. I have seen blokes held by their thumbs from the top of the toilet door severely beaten and made to eat their own excrement. This was common practice. The guys I was with were excellent soldiers, rough as hell, often ignorant, nothing else existed other than being a paratrooper. In an unreal situation of violence any enemy would do …[10]

Michael Asher, author of *Shoot to Kill,* described the violence he witnessed while serving as a paratrooper in Belfast in the early 1970s. There were many fights in the barracks:

> They were what happens in most exclusively male societies: fights to determine the pecking order and who can boss who. But they weren't the only exotic form of entertainment. One group of soldiers would hold so-called 'gunge' contests. They sat around in a circle and tried to outdo each other in acts of gross obscenity, like eating shit and drinking urine.[11]

The paratroopers came to despise the Nationalist community:

> During house searches they vented their anger on their victims, smashing down doors and breaking up furniture, kicking and rifle-butting anyone who resisted, making lewd suggestions to the women of the house and threatening the children. Some of them tormented the quiet Pakistani in the [regimental] shop until he threw a chip-pan of boiling fat at them. They battered to death a stray cat that wandered past the OP and held up its mangled corpse to the children who came looking for it.[12]

Asher knew paratroopers who were truly scraped from the bottom of the barrel:

> Several of them boasted of dragging a mentally deficient girl into the OP and forcing her to perform oral sex. They said she enjoyed it.[13]

Another ex-paratrooper, Harry McCallion, wrote about the mind-set of his colleagues in his book *Killing Zone*. He hailed from Glasgow and had joined the Parachute Regiment in 1970. Brutality was instilled in him from the outset:

> We were never left in any doubt about our primary role in life: to kill. On one simulated exercise we ambushed a patrol of terrorists, one of whom dropped near my feet, apparently wounded. I was told by the training major to interrogate him. I did and managed to get the location of the enemy base from him. I rejoined my ambush party.
>
> 'What are you going to do to him?' asked the training major.
>
> I hesitated and he kicked me in the ribs so hard I was bruised for weeks.
>
> 'You kill him. You understand? Kill him. We'll have no squeamishness here.'
>
> I shot him with my blank ammunition. It was a lesson I learned well.[14]

McCallion recounts another story which, had it come from anyone but a military insider, would defy belief. On 7 August 1971, a man called Harry Thornton was shot dead by paratroopers in Belfast after his van had backfired. Thornton had a passenger who was beaten up. One of the paratroopers kept a memento of the event: a piece of Thornton's skull; worse still, he used it as an ashtray.[15]

Asher felt the brutality of their training combined with the friction in Belfast transformed them into savages. They became 'a hurricane of human brutality ... a caste of warrior-janizaries[16] who worshipped on the high altar of violence and wanted nothing more'.[17]

According to him, the paratroopers itched for trouble.

> Often, standing for hours in the sopping rain, bored to death by the routine and the lack of action, we prayed for something to happen: for someone to shoot at us, for someone to make trouble. But the hours passed, and everything was stultifyingly normal. Our greatest dream was that the IRA would come out in the street and fight us like a proper army. But they were far too clever for that. Instead, we had to make do with shouting abuse at women and clipping the ears of the cheeky urchins who walked by us in the streets. The NCOs bore down on us to keep us in line.[18]

Yet, to Kitson, these soldiers were a fine bunch of men. He told the Saville Inquiry:

> I do not think that the Parachute Regiment in general or 1 PARA in particular went about their duties in an excessively forceful way and on many occasions members of the Regiment exhibited a natural compassion, comforting and assisting the victims of bombs and riots.[19]

If we were to believe Kitson, 1 Para should be remembered for having been 'heavily involved in community relations'.[20]

The Saville Inquiry was interested to learn how Kitson's 'tactics, special training and general philosophy impacted on the mind-set' of the troops who had fired on the unarmed citizens of Derry on 30 January 1972.[21] He deflected this probe by suggesting that the troops under his command probably did not think much about him. This contrasts sharply with what Gen. Michael Jackson, then serving as a captain and adjutant to the commander of 1 Para, Col Derek Wilford, stated when he described the awe in which he was held.[22]

Kitson was at pains to portray himself as someone who had been keen to ensure that his troops observed the letter of the law. There was no mention of the MRF which had been supplied with machine guns and put on the streets of Belfast to kill. Instead, Saville was told that:

> When a battalion arrived in Belfast I met and spoke to as many of the men as possible either with the whole battalion assembled or, where this was not possible, to the companies individually … I would then say briefly what the aims of the various groups in Northern Ireland were and explain what we were trying to do in order to establish law and order while the politicians were working out the longer term future. Throughout I would stress the need to keep law abiding people on our side and to pursue law breakers vigorously whilst keeping within the law ourselves.[23]

The activities of the paratroopers, however, while violent and reprehensible, did not represent the nadir of the clandestine counter-insurgency effort in Ireland. Far worse horrors lay in store for random members of the Nationalist community in Belfast.

8

Military intelligence Assets in the UDA

Kitson, Carver and Tuzo were of a mind to confront the IRA, and only the IRA. Carver revealed in his memoirs that 'a direct armed clash between the army and the UDA, when the former was already facing the IRA, was not a situation that anybody wished to provoke'.[1]

On 9 July 1972, Tuzo submitted a paper suggesting that the British government should 'acquiesce in unarmed UDA patrolling and barricading of Protestant areas. Indeed, it was arguable that Protestant areas could be almost entirely secured by a combination of UDA, Orange Volunteers and RUC.'[2] He also suggested that they be allowed retain weapons in the districts they controlled. Tuzo's views were aligned to those outlined in Volume III of the MoD's 1969 *Land Operations* which had advocated, 'Liaison with, and organisation of, friendly guerrilla forces operating against the common enemy'.[3]

On 1 February 1973, Eugene 'Paddy' Heenan, a fifty-year-old married Catholic with five children, became the victim of an appalling example of an operation involving 'friendly guerrilla forces'. Heenan, a builder, was on his way to work on a bus with fourteen colleagues when it drew to a halt at Kingsway Park to allow a man with what appeared to be a sore leg shuffle across the road. Suddenly, he turned and threw a paint pot at the bus while an accomplice broke a window with a hammer. After that, Albert 'Ginger' Baker lobbed a grenade through the broken glass killing Heenan and injuring many of his fellow passengers.

In July 1976 members of Baker's family revealed to the *Sunday World* that he had had a relationship with British military intelligence. Recently a former military officer who worked at Thiepval Barracks and read some files relating to him has confirmed that he was indeed a British agent designated with the codename 'Broccoli'.[4] What puts the matter beyond dispute is that in the 1980s Baker admitted to Ken Livingstone, former MP and lord mayor of London, that he had worked with undercover British military officers.[5]

Born in East Belfast, Baker earned his nickname 'Ginger' after the drummer of the rock band Cream. In March 1970, at the age of nineteen, he joined the Royal Irish Rangers in Belfast. He was sent for training in Ballymena, where he won prizes as a crack shot. From there he went to Warminster in England, where the Regiment's 2nd Battalion was based.

He returned to Belfast at some stage in 1972 to find a flourishing UDA taking control of Loyalist parts of Belfast. At his trial a year later, his counsel told the court that: 'He got into the company of UDA men and found that they had plenty of money. He was tempted to get money and joined the organisation.' He gained entry to the UDA by impressing some of its members in Belfast with his bravado during a bar robbery. He also exploited his army experience to train UDA volunteers. Soon he became a member of the

East Belfast UDA's so-called No. 1 Assassination Team led by Ned McCreery.

The man in charge of UDA assassinations was its vice chairman, Tommy Herron, a former security guard, who was a leading member of its Inner Council. Herron was acting in liaison with British military intelligence, probably an offshoot of the MRF or some other covert branch of intelligence controlled by 39 Brigade in conjunction with the RUC. Herron, who had a criminal record, was given a legal permit to carry a gun, ostensibly to protect himself.

Baker served as a bodyguard to the UDA's ruling 'Inner Council' when it met. He also protected Herron who sat on the body. By 1972, Herron enjoyed a high profile, often appearing on television. He ran for election as a Vanguard Unionist candidate in 1973. Baker has claimed that RUC officers provided Herron with guns, information and other assistance.

In a handwritten account Baker produced in 1986, he revealed that after his arrest in 1973, he had received a visit 'from Chief Insp. Carlyle and Det. Insp. Hamilton. I was questioned about the Vice Chairman of the Ulster Defence Association, Tommy Herron. I informed them that Tommy was the man directly responsible for all sectarian assassinations in and around Belfast as he was the person [whose] authority these assassinations were sanctioned by. You must remember that I am not [only] speaking about the assassinations I was involved in but all sectarian assassinations of Catholics'.[6] Baker described the activities of his gang as having included 'sectarian assassinations; armed robberies; riots; [and] the training of young Protestants to facilitate them to become the next generation of loyalist assassins ..."[7] In July 1988 Ken Livingstone interviewed Baker. During the interview, he explained how he had been recruited:

> **A.B.** I have never mentioned it to anyone before but as far as I and other members of the UDA were concerned, we were operating for the UDA, but we had close links with the British Intelligence Services.
>
> **K.L.** Do you remember any names?
>
> **A.B.** M was an operator. He was working for the British Intelligence Services.
>
> **K.L.** What makes you so certain of that?
>
> **A.B.** It was Tommy Herron, he told me and a couple of others to contact the British Intelligence controller who was a man named 'B'. We only knew his name as 'B', but the other one was M.
>
> **K.L.** Did you ever meet them?
>
> **A.B.** I met 'M' and we used to go to the centre of Belfast, then York Street, to a telephone kiosk and he phoned 'B', the controller. Other officers[8] in the inner circle of the UDA contacted 'B'.[9]

'B' was known to Baker as 'Capt. Bunty'. While no such person as 'Bunty' was listed as serving in Belfast at the time, there was a captain with a remarkably similar name who was listed as a 'Special Regular Officer' with the Army Education Corps.

***

Baker's first murder took place on 18 August 1972. Philip Anthony Faye, a twenty-one-year-old waiter, had been serving the Inner Council, at the Girton Lodge Hotel. He originally came from County Cavan in the Irish Republic. During his interview with Livingstone, Baker said:

> So the Inner Council was in this room and Faye came in with drinks. Tommy Herron found out the geezer was a Catholic and

ordered his assassination in case he'd overheard anything. I went down to Island Street and assassinated him.[10]

Faye was sleeping when Baker knocked on the door of his home at Island Street in the predominately Protestant East Belfast at about 3 a.m. After he opened it, Baker asked if he was a Catholic. When he replied in the affirmative, Baker told him to turn round and shot him twice in the back of the head with his .32 Browning automatic. As he lay dying on the ground, Baker fired three more rounds into the area below his ear.

Baker and his associates became known as the 'Romper Room Gang' after the torture chambers to which they took their victims. The venues were named after a television programme for children. Typically, they were located inside disused buildings, lock-up garages or rooms above pubs and drinking clubs. Once inside, a victim would be beaten and tortured as a prelude to murder. Baker was an active participant in a string of these gruesome murders. Davey Payne, a UDA brigadier, started this practice of kidnap, torture and murder.[11]

The second murder involving Baker took place on 26 September 1972 when Paul McCartan, a fifty-two-year-old barman was abducted by a UDA patrol as he made his way along the Newtownards Road in East Belfast. The gang went to a UDA club, where he was questioned about his religion. He was tortured, hooded and shot three times in the head by Baker.

The next assassination took place on 3 October 1972. It was purposeful as opposed to random. The victim was James

Patrick McCartan, a twenty-two-year-old forklift truck driver. Baker told Livingstone:

> He was interrogated. He was supposedly in the IRA. This was information passed on by Special Branch and CID officers to a UDA commander. We were sitting in a bar when we were told to drive off to the Park Avenue Hotel. We took him out of the hotel, interrogated him and then assassinated him.
>
> 'C' of CID and [the Conservative Party Secretary of State William] Whitelaw's special squad used to give us files. They were like a deck of cards. They were all joined together and there were photographs of every Republican. I used to sit and drink with 'C'. Half the assassinations in Northern Ireland in the early 1970s wouldn't have been committed without RUC backing. Half the people who died in those assassinations would be alive today if the RUC hadn't supported the assassination teams. The RUC knew the assassination teams – every single one of them.[12]

What happened to McCartan was far more gruesome than Baker's description suggests. McCartan had been at a disco at the Park Avenue Hotel. When he left, he was in the company of a girl. They were punched and kicked by Baker's gang who had lain in wait for him outside, but the pair managed to retreat back inside. McCartan tried to leave a while later with a Protestant friend, but Baker and his goons set upon him again. One of them told his Protestant friend: 'You have nothing to worry about, we [just] want McCartan …' before dragging him away.

Ned McCreery ordered the gang to take McCartan to a club with a 'Romper Room'. One was available at the back of a UDA club in Clermont Lane. According to testimony at Baker's trial, several UDA members and their girlfriends arrived to drink and watch the slow torture of McCartan.

He was conveyed around a number of 'romper rooms' in the Newtownards Road area – specifically in Finmore Street and Clermont Lane that night. He was stripped naked, hung up by the ankles and subjected to lengthy torture sessions at each club. At one stage, he was kicked and beaten with a pickshaft, while a dagger was used to stab him in the hands and thigh. All told, he received approximately 200 stab wounds. At one point during his ordeal, he was threatened with castration and dropped head first from the ceiling. McCreery finally gave Baker a pistol and told him to kill McCartan. The gang tied his hands behind his back and placed a bag over his head. He was taken to the Connswater River, where Baker shot him dead. 'I was probably asked because I had already killed one man with a pistol, or maybe because I had training with small arms and the British army', Baker said later.

McCartan's unrecognisable body was found on waste ground. Baker maintained McCartan was a wanted Republican based on the RUC information. In reality, he had no paramilitary connections.

McCreery was involved in another killing on 2 December, 1972. Baker was not part of it this time. The victim was later described as 'retarded', a thirty-two-year-old Catholic called Patrick Benstead from the Short Strand in Belfast. The coroner described it as the most horrifying he had ever dealt with. Evidence was given that his naked body had been found on the street with a cross burned onto his back. It had been put there with a hot iron. The word 'IRA' was burned onto him. There were other burn marks on his body, hands and feet. He was shot through the head after his ordeal.

The guns that Baker claims the RUC supplied to his gang came from Mountpottinger RUC station in the Short Strand, Belfast. Some of them were used during an attack on the Red Lion Bar near the Albert Clock in the centre of Belfast, which was carried out in the hope of assassinating a suspected IRA man. However, a police Land Rover had chanced by and the attack was abandoned. The weapons were handed to an RUC detective who was waiting in a civilian car in a nearby carpark. From here, Baker claimed, the detective drove the weapons back to East Belfast, where he returned them to Baker and his men. They had travelled across the city without any fear of being stopped and searched. Baker told Livingstone:

> ... the guns were taken and put in 'C's car and he drove them through the police and army checkpoints back to East Belfast where he handed them back to us. The assassination was carried out later using police guns and Sterling submachine guns.[13]

Adding general credence to these claims, Colin Wallace recalls 'a number of allegations in the 1970s that the RUC gave surrendered firearms to Loyalists, including William McGrath'.[14] McGrath was involved with the UVF, UDA and ran his own paramilitary group called Tara.

***

By the end of February 1973, Baker had become disillusioned with the UDA and returned to his regiment in England where he was later court-martialled and discharged.

Declassified British Army records help to confirm that Baker was a contact, if not a fully-fledged agent, of military intelligence. On 24 May 1973, Maj.-Gen. Frank King, the new GCO NI, met with the vice chief of the General Staff (VCGS), Sir David Fraser, in London. The record of the meeting reveals that: 'We have now got good intelligence on [Tommy] and the Protestant extremists'. As a bodyguard to the Inner Council, Baker was ideally placed to supply this information.[15] The fact that the army had 'good intelligence' on Herron indicates that they did not control him. Hence, he appears to have been more an ally than an agent.[16]

The document also reveals that Fraser brought GOC King 'up to date and discussed the problem of the protection of the "source of their information", someone designated "Agent Broccoli".' Again, Baker perfectly fits the bill as the 'source'. He certainly would have required 'protection' from his erstwhile UDA colleagues who by then must have suspected he was a spy after he disappeared from Belfast.

What King and Fraser did not know when they were having their discussion on 24 May 1973, was that Baker had, or was about to, walk into Warminster police station and confess to his crimes. The Warminster constabulary alerted the RUC and two RUC officers at Taunton police station interviewed Baker. After this, he was taken back to Belfast and held at Mountpottinger RUC Station, where he was questioned further.

Presumably, only a select number of the RUC knew about the use of Loyalist terrorists as allies and proxy assassins on behalf of British military intelligence. There was no love lost between many in the RUC and the UDA. The first RUC officer to be killed during the Troubles was Victor

Arbuckle who perished during a Loyalist riot in October 1970 involving many figures who became UDA leaders. Also, in the early 1970s, the UDA and RUC engaged in a number of violent street confrontations. Against this background, the RUC commenced the investigation of Baker's case in a normal fashion.

***

After his arrest, Baker made a number of allegations of collusion between named members of the RUC and Loyalist paramilitaries. These involved the theft of weapons by RUC officers from Mountpottinger RUC station in Belfast which were handed over to the UDA. In his handwritten account Baker described how, when he was being brought to Chichester Street Magistrates Court on one occasion, he:

> noticed a U.D.A. deep penetration officer who was also a member of the [RUC] Inner Circle Murder Squad. I turned back into my cell and pushed the door to. Sergeant McCoy observed that I was worried and agitated ... I informed him that one of his officers was a U.D.A. man and I was afraid of being driven into U.D.A. ambush. Well he was thunder-struck and told me not to worry ...[17]

Baker's handwritten account states that, 'This officer is B__ C____, who associated with Jim McC____ a lieutenant in the U.D.A ... Chief Inspector C_____ impetuously told me to keep quiet on this matter and say nothing to anyone else about it'.[18]

When he returned to Crumlin Road jail, Baker received a visit from Sgt McCoy and another RUC officer who had been a 'schoolfriend'. During the encounter he named another RUC officer who was colluding with the UDA while McCoy was questioning him 'about these missing weapons and asked me how I knew, I informed him, I [had seen the] RUC officer hand them over to Tommy Herron the Vice Chairman of the Ulster Defence Association at UDA headquarters. I was then asked by Sergeant McCoy if I would speak to the RUC corruption squad and I said I would [do so] willingly. Later I received a couple of visits from the RUC corruption squad and made a statement about Insp Mc_____ an RUC uniformed officer who handed over a sterling submachine-gun in the UDA headquarters to Tommy Herron. I do not think any action was ever taken against Insp Mc_____...'[19]

The picture that emerges here is one of a regular RUC team which continued to investigate his crimes, until they encountered a force more powerful than them. Such a power could have emanated from people such as King, Fraser and their subordinates, not to mention MI5 and MI6.

In August 1973, Baker was charged with eleven robberies, a number of firearms offences and the murder of four Catholics.

On 16 September 1973, a loose intelligence end was disposed of when Loyalist opponents murdered Herron as part of an internal UDA feud. Ian Paisley led prayers outside his home on the day of his funeral. According to Baker's handwritten account:

> I also informed the RUC that Tommy Herron was to be assassinated before I was sentenced ... I did not tell the RUC how I knew about his pending assassination nor was my evidence ever mentioned during the Coroner's Court Hearing.[20]

Baker's trial was the first to be heard before the Diplock courts which sat without juries. He pleaded guilty and, on 15 October 1973, was given a life sentence with a minimum of twenty-five years to be served. He was immediately taken to Musgrave Park Military Hospital, and from there to Aldergrove Airport, and finally to Wandsworth Prison in England. His family were also removed from Northern Ireland and resettled in northern England. None of the dirty linen linking the UDA to military intelligence emerged in court.

In February 1974, Baker gave evidence against McCreery and six other UDA men he had identified as participants in the torture of one of the men he had murdered. Again, he said nothing about 'Capt. Bunty' or British military intelligence or RUC complicity in the activities of his gang. The trial judge rejected his evidence as it was uncorroborated and because he was an accomplice in the crime. After the acquittal, McCreery and three of the other defendants were rearrested outside the court and interned.

Baker was released in 1992 and has maintained a low profile ever since.

***

On 27 April 2015, Kitson was cited as a co-defendant, along with the MoD, in an action taken by Mary Heenan, the widow of Eugene Heenan. Her action accuses the defendants of negligence and misfeasance in office on account of 'the use of Loyalist paramilitary gangs to contain the Republican-Nationalist threat through terror, manipulation of the rule of law, infiltration and subversion, all core to the Kitson military doctrine endorsed by the British army and the British government at the time'.

'I wasn't a policy maker', Kitson protested in response to the suit, 'I was a commander of troops. I have absolutely no knowledge of Mr. Heenan and I had gone from Ireland at the time of his death'.[21]

Kitson is correct in saying that he had left Ireland by the time Baker started killing people in Belfast. What is important, however, is what he knows about the relationship between the British military intelligence officers in Belfast under his command and Herron. It was Herron who was behind the UDA's assassination programme. It was Herron who put Baker in touch with 'Capt. Bunty'. What Kitson knows about this officer will be of great interest. At the time of writing, the Heenan case has yet to be heard.

9

PSYOPS

More than anyone at 39 Brigade, Kitson appreciated the value of the corrosive mind games the Psychological Operations [PSYOPs] teams across the field from him at Lisburn played with the IRA. The media manipulation programme they had set up had grown into a powerful locomotive which pulled a lethargic British and Irish media in its wake, often smothering the truth with the smoke of black propaganda.

In *Bunch of Five,* he explained the importance of ensuring that insurgents did not win the 'war for the minds of the people'.[1]

Kitson had regular meetings with the senior staff at Lisburn. Occasionally, after them 'he would call at my office for a brief chat', recalls Colin Wallace, the psychological warfare specialist from County Antrim, who had an office on the ground floor of the building. No one at Lisburn had his finger fixed more firmly on the pulse of what the press was thinking than Wallace. Part of his job was to monitor how they reacted to events, especially military initiatives. On these occasions, Kitson would pick Wallace's brain. 'As an individual, I do not fault him. Unlike some senior officers, he never summonsed me over to his side of the field. I had an old red armchair in the office and he would normally sit down in it before raising whatever issue he wanted to discuss. Usually, his questions related to how the press were responding to something, or what my view was on something. He was a very analytical thinker and would normally question what he was being told. I got the feeling that he would have little time for those who attempted to tell him what they thought he wanted to hear. It was very difficult, if not impossible, to work out what he was thinking, but, like him or dislike him, no one who talked to him would be left in any doubt about his total commitment to his role.'

Insofar as PSYOPs were concerned, Wallace recalls that he had 'a real interest in the information war and was very aware of what we [in the Information Policy Unit (IPU)] were doing. He was very conscious of the need to influence the public mind. Mainly, he did the listening. I always knew I had his rapt attention. He took everything in. He was a no-nonsense type of guy, a tough cookie. He used our encounters to test out ideas he was developing. If something was wrong, or wasn't likely to work, he wanted to know. I got on well with him. He had a thirst for knowledge and always wanted to get to the bottom of things'.

Farrar-Hockley was another officer who paid visits to Colin Wallace to discuss the information war.[2]

Kitson was directly involved in the dissemination of black propaganda about the people his troops were killing on the streets of Belfast. Simon Winchester, then a young *Guardian* journalist, has described how, after shooting incidents, he would often call Kitson. The brigadier, he revealed, was his 'principal contact at army headquarters'.

So I would drive to Lisburn, gates would open, sentries would salute, escorts would appear and by 11 o'clock I would be sitting before the dapper little brigadier, all brass, red flashes and obsequious batmen, while he explained the intelligence files, the special branch files, the electronic intercept files on the victim. I would write it all down, thank the good brigadier for yet another small scoop, race back out from Lisburn, screech to a halt outside the BBC studios on Ormeau Road.

When Winchester would appear on radio, he would tell his audience 'more or less exactly' what Kitson had told him, e.g:

the dead man had been the quartermaster/acting section leader/ordnance expert/senior marksman in an active service unit of C company or A company of the 14th Armagh or 9th Monaghan battalion of 2 Div or 6 Div of the Provisional IRA. And his death was a significant blow/stunning setback/mortal wound/lucky break, and would set the IRA's fighting ability back a week/month/year or, more likely, not one whit.

Winchester came to realise he had been misled by the wily Kitson because 'the army's intelligence was so rudimentary in those days ... that most of what I gaily rebroadcast was, if not a pure figment of the imagination of some superheated British army intelligence officer, then to a very large degree, wishful thinking'.[3]

Unlike most UK papers, the *Guardian* was a high value target for Kitson's machinations. Winchester had pondered why Kitson selected him as the *Guardian* was 'after all ... the enemy'.

Army memoranda came to light during the Bloody Sunday inquiry which referred 'official "disappointment"' that despite the best efforts of some, Winchester had been 'lost' and 'never recovered' – that he had remained critical of British army behaviour, and 'had refused to fall in with the line more often written for the readers of the conservative papers'.

Winchester suspects – and he is undoubtedly correct – that Kitson picked him because his reports 'would perhaps seem more credible, coming from a source less evidently tainted'. Winchester was unduly harsh on himself by adding the comment that by 'appearing so regularly on the radio, and offering a message that in fact was the message of the British army, I was for a brief while, very tainted indeed'.

Significantly, Kitson's manoeuvrings reveal that he was fully aware that his troops were killing at least some innocent people on an on-going basis. Why else would he have had to invent lies about them?

***

Some of the PSYOPs from this time are well-known. On 21 October 1971, the front page of the *Daily Mirror* ran with a headline claiming IRA HIRE RED KILLERS. Readers were informed that a 'Czech assassin' had been 'shot by troops' in Derry. 'The gunman had ambushed an infantry patrol. The troops stalked him and cornered him in a graveyard.' The source of the story was an anonymous 'Army Officer in Northern Ireland'. The killer had been 'dressed all in black' and had used a 'Czechoslovak rifle' to fire at the soldiers before being 'killed by a soldier from the 1st Battalion of the Royal Green Jackets'. Troops were ordered 'not to talk about the incident'.[4] This was fanciful nonsense: the sad truth was that the man they killed was a British photographer from West London who had been mistaken for a sniper.

Another opportunity to promote a fictitious Soviet-IRA link presented itself after a routine RAF maritime reconnaissance patrol spotted a Soviet conventional submarine which had broken down on the surface of the sea somewhere off Scandinavia. Pictures that were taken for strategic intelligence purposes found their way to MI6 and the IRD who realised their potential for black propaganda. They were sent to a Belgian news agency via one of their agents in the press. The pictures were sold to the *News of the World*, which put them on their front page in 1972. *Russia In IRA Plot Sensation* the headline declared. Readers were told that three KGB trained agents had been dropped off the coast of Donegal. The story was 'corroborated' by 'intelligence sources' and revealed that the Soviets planned to 'turn Ireland into a Kremlin-controlled Cuban-style republic'.

James Molyneux MP, leader of the Ulster Unionist Party (UUP), became a disciple of the story, maintaining for years afterwards that the Kremlin was supporting the IRA. The article had no discernible impact among the Nationalist community.

A smear story with more potential to inflict a wound began on 13 May 1972 when soldiers in Belfast arrested Louis Hammond, a Royal Irish Ranger deserter, at a barricade in the Slievegallion area of Andersonstown, West Belfast. Hammond, born in 1954, grew up in Andersonstown. Having joined the army in 1970, he disappeared after a visit home in 1972 and joined the IRA. He now opted to become an MRF agent instead of facing charges for desertion and IRA membership. After the IRA lifted two other MRF agents, Seamus Wright and Kevin McKee,[5] Hammond was spirited to Liverpool.[6] That should have been the end of Hammond's entanglement with the intelligence services. Hugh Mooney, however, an IRD officer who had been sent to Northern Ireland, drew him into an operation to sow dissent within the Provisional IRA. Mooney's plan was to plant stories that Republican leaders were embezzling the proceeds of IRA robberies.

A document was prepared which was made to appear as if a senior IRA prisoner held in Long Kesh had written it. The plan was to pretend that the security forces had intercepted it. It was addressed to the IRA's Belfast commander, Seamus Twomey, and named IRA members who had allegedly misappropriated funds. The forgery was passed to the journalist Chris Ryder, who alerted *The Sunday Times* in London. The paper assigned Ryder and Paul Eddy, another journalist, to investigate the story.

Hammond was brought back into play and ordered to contact Ryder and reveal he had been the Intelligence Officer of the Provisional IRA's E Company in Riverdale and was prepared to sell him information about IRA embezzlement. To Ryder, it appeared that Hammond was corroborating what was in the Long Kesh document.

Ryder published an article in *The Sunday Times* which quoted an unnamed former Intelligence Officer from E Company as the paper's source. The IRA quickly realised it was Hammond and ascertained that he was back in Belfast. He was lured to a house in the Markets district and interrogated for three days, after which he was shot three times in the head and once in the stomach. Somehow, he managed to survive, albeit partially paralysed and blind in one eye.

Ryder had been negligent in revealing that his information had come from a 'former Intelligence Officer from E Company'.

Following the publication of the story, the IRA considered killing Ryder. Ed Moloney has revealed on his Broken Elbow blog that they were talked out of this by a journalist – still alive and therefore unnamed – who advised them this would backfire on them by alienating the media. The intelligence services decided not to take any chance with Ryder's safety and moved him and his family to a house at Butlins Holiday Camp in Bognor Regis temporarily. They were then taken to Manchester for a number of years from where he continued to report on Northern Ireland.[7]

One of the reasons Mooney was pushed out of Northern Ireland by the Director and Co-ordinator of Intelligence (DCI) at the NIO was due to the Hammond fiasco. This happened despite Mooney's efforts then and later to distance himself from the debacle.

***

In early December 1971, Kitson became complicit in a media deception involving the worst atrocity to take place in Northern Ireland up to that point in time. He was implicated in a plot to blame the infamous attack on McGurk's Bar in Belfast on the IRA, when the UVF were responsible for it. Fifteen people died, including two children.

Broadly speaking, Colin Wallace points to the pressures with which Kitson had to cope to understand some of his transgressions, but offers no defence on this occasion. 'If I have a criticism of him,' he says, 'it relates to the McGurk's bar bombing. Why did Kitson, who was no shrinking violet, go along with the cover-up? Why did he not stand up and put a halt to the disinformation? Instead, he ordered the telephone operations room at 39 Brigade to direct queries to the RUC who were promoting the IRA "own goal" fabrication.'[8]

This was far from the last time that Kitson would play games with the truth.

10

Being Less than Frank

Since the early part of this century, Kitson has tried to minimise the role he played in policy formation in Ireland between 1970 and 1972.

For a start, he has tried to conceal his participation in the political dimension to his assignment to Northern Ireland. Yet, some of it has now come to light. In a paper he submitted to his superiors on 4 December 1971, he spoke of how operations in Belfast since internment 'have been carried out on the basis of so weakening the IRA that a future political initiative can be launched under favourable circumstances'.[1]

The document, which passed through the hands of the MoD and the Home Office, appears to have been withheld from the Saville Inquiry, or if it did acquire a copy of it, no use was made of it. Had it been produced to cross-examine Kitson, a more accurate portrait of the man might have emerged.

The fact that the British army was prepared to engage in a secret 'shoot to kill' programme against the IRA in 1972 via the MRF is something else that Kitson has never spoken about in public. Equally, he has said little or nothing about the inadequacies of the RUC. He did, however, mention both the MRF and RUC in his once secret 4 December 1971 paper. In it he described how:

Despite the clumsiness of the Security Forces machine good progress was made in September, October and November [1971], largely because both wings of the IRA were also clumsy, and indeed much too big for the purpose for which they were designed to fulfil. It is likely that having fined down the enemy organisation to the extent that we have done, future successes will be increasingly hard to achieve from an operational point of view, unless we are able to make our own organisation very much more efficient. As you know we are taking steps to do this in terms of building up and developing the MRF and we are also steadily improving the capability of [RUC] Special Branch by setting up cells in each Division manned by MIO/FINCOS and by building up Special Branch's records with Int Corps Sections.[2]

Carver not only shared Kitson's exasperation at the RUC, in his memoirs he wrote about how the military's frustration:

led to gradual and increasing pressure that it should rely less on [RUC] Special Branch and do more to obtain its own intelligence, a tendency I was initially reluctant to accept, all experience in colonial fields having been against this and in favour of total integration of police and military intelligence. However the inefficiency of the RUC Special Branch, its reluctance to burn its fingers again [after the Compton Report which had been critical of its methods], and the suspicion, more than once proved, that some of its members had close links with Protestant extremists, led me finally to the conclusion that there was no alternative.[3]

Despite all this, Kitson told the Saville Inquiry that at 'this time the Army relied on the RUC for intelligence ...'[4]

Other dubious claims continued to trip off his tongue at the Saville Inquiry. One need only recall how he had told it that he knew nothing about the 'political decisions which governed security policy' and very little about the 'situation elsewhere in the Province' (*sic*).[5] Yet, in addition to laying the security groundwork designed to lead to a 'political initiative', he deigned to furnish his views on various scenarios that might be adopted as a precursor to an 'ultimate union between the North and South of Ireland'.

Kitson pointed out the danger of allowing 'left-wing' elements take control of the situation via 'revolution'. All this from a man who swore on oath that he had no interest in anything beyond the area controlled by 39 Brigade. Kitson furnished the paper to either Tuzo or Ford, probably to the latter, as Kitson reported directly to him. According to Kitson, the purpose of his paper was 'to outline various possibilities and to elicit guidance'. A cynic could be forgiven for suspecting that one of the purposes of the paper was to plant the seeds of his own ideas in the heads of his superiors.

When the GOC and CLF met with Howard Smith, the UK Representative (UKREP) to Northern Ireland later that month, they mentioned Kitson's paper in the course of their discussion. (The UKREP was the equivalent to the head of the Northern Ireland Office before Direct Rule was introduced in 1972.) Ford subsequently furnished a copy of it to Smith. In turn, Smith forwarded it to Philip J. Woodfield at the Home Office in London, mentioning that he thought he would be 'interested to see' it and asked him to 'restrict it to the Department'.

Smith also drew attention to the first paragraph of Kitson's paper, which expressed 'a cautious view about prospects of success in dealing with the IRA'. Smith linked Kitson's concerns about this to a paper from the Joint Intelligence Committee that had addressed the 'current state of the IRA' and suggested that 'we have a long way to go on that front; I find the picture it presents a pretty gloomy one, and I shall probably be writing separately about that'.

Why was Kitson so coy at the Saville Inquiry decades later? Why did he strive to deny the policy concepts he developed and the influence he had commanded in the early 1970s?

Although not addressed in his 1971 paper, Kitson was aghast at what was going on in 'Free Derry' where the IRA was a law unto itself. So too were Gen. Ford and Col Derek Wilford, the commander of 1 Para. The prospect of wearing down the IRA to the point where they would be amenable to a political solution was unlikely to materialise while they enjoyed the freedom to make bombs untroubled by the police or army and then smuggle them out to attack the commercial heart of Derry city at will. It was against this background that a conspiracy entitled, *Operation Hailstone* came into being.

11

THE FAILURE OF *OPERATION HAILSTONE*

To the intense dissatisfaction of Carver, Tuzo, Ford and Kitson, the queen's writ did not extend into parts of Derry. 'Free Derry' came into existence at the end of the 'Battle of the Bogside' in August 1969 when Nationalists had brokered a truce with Lt-Col Todd of the British army. The Bogsiders had not fought the British army, rather the RUC and B Specials.[1] The agreement with Todd heralded a 'honeymoon period' during which the relations between Nationalists and British soldiers were harmonious. At the time, squaddies were seen as the saviours of the minority. By 1971, however, this period of relative calm had turned sour.

Militarily, the city was under the command of Brig. Alan Cowan of 8 Brigade. Since August 1969, parts of it had become largely off limits to the RUC and British army with thirty or more sturdy barricades acting as a *de facto* border. A Tricolour flew over the enclave. Behind the barricades, the two factions of the IRA, the Officials and Provisionals, sank their roots into the community. To the dismay of Unionists, the radius of the 'no-go' area seemed to be pushing outwards. The commercial heart of the city, which was largely run by businessmen loyal to Stormont, was being systematically reduced to rubble by IRA bombers who ventured forth at will from 'Free Derry'. Ford was under great pressure to bring about an end to the destruction.

The flashpoint in Derry was a piece of waste ground known as 'Aggro Corner' on the edge of the Bogside, which Mike Jackson recalled was 'openly patrolled by armed and hooded IRA men' while a 'community alert system' existed to 'mobilise the IRA to repel incursions by the Security Forces. Women would sound the alarm by banging dustbin lids. The Irish flag flew over "Free Derry", which to all intents and purposes was no longer part of the United Kingdom'.[2]

The army's street maps showed a big black dotted line, known as the 'containment line', beyond which the police and the army hardly ventured. As Jackson recalled, 'young hooligans considered it good sport to come in the early evening and "brass up" the troops holding the containment line, hurling stones and petrol bombs, anything they could find. This became known as the "5 o'clock follies".'[3]

Unlike Kitson, Jackson was not afraid to admit that he had been an observer of what was taking place in Derry:

> You could see it on television, night after night, soldiers wearing shin guards and carrying big shields, standing there and getting pelted. Some referred to these as matinee performances, because they seemed so obviously staged. As in Belfast, there were occasions in which snipers exploited such riots in order to fire at soldiers. On the very morning of Bloody Sunday, a young officer died of wounds received from such a sniper attack days before.[4]

When Kitson appeared at the Saville Inquiry in 2002, he was probed about the barricade dismantling tactics he had overseen in Belfast as compared to the softly, softly approach in Derry. An extract from *Brits: The War Against the IRA* by Peter Taylor was read out to him: 'With Kitson commanding the Army's 39 Brigade in Belfast, there was to be no nonsense.[5] When

Republican barricades went up, they were immediately taken down, giving the IRA no chance to seal off and make them no-go areas.' Kitson had no difficulty confirming the accuracy of this and added that the policy was to give Nationalists 'no chance to seal off and make them no-go areas ... we did not have places blocked in Belfast'.

Later, he was asked if another passage from Taylor's book was accurate: 'As far as [Kitson] was concerned there was no part of the realm in which the Queen's writ did not run, at least in the Belfast area that he controlled.' In response Kitson said:

> I did not think of it in those terms, I thought of it in terms of HQ Northern Ireland policy is not to allow barricades in Belfast or most of Ireland, in fact.

When it was suggested to him that the paratroopers 'plainly would have been aware that [the dismantling of barricades] was the policy in Belfast' and one endorsed by him, he replied:

> It was the policy throughout the Province (*sic*), exclusive of Londonderry, and of course it was endorsed by me, I could not have unendorsed it, it was Gen. Tuzo's policy. [6]

He did make a concession about the ferocity of 1 Para in dealing with the presence of Nationalist barricades. A quote attributed to Jackson, which appeared in Peter Taylor's book, was put to him:

> Those barricades would be defended by the IRA and their supporters. We would be going in to restore law and order and to remove the so-called 'no-go' areas and we would be resisted. It

is not a situation in which half-hearted measures are going to be successful. If they were half-hearted, you would be taking inordinate risks with the lives of your own soldiers. Belfast was run in a no-nonsense way.

The barrister asked him if this reflected what had 'been called the mind-set of the time, in Belfast by paratroopers?' Kitson replied:

It records the reality of the situation by all the battalions in Belfast ...

It is hardly likely that he felt any less hostile toward the 'no-go' area in Derry or that robust measures would not also have been appropriate to deal with the problems it too presented.

***

The businessmen in the city centre were warning Gen. Ford that the commercial heartland of the city was on the verge of collapse due to the IRA bomb campaign and that he had to act. Some of them wanted the army to sweep aside the barricades and occupy the Bogside and Creggan, implement a shoot-on-sight curfew and evict the 5,000 residents of the Rossville Flats. Ford knew that this was irrational. Instead, a subtler scheme, *Operation Hailstone*, evolved to lure the IRA out of the 'no-go' area so that British soldiers could crush them. It was formulated under the auspices of 8 Brigade but was handed over to 1 Para to implement. This notwithstanding the fact 1 Para was assigned to 39 Brigade area.

The plan was to entice the rioters into a trap. Two 'reinforcing battalions' were to be transported to Derry where a 'target area' would be established.[7] Under the heading 'Peripheral Operations', the order prescribed that: 'Units must be prepared to deal instantly with gunmen who may try to interfere with the operation.'

Ominously, the order stated that if 'in the event, there are no "spontaneous" attacks on Bligh's Lane during the evening and night of 17/18 July, it will be necessary for 1RS [i.e. the 1st Battalion of the Royal Scots][8] to offer targets or to arrange circumstances which will lure mobs into the target area and attract gunmen to the periphery'.[9]

Operation Hailstone commenced on 17 July and drifted over to the next day. According to Jackson, the hooligans and IRA did not raise their heads above the parapet. A week before Bloody Sunday, Jackson spoke about it to journalists from the *Sunday Times*. According to their notes, he said *Hailstone* had been aimed at arresting rioters but:

> The bloody July [1971] operation never got off the ground, an officer [i.e. Jackson] recalled ... We were sitting up behind the reservoirs and they kept putting it back 30 minutes and another 30 minutes until it was dark. We could not get the yobbos out. They had been throwing stones for weeks, but as soon as we turned up our luck goes. According to the Para officer his men tried very hard last July to provoke confrontation. We tried a bit of Aggro Corner searches and things to bring them out. But they were not falling for it.[10]

When the quote from *Sunday Times* was put to Jackson at the Saville Inquiry the he tendered a more circumspect characterisation of *Hailstone* alleging:

> All I can say is that in general terms there was a feeling that Londonderry was getting out of control. This was not only a feeling

of 1 Para, but a feeling in political, media and military circles generally. I cannot recall saying anything like this .. there was no attempt to provoke confrontation in the July 1971 operation. It was simply an abortive arrest operation. If such things were said by me then I suspect they were the bravado of a young officer ....[11]

Kitson professed to have no memory of *Operation Hailstone*. The Saville Inquiry had written to him asking about it:

Paratroopers were in 'Derry' on 17/18 July and conducted what was described at the time by Ivan Cooper MP as a 'high powered campaign of provocation carefully calculated in my opinion to outrage the entire Catholic Community'. The climax of this campaign came on Saturday 17 July when the soldiers searched twenty houses in the Creggan and Bogside. What comments does Sir Frank Kitson have in relation to Ivan Cooper's comments?[12]

Kitson's written response was:

I have no knowledge of the operation that took place in London-derry on 17/18 July 1971, which is not surprising as it took place outside my operational area. I do not know Ivan Cooper MP and cannot comment on his comments.

***

The situation in Derry deteriorated after *Operation Hailstone*. On 10 August 1971, in the wake of the turmoil created by the introduction of internment, Bombardier Paul Challenor, of the Royal Horse Artillery became the first British soldier shot dead in the city as he repaired a perimeter fence at Bligh's Lane observation post. A shot from a .303 rifle took his life moments after a car carrying a group of IRA men drove by warning pedestrians to keep away.

In an attempt to dampen the smouldering fires, Gen. Tuzo and UKREP Smith met with a delegation of promi-nent Nationalists, all moderates, at a hotel outside the city towards the end of August. In response to complaints from the delegation about the conduct of the British army, Tuzo offered to halt all military operations for one month if they could deliver peace.

The delegation did not represent the IRA but it was agreed that they would use their influence to see if they could procure a truce and they enjoyed a modicum of success. In response, the British army began to ignore the barricades and the sniping against the British soldiers diminished, although the bombing campaign in the commercial centre of the city continued.

By the late summer of 1971, Ford acknowledged bleakly that the security forces were facing 'an entirely hostile Catholic community'.[13]

The peace initiative collapsed completely on 6 September after locals blamed the British army for shooting a fourteen-year-old girl, Annette McGavigan. More than 10,000 mourners attended her funeral. The rioting that followed her burial lasted for several days.

Col Wilford, commander of 1 Para, gave the Saville Inquiry the impression he knew nothing about *Operation Hailstone* as it occurred 'before his time'. Wilford, a lean fit 38-year-old, led 1 Para during the Ballymurphy massacre in August 1971 and in Derry on Bloody Sunday. He had served with the SAS for two years and trained with American paratroopers at Fort Bragg, the US Army Special Forces School. He was also a veteran of Malaya and Aden. In 1969, he had joined the Parachute Regiment as a company commander. Perceived as a bit of a loner, he was given to reading books including the classics in their original Latin. What Wilford did not stress was that he took over 1 Para on 21 July 1971, literally days after the failure of *Operation Hailstone*. It is difficult to accept that he did not read himself into his brief and talk at length to his commanders about the situation on the ground. It is unlikely in the extreme that he possessed no curiosity about the strength of the IRA outside 39 Brigade area. Nonsensically, this would also mean that he never spoke to his adjutant, Capt. Jackson, who was talking so freely to the press about *Hailstone*. Jackson sat right outside his office and assisted Wilford in every step he took at Palace Barracks. The alternative is that Wilford was lying about his lack of knowledge of *Hailstone*. If so, what was there to hide about the tactics which underpinned it, that inspired such deceit? It is not fanciful to speculate that he did not want to acknowledge in public that 1 Para had gone to Derry on a mission to 'attract' IRA 'gunmen to the periphery' and take them on in open battle. That was precisely what some accuse 1 Para of having done on Bloody Sunday, when the Support Company of 1 Para slaughtered thirteen unarmed citizens in a cynical and pitiless attempt to provoke the IRA to react in kind.

Wilford's dubious account of his lack of knowledge about *Hailstone* at the Saville Inquiry was as follows:

> I have been asked by Eversheds [for the inquiry] about previous 1 PARA Londonderry operations. As far as I can recall the Battalion had been alerted for a previous operation in Londonderry, but what it was I do not know as it predated my command. My recollection is that elements of the Battalion made a reconnaissance; I do not think the Battalion was in the event deployed to Londonderry.[14]

The last sentence was entirely erroneous for 1 Para had in fact been deployed to Derry where they had, *inter-alia*, conducted provocative house searches.

In Belfast, meanwhile, Kitson, Wilford and 1 Para were about to learn that they could shoot non-combatant civilians, provoke the IRA into retaliatory gunfire and quite literally get away with murder.

12

OPERATIONS *LINKLATER, DEMETRIUS*

AND THE BALLYMURPHY MASSACRE

In July 1971, Maj.-Gen. Tuzo drew up a plan which became known as *Operation Linklater*. On the surface, it involved a series of search operations designed to disrupt the IRA while providing reassurance to the public that the British army was taking the battle to the terrorists. But there was more: a soldier who served with 2 Para in Ballymurphy told the military historian (and former clerk to Kitson) James Kinchin-White that *Linklater* had a 'deception' dimension designed to enable his battalion to arrest people and ascertain the identities of Republicans who lived in the housing estates around them.[1] With this information, the army hoped to place themselves in an enhanced position to sweep up active Republicans when internment took place. At the time, 2 Para's intelligence was 'poor', as, no doubt, was that of other regiments.

There was, as yet, nowhere to place the *Linklater* targets. On 19 July, it was resolved that they would not be taken into custody until after the Apprentice Boys annual march in Derry the following month. Kitson was about to go on leave and hence could expect to be back in plenty of time to deal with the action. Before he departed, he talked to Farrar-Hockley only to be advised that arrests were imminent but he was not told the reason why. 'I thought this was crazy,' Kitson told the military historian Jonathan Riley, 'as we had nowhere to keep them'. If we are to believe Kitson, he told Farrar-Hockley that the suspects 'had not so far done anything illegal and it would make things harder for us if we do bring in internment'.[2] Farrar-Hockley, who was second in the pecking order at HQNI, agreed with Kitson but asserted that there was no alternative.

Operation Linklater was launched on Friday 23 July while Kitson was on leave in England. The army was reported to have arrested forty-eight people but that figure may have been an over-estimation. Kitson, apparently, first read of the development in the Sunday newspapers while in England. He rang Carver who 'asked him to come by for a drink after church. On the doorstep, Carver said, "what is going on in Belfast?" Kitson replied, "I thought you were going to tell me"!'[3]

In excess of 100 houses and workplaces were searched. Radio equipment, some explosives and documents were confiscated. Further searches on the 26 and 27 July led to the confiscation of a small number of weapons and more documents.

The politicians highlighted the other dimension to *Linklater*, the harassment and disruption of the Officials and Provisionals. The Home Secretary, Reginald Maudling, told the Commons that the operation demonstrated that the security forces would henceforth 'search out the men and organisations responsible' for the violence in Northern Ireland. Inevitably, it also put the IRA on high alert. When internment was introduced a few weeks later, most of the more senior members were not at home and evaded detention.

***

Operation Demetrius was the code name ascribed to internment. It commenced on 9 August, 1971. Kitson, who was favourably disposed towards it, was, however, aghast at how it was mishandled. He believed it was implemented before the army and RUC had identified the key IRA players and their whereabouts and likely boltholes. The army had been directed to carry out the swoops too early due to political pressure exerted by Brian Faulkner on Heath. Shortly after the swoops had begun, Kitson attended a meeting of officers from all parts of Northern Ireland. One of them recalled how he rose to his feet and berated his 'astonished colleagues with a withering indictment' of the endeavour. 'I think he was jolly nearly sacked for what he said,' the officer remarked. 'He told them that it had been done in the wrong way, at the wrong time and for the wrong reasons. Didn't seem to go down terribly well!'[4]

342 people were swept up on 9 August 1971, and taken to makeshift camps in a series of dawn raids by the British army. 105 were released after two days. Instead of restoring law and order, the arrests sparked an eruption of violence. During the upheaval that ensued between 9 and 11 August 1971, paratroopers murdered ten civilians in Ballymurphy, Belfast. Kitson must shoulder the lion's share of the blame for this. As late as 1989, Carver was still prepared to praise what he perceived as Kitson's decisive response to the upheaval. He did so in his memoirs where he described how

Belfast had fallen quiet by 12 August 'after some rioting and burning, thanks to the energetic action of Frank Kitson, the brigade commander there'.[5]

Byron Lewis, a former paratrooper with Support Company of 1 Para, provided a more accurate appraisal of it:

> I recall before internment great efforts were made on the part of the army to communicate with the local populace, one of the several projects was a club set up on the Falls Road (Pegasus Club?), which came under the heading Hearts and Minds which demonstrates the effort which was made to smooth relations between the army and public. When August 9th arrived, the day of internment, all this went by the board. The initiation from my battalion was a prolonged gun battle on the first day from a sand-bagged Henry Taggart Hall across the Springfield Road to Ballymurphy. A child[6] was killed during this incident which was the start of the 'Tit-for-Tat' vendettas which were to escalate over the months to enormous proportions.[7]

The infamous Ballymurphy massacre began after Loyalist gangs came out in force to take advantage of the upheaval. On 9 August, a group of them launched an attack on Nationalists at Springfield Park causing an exodus from their homes. During it, a group of people fled across a wasteland to get away from them. This sparked a series of shootings and murders from 9 to 11 August. Kitson's paratroopers shot many of those killed or injured in the back. The official inquest into the atrocity concluded – nearly fifty years later – that all ten of the victims were innocent of any form of wrongdoing, adding that there was no justification for their deaths. The coroner, Mrs Justice Keegan, added that none of the killings were properly investigated at the time.[8]

What did not emerge during the inquest was that two of

the paratroopers – including the infamous Soldier F – who had participated in the activities of 1 Para between 9 and 11 August in Belfast received commendations from their superiors for gallantry.

13

KITSON'S 'GALLANT' KILLERS

One of the paratroopers who served during the internment swoops, a lance corporal, was designated 'Soldier F' at the Widgery and Saville Inquiries. He was a small man who had joined 1 Para in 1966. In 1971, he was attached to 1 Para's Support Company. His military number was 24093491.

Soldier F was 'mentioned in despatches' for his valour in Belfast in August 1971. A soldier receives this honour for gallant or meritorious action in the face of the enemy after an official report is written by a superior officer and submitted to the high command. This means that someone such as Maj. Edward Loden of Support Company, Col Wilford, or perhaps even Kitson, furnished such a commendation for his gallantry during the turmoil of the internment swoops to Gen. Ford and Gen. Tuzo. In turn, they would have passed it to Carver in London. If Kitson was not the instigator and author of the recommendation, he most certainly approved the one passed to him by Loden or Wilford.

Soldier F's 'mention in despatches' was published a few weeks after Bloody Sunday. Presumably, the lance corporal knew all about the honour before he went to Derry and became a key figure in the massacre that would occur there. Soldiers mentioned in despatches are often seen as leaders of men with a bright military future ahead of them. Wilford and Kitson were earmarking him for what lay ahead.

Kitson had once written that no operation 'can succeed until the men are really keen to get to grips with the enemy and destroy him utterly'.[1] In Soldier F, Kitson seems to have found just such a man.

It is possible that Soldier F and his comrades, Soldiers E, G and H, were involved in the shooting of unarmed and innocent civilians during the Ballymurphy massacre of August 1971.

Soldiers from Support Company 2 Para were involved in some of the killings in Ballymurphy. It is not clear if soldiers from one support company could have been assigned temporarily to another.

A second paratrooper, a private in 1 Para Support Company, was also 'mentioned in despatches' for his activities in Belfast in August 1971. Like Soldier F, he too went on to participate in the Bloody Sunday massacre of January 1972.

It is possible to discern a disturbing picture here, one involving a group of handpicked paratroopers attached to the support companies who were prepared to exterminate civilians, even in circumstances where they posed no threat to the British army. As part of any grooming to de- humanise them – and keep them in that condition – they would have been reassured that what they were doing was necessary and in the best interest of the crown. Hence, some of them were 'mentioned in despatches', a lowly honour that costs the state nothing.

Another technique to keep these assassins in play was

to ensure that the police did not investigate their activities. Instead, they were questioned – if questioned at all – by a compliant Royal military police which always let them off the hook.

What is not in doubt is that Soldier F was a cruel, cynical and clinical killer. What lay in store for the people of Derry would reveal the full extent of his ruthlessness. While not wishing to disrupt the chronology of this narrative, it is imperative at this point to note that Soldier F went on to shoot a number of peaceful and unarmed people, including Patrick Doherty and Barney McGuigan, the following January in the Bogside. For present purposes, all that is necessary to record is the callous nature of these murders. One of soldier F's rounds struck Doherty in the buttock while he was on the ground crawling away from him. As Doherty lay crying out in pain, his life draining away from him, Barney McGuigan, an exceptionally brave and humane man stepped forward waving a white handkerchief looking to help Doherty. Soldier F reacted by dropping to one knee to aim his rifle and shot McGuigan in the head. There is no reason to believe that Soldier F was not a cold-hearted killer in August 1971 but somehow mutated into one by January 1972 when Bloody Sunday took place

The Saville Inquiry found that on Bloody Sunday 'none of the soldiers fired in the belief that he might have identified a person in possession of or using or about to use bombs or firearms'. This is exactly what happened in Ballymurphy in August 1971.

In July 2021, Colum Eastwood MP, the leader of the

SDLP, named Soldier F in the House of Commons, under privilege. Soldier F had been facing murder charges for his actions on Bloody Sunday, which had just been dropped. Eastwood said that, 'For 50 years he has been granted anonymity and now the government want to grant him an amnesty. No one involved in murder during the Troubles should be granted an amnesty.'

After his speech, Eastwood told BBC NI that: 'Over the past couple of weeks his name has been plastered on Free Derry Corner, it has gone viral on social media. The people of Derry know his name. There is no reason for him to be granted anonymity. No other perpetrator involved would be given anonymity, for some reason Soldier F is a protected species.' One answer to Eastwood's question is that he became a member of a 'protected species' because he had been trained by Kitson to engage in ruthless activities that could – and did – result in the slaughter of unarmed civilians and that this cannot be allowed come to light.

***

If we are to believe Kitson, the Ballymurphy massacre made no impression on him. When he appeared at the Saville Inquiry on 24 September 2002, he was asked if he could 'recall an incident on 10th August, in the early hours – a series of incidents, I should say, in the early hours of the morning of 10th August in Ballymurphy where 1 Para was involved in the shooting dead of five people?' Kitson replied: 'No, I do not – the whole of, I think I am right in saying the 10th August came very soon after internment started.'[2]

The barrister prompted him saying it was 'the day after, in fact really the night and early morning of the day of the introduction of internment'. 'The answer is, no, I am afraid I do not,' Kitson replied.

'If I were to mention to you the names of two of the … people who were killed: Father Hugh Mullan, a Catholic priest, and Mrs Joan Connolly, a fifty-year-old woman; does that help to jog your memory at all, so that you remember it?' To this Kitson relied: 'No, I am afraid I had not looked at any of that. A lot of what we have been talking about in January 1972, one's memory, as you put it, has been jogged, but I have not been back over the period of the previous year at all.'

The barrister tried again: 'If I were to tell you that the … deaths were a matter of considerable public controversy and that it was alleged that the members of 1 Para had quite improperly shot and killed these people; does that assist you?' It didn't.

After Kitson was told that no criminal prosecution had taken place, he was asked if he was aware of any type of courts martial that might have taken place. He replied he was not.

When asked if he had disciplined any of the soldiers, he took refuge in jargon and arid points of procedure:

> Well, they would not have been disciplined by me. The system of what you might call court's martial action is in any theatre, it is not typical of Northern Ireland. It goes from the battalion to the division, that is to say the two-star level have the dealing with this and it goes to HQ Northern Ireland.
>
> So if there was a prosecution it would have been ordered in that way, by 1 Para and thence to – HQ Northern Ireland would have produced the military part of the investigation and then that would have led, if it did, to a prosecution.

Kitson could not recall any form of discipline or rebuke that was meted out to any of the paratroopers linked to the carnage.

Wilford did not appear at the Ballymurphy inquest. Instead, he sent a statement purporting not to recall the atrocity. 'This comes as a complete surprise to me ... None of that information came my way. Had it come my way, it would've been quite serious.'

What neither man revealed was that there was a secret procedure in place to block criminal investigations into killings caused by British troops in Belfast. In 2021, two paratroopers were belatedly prosecuted for the shooting of Joe McCann, an Official IRA volunteer, in April 1972, while he ran away from them. Judge James O'Hara pointed out that at that 'time, in fact until late 1973, an understanding was in place between the RUC and the army whereby the RUC did not arrest and question, or even take witness statements from, soldiers involved in shootings such as this one. This appalling practice was designed, at least in part, to protect soldiers from being prosecuted and in very large measure it succeeded.'

This procedure was probably organised by Kitson and his allies in the RUC.

14

The Music Box

Sir Dick White, the Intelligence Coordinator at the Cabinet Office, 1968 to 1972, sat at the summit of the intelligence community. Uniquely, he had served as both director-general of MI5 and chief of MI6. Born in December 1906, he had been a schoolmaster at Whitgift School in Croydon. He became an expert at interrogation during the Second World War at the infamous Camp 020 at Latchmere House, London, where torture and brutality was commonplace. Equally severe methods were deployed at a prison he had run at Bad Nenndorf in Germany after the war ended. He went on to become director-general of MI5 and was in charge during the atrocities his officers oversaw and tolerated in Kenya. White was central to an intelligence overhaul which took place in Northern Ireland in the early 1970s. Black propaganda was another of his specialities and he participated in setting up the anti-IRA campaign in the early 1970s.

Most, if not all of the important figures in the IRA, had avoided the internment dragnets, having surmised that internment was imminent. Some blame for this fiasco was laid at the feet of MI5 and the RUC Special Branch, neither of whom had been able to identify the real players in the IRA. Ted Heath complained in his memoirs that the intelligence supplied by the RUC Special Branch had been 'hopelessly out of date'.[1]

The codename given to the interrogation programme was *Operation Calabra*. The first wave of interrogations was carried out by the RUC and proved unproductive. Subsequently, a decision was taken to bring in military advisers who had developed techniques that are more sophisticated. According to Carver, the methods they deployed during it owed 'their origin to the experience of the Korean War, when British servicemen who had been captured were subjected to prolonged and sophisticated methods of interrogation. As a result, training in resistance to this type of interrogation had been instituted in the Services generally, and specifically for those most likely to fall into enemy hands. Turning this experience inside out, the methods used for training had been employed for actual interrogation with considerable success in Malaya, Kenya, Borneo and Aden. In the last-named, they had given rise to allegations of torture, and, as a result of the Bowen [Report] (November 1966),[2] the rules governing their use had been revised and specifically endorsed by the Defence Secretary at the time, Denis Healey'.[3]

This was only half the truth. The brainwashing techniques had not fallen into Britain's lap by accident as Carver suggested. However, this sleight of hand allowed him to conceal the brutal methods that White and his colleagues had developed both during and after the Second World War, and which were now incorporated as part of the tactics inflicted upon the Irish prisoners. During the two years (June 1945–July 1947) in which Bad Nenndorf Interrogation Centre was open, 372 men and 44 women passed through its gates. They received severe beatings, sometimes involving whippings. 'Shin screws' which had been confiscated from a Gestapo prison in Hamburg were put back into use. Some prisoners were forced to stand for twelve hours at a time and threatened with execution. Inmates were doused in water despite sub-zero temperatures. One man was forced to stand in a cell in cold water for eight days. At least one inmate was told that his wife was being brought in for torture; another was suspended by his wrists and beaten by men wielding rubber truncheons. A few died from this maltreatment. A doctor in a nearby hospital complained about the number of filthy and confused patients he was required to treat. Many were suffering from multiple injuries and frostbite; others were painfully emaciated after months of starvation.[4]

The 'deep interrogation' aspect of *Operation Calabra* commenced at 05:32 hours on Wednesday, 11 August and lasted until 11:30 hours on Tuesday, 17 August. It was an attempt to use modern psychological techniques to break prisoners and get them to talk. A subgroup of a dozen prisoners was flown to Ballykelly for 'deep interrogation'. Together with another two who were selected the following October, they became known as 'the Hooded Men', or 'the Guineapigs'.

The 'Hooded Men' were flown to Hut 60 at Ballykelly by helicopter. They were taken on a circuitous route with a flight time of one hour to simulate a long journey, and so most suspects believed they were being questioned in England.

When they landed at Ballykelly, they were stripped naked, photographed, and examined by doctors with English accents. Shortly afterwards they were subjected to the 'five techniques' which were later described by the European Court of Human Rights (ECHR) as follows:

* wall-standing: forcing the detainees to remain for periods of some hours in a 'stress position', described by those who underwent it as being 'spread-eagled against the wall, with their fingers put high above the head against the wall, the legs spread apart and the feet back, causing them to stand on their toes with the weight of the body mainly on the fingers';
* hooding: putting a black or navy coloured bag over the detainees' heads and, at least initially, keeping it there all the time except during interrogation;
* subjection to noise: pending their interrogations, holding the detainees in a room where there was a continuous loud and hissing noise;
* deprivation of sleep: pending their interrogations, depriving the detainees of sleep;
* deprivation of food and drink: subjecting the detainees to a reduced diet during their stay at the centre and pending interrogations.

Interrogation sessions took place after the 'techniques' had been used to soften the prisoners up. The British government never contested that all this happened, merely that it did not amount to a system of torture.

Officers from the Joint Services Interrogation Wing (JSIW) of the British army were flown to Northern Ireland to supervise the interrogations.

The interrogators referred to the room where prisoners were subjected to excruciating and corrosive 'white noise' as the 'music box'.

Carver professed ignorance about what was afoot and blamed his subordinates. He claimed that after his return from leave he had enquired 'more deeply into what the details of the methods had been, who had carried them out and the extent to which this had been explained to and authorised by Ministers …' He received what he described as 'evasive answers. With some difficulty I obtained a description of the methods – wall-standing, hooding, noise, and bread and water diet – later given in detail in the Compton report'.[5]

If Carver was truly ignorant of the methods deployed, and was unhappy about them, it is difficult to understand how the abuse continued while he was still in overall charge of the military. Over the months that followed, prisoners were subjected to at least one of the five techniques. Others were subjected to more traditional methods of torture, reminiscent of those used in Palestine, Kenya and other British colonies such as waterboarding; the whipping of the soles of feet; electrocution, burning with matches and candles. Some internees spoke about being forced to stand over electric fires while they received beatings; more again about having their genitals squeezed; some revealed they had objects forced into their anuses. Others claimed they were given injections and subjected to games of Russian roulette. Alsatian dogs menaced and bit others of their number.

***

An article appeared in *The Daily Mirror* after evidence of the abuse of the prisoners emerged. It asserted that Kitson had developed the 'five techniques' in Kenya. This was wide of the mark. The senior civil officials inside Thiepval Barracks and at Whitehall knew the paper would not be able to stand over the allegation. Kitson threatened to sue for defamation if the record was not corrected. One insider who worked at Lisburn believes that Kitson was pushed into this position by the MoD who wanted a correction and an apology so they could 'kill the story'. *The Mirror* duly apologised.

The story, however, did not die. In 1974, John McGuffin published a highly regarded book about it, *The Guineapigs*.[6] Also that year Denis Faul and Raymond Murray published *The Hooded Men*.[7]

The Irish government took the British government to European Commission on Human Rights over the abuse. There was plenty of hostile reporting and legal action. Indeed, some of the 'hooded men' who are still alive are currently pursuing an action against the British government for their ordeal. Their lives were blighted by post-traumatic stress disorder and physical ill health directly related to *Operation Calabra*.

15

'Your Fucking Minute's Ticking Away'

Lord Carver felt that the 'combination of internment and interrogation, and the allegations to which they both gave rise, greatly antagonised the Catholic population of Northern Ireland and the Government and public opinion of the Republic. It was very different from the days of August 1969, when the army had been welcome in the Catholic areas as an alternative to the RUC and B Specials. We were now Enemy Number One.'[1] If Carver truly felt that there was a problem with the behaviour of his army, he proceeded to do little to remedy the situation. The violence and abuse of Nationalists continued unabated.

Internment also exposed the gaps in the knowledge of RUC Special Branch. To remedy this, Kitson decided to develop the army's own intelligence gathering networks. Carver gave permission to proceed for 'there was no alternative'.[2]

Foot patrols were instructed to gather 'contact-information', and to assemble a detailed, comprehensive profile of their area of operations and its inhabitants. In addition, the British army routinely stopped and questioned pedestrians and motorists on the streets and carried out house searches. These encounters often involved violence, some of it extreme. Kevin Myers, the former RTÉ broadcast journalist, has written about how one evening in September 1972, he was:

stopped by a para patrol, led by a fat Scottish sergeant. I showed him my RTÉ accreditation and told him I was making a social visit. He told me I had one minute to leave the area, otherwise he would shoot me. I said I had to tell my friend that we would not be going out that night. 'Your fucking minute's ticking away', he replied.

Having told my friend that I was leaving immediately, I ran back to my car just as a singing drunk was passing by. Without saying a word, the Paras beat him about the head with their rifle-butts, and then repeatedly kicked him on the ground. I said: 'Sergeant, you've got to stop that,' pronouncing his rank as 'sarnt', which suggested a certain military authority.

'Fuck. You still here? Your minute's nearly up. You want to be very fucking careful, or you'll end up like this poor fucking cunt here.'

Then he walked over to the figure on the ground and kicked him very hard in the groin.

I got the victim – named John Kelly – into my car. He was cascading blood and I took him down to the Royal Victoria Hospital where about twenty-five stitches were put in his head (though clearly, he should have been admitted). Four hours later, I drove him homeward, along with a teenage hitchhiker I'd picked up on the Falls. On the Whiterock Road was a checkpoint: yes, the same Scottish sergeant.

We three were taken from the car. The two others were given a terrible hammering – John Kelly's second of the night – while I (presumably in deference to my accent) was put with my finger-tips against the wall of City Cemetery while I was punched in the back and my feet were repeatedly kicked apart.

'Is there any fucking reason why I shouldn't blow your fucking brains out, you cunt?'

'I've told my office about you, and they've notified 39th Brigade watchkeeper,' I lied (quite inventively, I must admit). 'If any harm comes to me, it'll come to you too.'

That did it. The three of us were released, the other two in a terrible shape. I drove them home, despite being warned not to. We all three of us expected to be riddled as we left.

The people of Ballymurphy had to put up with conduct like that every day during those times. One of the victims was nineteen-year Liam Holden, who was beaten, tortured and even water-boarded by paras into admitting shooting a soldier, and then served seventeen years in jail for a crime he did not commit.[3]

The ruthless methods to which Belfast had been subjected during 1971 were about to be exported to Derry. The existence of the 'no-go' area known as 'Free Derry' was a source of exasperation, if not fury, to the top brass at Lisburn. According to Ford, Kitson repeatedly asked him how he was going to deal with the challenge. In response, Ford probably shared a ruthless policy idea he was exploring and would commit to paper early in the new year.

16

'Shoot Selected Ringleaders'

From a military perspective, 'Free Derry' fell within the jurisdiction of 8 Brigade. It had been sealed off from the police and military periodically during 1969, 1971 and 1972 by the erection of up to thirty sturdy barricades. Some of these could even withstand a battering from the army's one-tonne 'pigs'. The entrance to it was via the Bogside which was overlooked by Derry's wall, an edifice originally built by the Honourable Irish Society between 1614 and 1618. Local residents manned the barricades around-the-clock employing searchlights at night. When the military or police attempted to breach the no-go area, loud alarms were raised. By 1972, those manning the barricades had become bored and handed over some of the night shifts to local alcoholics who were happy to do the job for some liquor. They were even given radios. British soldiers on the city's walls monitored all of these activities.

On 27 October 1971, a forty-six-year-old officer of the Coldstream Guards, Brig. 'Pat' MacLellan assumed command of 8 Brigade. He was appointed after a spell serving on the army Staff Command in Cyprus. Unlike Carver, Tuzo, Ford, Kitson and Wilford, he had not engaged in counter-insurgency wars. Carver described him as 'a quiet man, in some ways un-assuming. I had known him in a previous job but I cannot now recall what it was. He is very different to Frank Kitson. He was probably the sort of man to take the safe course. He provided a steady reliable pair of hands'.[1]

MacLellan had access to reliable sources inside 'Free Derry' through RUC Chief Superintendent Frank Lagan, the most senior police officer in the city. Lagan, a native of Derry, had spent thirty years in the police. A Catholic, educated at St Columb's, he understood the Nationalist outlook and was in contact with people ranging from constitutional Nationalists such as John Hume on the one side, to militants on the other. Earlier in his career, Lagan had commanded the RUC squad which removed the Tricolour from the window of Sinn Féin's election HQ in Belfast during the 1964 UK general election thereby sparking the Divis Street riots. He later returned to Derry and established an information network that reached into the Bogside and Creggan, which provided him with an accurate picture of what was afoot in January 1972. He is one of the unsung architects of the peace process, a labour at which he toiled for decades. He put British spies and the IRA together, leading not just to the 1974–75 ceasefire but to the successful process that culminated in the Good Friday Agreement. The go-between was Brendan Duddy. The IRA appreciated Lagan's good faith in what was akin to walking a tightrope and issued orders that he was not to be targeted. He enjoyed his retirement living on the Nationalist side of Lough Foyle, not far from the Bogside and Creggan.

MacLellan and Lagan worked well together. The RUC man would often drop in unannounced at Ebrington Barracks, the 8th Brigade's Victorian HQ in the Waterside, where MacLellan had his office; and the brigadier was welcome without appointment at the RUC HQ in the city. MacLellan's wife had Irish roots with relatives in Kinsale, County Cork. He appreciated that the Bogside and its environs were Nationalist and had no desire to aggravate the deteriorating and volatile relationship between the community and the British army. He fell into the role of maintaining the peace as best he could, while the politicians searched for a peaceful solution.

There were those in the British army who felt MacLellan was not being sufficiently robust. They included Ford, Kitson and Wilford. Almost certainly, Carver and Tuzo held the same opinion.

According to Wilford's adjutant, Capt. Jackson, although the circumstances:

> in Londonderry were quite different from those prevailing in Belfast, there was a sense in 39 Brigade [in Belfast] that 8 Brigade [in Derry] hadn't been firm enough. We were very disapproving of the fact that a 'no-go' area had been allowed to come into being. The violence would never end unless the perpetrators [who lived inside it] were arrested.[2]

In Belfast, Wilford's troops had taken on the rioters and dismantled barricades earning themselves a fearsome reputation in the process, something Wilford relished: 'Of course my lads are tough,' he once boasted to a reporter. 'They are known around the world for that.'[3]

Although there had been an outcry at the behaviour of the paratroopers in Ballymurphy, the fact that the IRA had come out fighting gave the British propagandists the ammunition they needed to distract attention from the cold-blooded killings that had taken place. The lesson the hard men of the British army undoubtedly drew from this was that they could shoot unarmed civilians and get away with it, if they could manage to provoke the IRA to engage in battle with them. And if they could flush the IRA out into the open, they would always have a chance to crush them.

The politicians in London were concerned about 'Free Derry'. Carver attended a ministerial meeting early in January 1972 where he was questioned about:

> what would be involved if it were decided to carry out an operation to clear the 'no-go' area of Londonderry, where the barricades were still up, I estimated that it would need seven battalions to clear it and four would have to remain to keep it clear. Such an Operation was likely to involve a considerable number of civilian casualties and would therefore harden the Catholic attitude against the security forces. It was agreed that it might eventually have to be done, but that it should be avoided while hope of a political initiative was being pursued.[4]

Carver also revealed that from his perspective one of the 'major problems of Londonderry at this time was the unruly and obstreperous hooligan element who threw bottles, stones, bricks and petrol bombs and other missiles at the security forces'. It annoyed him that they could 'seldom be arrested, and, even when they were, received light sentences'. William Street was their favourite area, which they had reduced 'to almost rubble'. There was 'mounting pressure from the Protestants for their arrest and punishment'.[5]

Gen. Ford was ready, willing and prepared to take a hard line. A tall, imposing and energetic man, he hailed from a military family and had seen plenty of action before his arrival in Ireland. Born on 29 December 1923 at Yealmpton, Devon, he received his education at Musgrave School, Gateshead. He served with distinction during the Second

World War, and was a veteran of Palestine and Aden. Ford concluded that a course change was mandated. In a memo dated 7 January 1972, he contemplated shooting the 'ringleaders amongst the DYH' i.e., so-called 'Derry Young Hooligans' in certain circumstances. The DYH consisted of gangs, he wrote:

> of tough, teenage youths, permanently unemployed who have developed sophisticated tactics of brick and stone throwing, destruction and arson. Under cover of snipers in nearby buildings, they operate just beyond the hard-core areas and extend the radius of anarchy by degrees into additional streets and areas. Against the DYH ... the Army in Londonderry is for the moment virtually incapable. This incapacity undermines our ability to deal with the gunmen and bombers and threatens what is left of law and order on the west bank of the River Foyle.[6]

The passage about shooting the DYH ringleaders appeared in the next paragraph:

> I am coming to the conclusion that the minimum force necessary to achieve a restoration of law and order is to shoot selected ring-leaders amongst the DYH, after clear warnings have been issued. I believe we would be justified in using 7.62-millimetre but in view of the devastating effects of this weapon and the danger of rounds *killing more than the person aimed at* [*my emphasis*], I believe we must consider issuing rifles adapted to fire HV.22-inch ammunition to sufficient members of the unit dealing with this problem, to enable ring-leaders to be engaged with this less lethal ammunition. Thirty of these weapons have been sent to 8th Brigade this weekend for zeroing and familiarisation training. They, of course, will not be used operationally without authorisation:[7]
>
> If this course is implemented, as I believe it may have to be, we would have to accept the possibility that .22 rounds may be lethal. In other words, we would be reverting to the methods of internal security found successful on many occasions overseas, but would merely be trying to minimise the lethal effects by

using the .22 round. I am convinced that our duty to restore law and order requires us to consider this step.[8]

Ford advocated the use of self-loading rifles modified for the less powerful .22 bullets for the task.[9]

At the Saville Inquiry Ford professed to having no memory of this memo.

Kitson said he had no knowledge of it either, having never been consulted about it. One of the barristers asked him, 'do I understand correctly that before you were shown this document by Eversheds, the solicitors to the inquiry, you had, so far as you recall, never seen it?

No, I certainly had not seen it before ...[10]

Kitson was asked if, regardless of whether or not he had seen the memo, he was aware in January 1972 that Ford had come to the conclusion that the minimum force necessary to achieve a restoration of law and order was to shoot some of the ring-leaders of the DYH after clear warnings had been issued?

No, I do not remember this being discussed in any context.[11]

The barrister highlighted the passage which referred to the British army as 'reverting to the methods of internal security found successful on many occasions overseas' and asked if this might be a reference to some of the methods referred to in Kitson's book. 'Do you recall discussing that with Gen. Ford?' Kitson was asked. Instead of providing a straight answer, he set off on another of his peripheral meanderings:

No, but I do – I mean, it was the general system for dealing with riots up to a certain time. I mean, I think that the pamphlet that was issued in 1930 something, that was the system and you had a platoon and they deployed, and in the colonies they would say 'over now to the military Commander' and a banner would be extended in whatever language you were in, saying 'disperse or we fire' and then a fellow would say to one of the riflemen 'you see that man dancing round out there, fire one round at him', and then there would be pictures taken. This was all the formal system of internal security and duties in aid of the civil power that had at one time existed. It was not used in Northern Ireland.[12]

Kitson and Ford's recollections of the memo of 7 January are far from convincing. It is likely that Ford discussed his ideas with Kitson who was eager to learn what he was going to do about Derry. In an undated document discovered by the Saville Inquiry which emanated from circa 1972, Ford stated of Kitson that he 'used to say to me why can't you sort out Londonderry?'[13]

17

Kitson's Poor Recollection

of the Order to send 1 Para to Derry

In December 1971, Gen. Carver visited Derry where he held discussions with RUC Chief Superintendent Lagan and Gen. Tuzo about an anti-internment march which the Northern Ireland Civil Rights Association (NICRA) was planning for the following month. According to Carver, Lagan 'did not even want to stop the march going into the centre of Londonderry, but he was indecisive at the best of times'.[1]

At the start of the new year Brian Faulkner banned all parades and marches in Northern Ireland. In defiance of this edict, NICRA decided it would hold its protest in Derry on 16 January 1972, although subsequently rescheduling it for two weeks later. A week before 30 January, a group of protesters, including John Hume, attempted to march to an internment centre adjacent to Magilligan Strand. On their way, they encountered members of the parachute regiment who opened fire on them with rubber bullets. Decades later John Hume told the Saville Inquiry: 'if they were firing rubber bullets and gas on the beach where there could not be any form of violence … I thought "good Lord, what would they do on the streets of the town and what trouble would they cause".'[2] Hume advised those intending to attend the NICRA march the following week not to do so. He would not join it himself.

The reaction inside HQNI could not have been more polar. There, the focus was on the humiliation occasioned by TV footage of a woman beating one of the paratroopers on the beach. Its effect was emasculating. If that was how HQNI perceived it, one shudders to think how it was received inside Palace Barracks.

In response to the larger NICRA march expected to proceed through Derry, Ford asked Brig. MacLellan to produce a plan to block it. While MacLellan was working on this task, Ford sent a memo to Tuzo stating that he was 'disturbed by the attitude of both the Brigade commander [i.e., MacLellan], and also, of course, by Chief Superintendent Lagan.'[3] He told Tuzo he had issued MacLellan with 'very firm directions' and that he was 'to take all possible steps within his capability to inhibit and deter the operations of the bombers'.[4] The military plan that evolved became known as *Operation Forecast*.

On 24 January, MacLellan reported to Ford that Lagan feared that the consequences of stopping the march would be significant. According to Ford, 'Brigadier MacLellan agreed that the consequences would be serious and indicated that if the events anticipated by Superintendent Lagan transpired, his existing forces would be inadequate. I therefore alerted my Province Reserve, 1st Battalion the King's Own Border Regiment, which had become operational on 13 January 1972 but had not yet taken part in any operation. I also telephoned Brigadier Kitson, Commander 39 Brigade in Belfast, to inform him that I would require 1 PARA (his Brigade Reserve and only uncommitted battalion) for the forthcoming operation in Londonderry. I warned him that the battalion might be away for up to four days and he agreed that for this period of time he could – just – spare them. I assume I told him what the likely role was for 1 PARA but I have no records to support this.'[5] There are reasons to believe that this is a tissue of lies and that Ford, Kitson and Wilford had been drafting plans to deal with Derry in their own way long before this.

Ford had a high opinion of the paratroopers despite all the criticism being heaped upon them. 'I had confidence in Brigadier Kitson and 1 Para', he told Saville. 'I knew Brigadier Kitson very well and I had seen 1 PARA operating on earlier occasions. I knew Kitson's view of that particular Battalion; he thought they were very good and he depended on them'.[6]

Tuzo was party to the on-going discussions. The plan that evolved was that the NICRA march would be blocked when it reached the William Street area. According to Carver, 'over the previous month or so hooligans had been reducing William Street to utter ruin. None of these hooligans had been arrested or convicted. We therefore decided that the opportunity should be taken, at the march planned for 30 January, to arrest them if possible. This march was bound to have a hooligan element and something needed to be done. I think that this was Tuzo's suggestion. Hooligans were to be arrested if possible but there should be no direct conflict between the soldiers and the hooligans'.[7]

One of the assessments made by 8 Brigade predicted that the 'hooligan element' would be present from the start and that some 'gunmen are certain to be sheltering behind the hooligan ranks'.[8] The top brass at HQNI Lisburn shared these concerns and feared that the IRA would exploit the march to provide cover to snipe at the soldiers stationed at the barricades and observation posts. Yet, Lagan did not put particular weight on the sources that were generating these concerns.

According to Jackson, the 'basic plan' that developed involved deploying soldiers from 1 Para to protect the commercial heart of the city from the marchers by holding them behind the containment line and 'snatching' some of the rioters:

> The main difficulty was to stop people running away: put a cork in the bottle. We had evolved the tactic of going in behind the crowd or of coming in at the flank to cut them off. Clearly this was a large operation which would require a large number of troops. We envisaged using three companies, in a pincer movement, to surround the rioters and cut off their retreat, arrest them, bundle them into pigs [British army vehicles] and take them off for handover to the RUC.[9]

Kitson claimed that he had no recollection of the arrangements that culminated in the dispatch of 1 Para to Derry for *Operation Forecast*:

> I do not remember when the decision was made to reinforce 8 Brigade for the illegal march in Londonderry that had been arranged to take place at the end of January 1972. Commander 8 Brigade [MacLellan] must have felt that he needed to be reinforced and the GOC [Tuzo] and CLF [Ford] must have decided to send the province (*sic*) reserve battalion and 39 Brigade's reserve battalion (1 Para). In making this decision they would have considered the risk involved in removing 1 Para from Belfast for the short period concerned. It is probable that CLF would have asked for my assessment of the risk and it is unlikely that I would have objected to the move, as Belfast was relatively quiet at the time apart from bombing and isolated attacks on soldiers. If any battalion had to go from 39 Brigade it would have

to be the brigade reserve as my other battalions were deployed around Belfast and could not easily be extracted.[10]

Clearly, Kitson knew that 1 Para was going to Derry and had sufficient time to talk to Wilford. Yet, in his written statement to the Saville Inquiry he tried to distance himself from this possibility, even raising the prospect that he had not spoken to Wilford about the deployment to Derry at all. His exact words were that:

> It would have been the responsibility of HQ 39 Brigade to pass on the order to 1 Para for their move to Londonderry. If it had come through before I went on leave, I would almost certainly have spoken to Lt Colonel Wilford myself. I have no recollection as to whether or not the order came through before I went on leave or, if it did, of any conversation I may have had with Lt Colonel Wilford. The employment of 1 Para once they were under command of 8 Brigade would of course be a matter for Brigadier MacLellan.[11]

The role of MI5 has received little analysis in the context of Bloody Sunday despite its crucial contribution to the tragedy. At the time of Bloody Sunday, the overarching director of intelligence in Northern Ireland was an MI5 officer who had served as a paratrooper during Second World War. His career in Northern Ireland failed to live up to the standards he had displayed as a young man who had put his life on the line for his colleagues in the war against Nazi Germany. In Ireland, he oversaw some of the most reprehensible and abhorrent clandestine operations of the entire 'Troubles'.

18

MI5'S SPY IN FREE DERRY

In 1972, David Eastwood of MI5 was in overall charge of the sprawling intelligence apparatus in Northern Ireland. He was the 'David' who appeared at the Saville Inquiry in 2000 revealing that he had initially been sent to Belfast in 1970 as a security liaison officer.

Eastwood was a decorated Second World War veteran. Born in Bangor, Wales, on 27 January 1919, he received his education at All Saints, Bloxham, and St Edmund Hall, Oxford. He joined the Oxfordshire and Buckinghamshire Light Infantry and was posted to India where he carried out internal security duties until the outbreak of the Second World War. His unit was recalled to England to form part of the 31st Independent Infantry Brigade Group and later the 1st Airlanding Brigade Group. He took part in the Allied landings in Sicily in 1943. After he returned to England, he was called upon to advise the D-day planners about the lessons that could be drawn from that campaign.

After D-Day, Eastwood served with the 21st Independent Parachute Company where his exploits earned him a Military Cross. His company landed in France on 17 September 1944, to secure and protect drop zones designated for the arrival of 1 Para at Arnhem. At the time, he was a platoon commander and it was his task to lay out navigational aids at the supply drops. Before he could accomplish this, he had to kill or capture the German soldiers in the zone. When, two days later, Polish gliders appeared, Eastwood and his colleagues protected them from the German troops surrounding the area. Although he was cut off, he managed to lead his platoon through German lines and reach the outskirts of Arnhem. Over the next four days, he and his colleagues held the line near the Schoonord crossroads, where they were exposed to constant attack. In the face of incessant heavy enemy fire, Eastwood moved from one sector to another raising the morale of his troops. The soldiers held their ground until they were ordered to withdraw back across the Rhine. Clearly, Eastwood was not the type of man who was indifferent to the risks to which his comrades were exposed. His record shows that their survival was always of paramount concern to him, even at a risk to his own life.

When the Second World War ended, he joined the civil service in Malaya where he learned to speak fluent Malay and served as a district commissioner during the suppression of the revolt led by Chinese communist guerrillas. He met and married his wife Margaret, who was working at the military hospital in Kuala Lumpur. Malaya achieved its independence in 1957. Officially, Eastwood is recorded as having joined the MoD in 1959 but this was probably a cover for his admission to MI5. His duties took him to Jamaica, where he was first secretary 1964–1965. His next overseas assignment was to Northern Ireland where he spent approximately four years.

Three months after his arrival in Northern Ireland, he was promoted to the influential post of Director of Intelligence. He was stationed at Thiepval Barracks alongside the military top brass and given the rank of major-general. His department included a number of army officers but only one, his deputy, was from the army Intelligence Corps. Despite the fact that a post such as this had come into existence during many of Britain's colonial wars, Eastwood found that there was no established procedure which outlined how he was 'supposed to operate'. According to his uninformative testimony at the Saville Inquiry, his task became that of coordinating the intelligence gathering efforts of the various intelligence forces in Northern Ireland and overseeing a department consisting of MI5 and military officers. He also liaised with the police, particularly the RUC Special Branch:

> The people in my department both received intelligence from the RUC and obtained intelligence themselves. The intelligence was collated and assessed for inclusion in reports that were then disseminated within Whitehall and the intelligence community. A lot of the documentation would be addressed to me as Director of Intelligence but such was the volume at the time that there was much that I would not have seen. It was my job to ensure that this collation and dissemination was done as efficiently as possible.[1]

Eastwood's claim that 'there was much that I would not have seen' has the ring of something he contrived to distance himself from many of the embarrassments that had emerged about the Dirty War in Ireland by the time he made the comment. When he testified at Saville in 2000 the following scandals were in the public domain: collusion with Loyalist paramilitaries, the deployment of MRF hit squads, the management of brothels and the exploitation of children in care homes during MI5 and MI6 sexual entrapment operations.[2] All of these turpitudes had taken place on his watch. It is neither unrealistic nor naïve to suggest that junior MI5 and military intelligence officers could have run these operations without his knowledge. Such lower-level operatives could not have financed the establishment of the Gemini and Gardenia brothels in Belfast (and others perhaps elsewhere). If, somehow, Eastwood had not known about the brothels, he would certainly have learned about them after the attack on the Gemini by the IRA on 2 October 1972 in Belfast which was reported in the press.

Eastwood wanted to convey the impression that his priority had been to 'improve Special Branch where necessary through the provision of training and assistance'. He also tried to ensure that the army and special branch 'did not fall over one another in their operations'. In addition, he was occupied 'assessing security and ensuring that agents were not killed through sloppy handling'. Again, this raises questions about what he left unsaid. William McGrath had been an agent of MI6 and later MI5. He ran the paramilitary organisation Tara and was housefather at Kincora Boys' Home. Young residents of the home were raped and supplied to men on both sides of the border in Ireland. Some were trafficked to London for abuse. The Hart inquiry into Kincora reported in 2017 that MI5 was advised of McGrath's sexual proclivities on 7 April 1972 yet did not report them to the police, despite an obligation so to do. As the most senior officer, Eastwood must shoulder the primary blame for that act of concealment.

There were other Loyalist paramilitaries on Britain's pay sheet. If Eastwood's role was to ensure their safety and avoid 'sloppy handling', he must have been aware of their activities. McGrath in particular was suspected of being a British agent, not least because he boasted privately that he was such to associates. He was involved in forming the UDA and once enjoyed extremely close links to the UVF. He remained close to John McKeague, the leader of the Red Hand Commando. On the political front, McGrath had been close to Ian Paisley for decades.[3] It was important that agents like McGrath did not become the victim of 'sloppy handling'.

Albert 'Ginger' Baker was another agent whose reports undoubtedly reached Eastwood's desk. What did Eastwood know about the links between Baker, British military intelligence and the RUC? The answer is that he probably knew everything, especially after Baker handed himself over to the police and became a potential scandal of massive proportions that needed burying.

Eastwood told Saville that, in his view, the RUC Special Branch was 'a lot better at intelligence work' than was commonly believed, a view not shared by the likes of Carver and Kitson. So who was telling the truth?

These questions are important because they raise issues about Eastwood's credibility. If he could airbrush McGrath, Kincora, Baker, the MRF and collusion with UDA murder gangs from his account of his career, it is possible he concealed the full extent of what he knew about MI5's espionage activities inside 'Free Derry' too.

In place of substance, he provided dreary details about the various meetings he attended including those each morning with senior military officers and civilians from the MoD.[4] From time to time, he attended Faulkner's Joint Security Committee (JSC) at Stormont. He was not a 'formal member' although he and the head of the Special Branch attended it by invitation when 'intelligence input was required'.[5]

What is known, however, is that he also attended the Director of Operations' Intelligence Committee meeting which was responsible for 'pulling together all the intelligence received in the previous week and looking ahead to the next one'.[6] Since information was flowing in from informers in the UDA, UVF and TARA, he must have known about their recruitment and what they were doing on the streets of Belfast.

***

One of the most important agents feeding the intelligence machine over which Eastwood presided was the spy designated 'Observer B' at the Saville Inquiry. He had been reporting to the army since 1970. In July 1971 he became an asset shared with MI5 and fabricated information which he fed to his handlers.

Two military intelligence handlers looked after him for the army. Decades later they would both acquire bland codenames, IO1 and IO2 (Intelligence Officers 1 and 2) at the Saville Inquiry. Two MI5 officers, known as James and Julian, managed him for their service.

The information he submitted was fed up the chain of command and helped shape the response of the army and MI5 to threats – real and imaginary. One of his fabrications was that the IRA intended to fire shots at the British army from the Rossville flats in Derry on 30 January 1972. The Rossville flats consisted of three blocks which accommodated thousands people living on nine floors. It had served as an urban fortress during the Battle of the Bogside.

Observer B claimed he had been in the vicinity of the flats on 25 January, the Tuesday before NICRA's ill-fated Bloody Sunday march, where he noticed a group of about forty men between 'the ages of 18 and 30 dressed in civilian clothing'. One of them, a man aged about twenty-eight, 'with a pale complexion and dark hair, began to issue orders to others'. The men lined up, he claimed, in three rows in front of him as he shouted commands at them in Irish such as 'attention!' and 'at ease!' Observer B claimed they were IRA auxiliaries whom he had seen before.[7] It is implausible that a conspiratorial organisation which valued the anonymity of its recruits would mobilise so many members so publicly. There is no documented precedent for anything of this kind occurring in Derry.

When Observer B described the IRA's auxiliaries, he said they tended to 'be made up of men who wanted to contribute to IRA operations but were not considered to be suitable material for the IRA's active service units'.[8]

A short while later, he claimed he saw the men march across Rossville Street before filtering into the flat complex.

Within minutes, he alleged, he encountered another individual referred to as 'X'. Persisting with his deceit, Observer B claimed he had asked 'X':

> 'What is going on?' ['X'] replied 'You have noticed them.' I said 'I have noticed them, I've seen them practising. What do you think they are up to? X replied, 'They are practising for Sunday [30 January]. They were here yesterday at the same time.' I said, 'The best thing for you to do is to keep your head down and get on with what you're doing.' X replied that that was exactly what he would do.[9]

Observer B next claimed the imaginary formation split up and spread out along the three landings of Block 2 of the flat complex where they appeared to be engaged in some sort of a paramilitary drill. At first, they stood on the inside edge of the balconies with their backs to the doors of the flats. On command, they moved forward to the outside edge, keeping just to the left of each of the columns that were located on the outside edge at intervals. Observer B reported that he thought their manoeuvres were designed to conceal them from the army's observation posts located on the city walls which could peer into the flats. A little later, he claimed he saw 'X' again:

> I said to him 'what on earth do you think they were practising for?' X and I then discussed the possibility that the Fianna were planning to attack the Army to draw them into the area and then fall back, leaving the soldiers vulnerable to sniper fire.[10] I'd seen this tactic employed before on a couple of occasions but concluded that given the amount of people likely to be present on the march, they would not do such a thing. X said words to the effect that he would not rule anything out ... I telephoned [Intelligence Officer 1] that evening, describing what I had seen

and informing him that I thought there was going to be serious trouble at the march on Sunday ... IO1 replied 'we are going to have to think on this one – ring me again in the morning [Wednesday 26 January].' The next morning I telephoned him again. I repeated what I had seen and he asked me 'Do you think they will do it every day?' I took this to mean practise every day. I said that I did not know.[11]

On Thursday 27 January, Observer B claimed the auxiliaries had carried out an identical drill after which he encountered 'X' again:

I said to him: 'They're still at it' and he replied, 'Every day this week'. I telephoned IO1 telling him what I had just witnessed. He said he was looking into it. He seemed very excited by this information.[12]

The claim that IO1 was 'excited by the information' was probably the only true fact in Observer B's entire yarn. Beyond question, this information would have been relayed upwards to senior military intelligence officials and thence to Carver, Tuzo and Ford. Kitson was surely brought up to speed too, as his troops in 1 Para had already been assigned to go to Derry the following Sunday. Since Heath and Carrington were being kept up to date about the march, it is likely they also were told about this development.

As Observer B was a shared asset with MI5, the information would have made its way to them also.

***

The reality of what was taking place behind the barricades was far less dramatic. Reg Tester, the Official IRA quartermaster in Derry, told the Saville Inquiry that no Official IRA volunteers or auxiliaries had drilled near the Rossville flats in the days preceding the march.

Martin McGuinness stated that the Provisional IRA would never have countenanced the deployment of auxiliaries to fight the British army. Under no circumstances would any of them have been given a gun by the IRA. They were not people in a position to be physically in charge of a weapon or in charge of operations attacking British military forces.[13]

Significantly, none of the soldiers occupying the various observation posts which targeted the Rossville complex, or anyone flying above Free Derry in a helicopter noticed anything that resembled the paramilitary drilling described by Observer B.

What really puts the case that Observer B was lying beyond any doubt is that not a single person in Derry has ever spoken of anything even remotely resembling his description of these events.

Both wings of the IRA were adamant they did not launch any sort of an offensive action on the day of the march. Instead, McGuinness confirmed to Saville that, on Thursday 27 January, representatives from NICRA approached the IRA requesting that it should be allowed to proceed peacefully. The following day, the IRA, having observed a substantial build-up in the city, agreed to keep away from it. This was consistent with the way they behaved in the recent past. In July 1971, the DYH and the IRA in Derry avoided the temptation to engage with 1 Para when it was ferried to the city to provoke them into open confrontation as part of *Operation Hailstone*. The following month the IRA had responded in a similar cautious manner when they noticed the military build-up before the introduction of internment in August 1971. On that occasion, many of its leaders left their homes to go into hiding.[14]

Wilford told the Saville Inquiry that he was not aware that the IRA had agreed to avoid the march:

> I have been asked by Eversheds [solicitors for the Tribunal] if I have any recollection of a suggestion that the IRA had agreed to stay away. I do not.[15]

***

The Saville Inquiry asked Eastwood for a statement on whether or not there had been any intelligence of which he was aware that specifically predicted the IRA would attempt to exploit the NICRA march on 30 January, 1972, as cover for attacking the army. He replied:

> I do not remember any intelligence specific to the march in question to that effect but I do remember that it was endemic at that time that the IRA would join marches, demonstrations and any civil disturbance to exploit opportunities to cause trouble to the security forces. In any event [the RUC], Special Branch Londonderry would more than likely have collected what intelligence there was on the march at a local level at the time and would have given information directly to the local Brigade commander [MacLellan] without it ever coming to my attention.[16]

When he gave his evidence at Saville in person, Eastwood was asked some questions about Observer B:

> Q: We have understood from other evidence that Observer B was an informant who did not live in Londonderry, but who visited Londonderry from time to time. Do you now have any recollection of an agent or informant who answers to that description?
> A: No.[17]

He was also asked:

> **Q:** The Observer, Observer B from whom this information was obtained, has now died. But before he died he gave a statement to this Tribunal in which he said that he was in Londonderry two days (*sic*) prior to the march and saw a group of what he took to be IRA auxiliaries drilling in an area called Glenfada Park and later saw them on the landings of Block 2 of the Rossville Flats, apparently planning how to direct sniper fire at the Army. Do you now have any recollection of any intelligence about people being seen drilling or practising sniper activity?
> **A:** No.[18]

It is difficult to believe that this was a truthful answer for it would mean that military intelligence did not share this alarming information with Eastwood or his associates at their regular meetings. If military intelligence withheld this information, it could only have been done on foot of orders from someone as senior as Carver, Tuzo or Ford. If so, they must have had a very good – or rather very bad – reason for ordering such an act of concealment.

If Eastwood did receive the information and committed perjury at the Saville Inquiry by claiming not to have known about it, he must have had a deeply nefarious reason for so doing. For a start, it would mean he had endangered the lives of the troops under the command of 8 Brigade, including the paratroopers on loan from Palace Barracks.

There was one man, however, who was unquestionably entitled to a full account of the intelligence provided by Observer B but to whom such a briefing was denied.

19

KEEPING THE BRIGADIER IN THE DARK

Observer B's information was passed to his handler on the evening of Tuesday 25 January 1972. It should have been passed on to 8 Brigade in Derry but was not.

David Eastwood, the central intelligence chief and former paratrooper, did not admit that he had received the information at the Saville Inquiry. But his word cannot be taken at face value. The odds are that he did receive it. If so, he was guilty of gross negligence for not passing it to 8 Brigade. The fact that the information was false is immaterial: at the time, Observer B was perceived as a valuable and reliable asset and his information should have been passed to MacLellan. Precisely the same applies in circumstances where Tuzo, Ford and military intelligence were possessed of the information yet failed to relay it to MacLellan.

Meanwhile, Frank Lagan had his finger on the real pulse of Nationalist Derry. He had established a line of communication to the militants in the 'no-go' area, including the Official IRA. Unsurprisingly, he was told nothing by his sources about a forty-man IRA ambush party. Clearly, he was not told about Observer B's claims by either MI5 or military intelligence for, if he had been, he would surely have challenged them based on the information he was receiving from inside the Bogside.

***

Derry was on a knife-edge. The RUC and the business community were afraid that the march would reach the commercial heart of the city. The original NICRA plan was for it to culminate in a rally at the Guildhall in the city centre. At this point in time, Lagan wanted to let the march proceed while photographing the organisers so they might be prosecuted later.

According to Carver twenty-six barriers were to be set up, with 'knife-rests of dannert wire secured by concrete blocks, each manned by a platoon of soldiers' with an RUC constable present.[1] Two battalions were to be sent as reinforcements of which one would be 1 Para. The army did not believe that the NICRA organisers would be able to control the hooligans and hence an arrest force 'was to be held centrally, provided by the Parachute Regiment, and its operation order described its task as to maintain a brigade arrest force to conduct a "scoop-up" operation of as many hooligans and rioters as possible'. Crucially, the sweep was only to be launched, 'in whole or in part', on the orders of Brigadier MacLellan. 'The order stated that it was expected that the arrest operation would be conducted on foot.'[2]

On Monday afternoon, 24 January, MacLellan, Lagan and his deputy superintendent McCullagh, met at Ebrington Barracks to decide how they would deal with the march. The following Wednesday MacLellan submitted a plan to Ford.

Lagan's estimation was that 8-12,000 people would take part. According to a report MacLellan sent to Ford, the RUC man believed that a massive confrontation 'with the security forces would ... shatter such peace as is left in the city; and remove the 'last vestiges of moderate goodwill ...'[3] Since MacLellan had been left in the dark about Observer B, his plan for controlling the march did not address the prospect of the troops under his command coming under fire from a phalanx of gunmen.

MacLellan did receive a warning of sorts in a signal sent by Eastwood at 10.10 a.m. on 27 January reciting that a 'source known to you has provided the following information about plans for the march on 30th January as at about noon on [Tuesday] 26th January.'[4] The information was inaccurate:

> that the marchers will be armed with sticks and stones and he expects that the IRA will use the crowd as cover. The organisers are determined to have their revenge to what they regard as a humiliating defeat at Magilligan ... they are determined to get to the Guildhall, come what may.[5]

MacLellan was asked at the Saville Inquiry if Eastwood's signal had alerted him to anything 'which you did not either know or anticipate as a possibility'?

> A. No, I do not think so. The source was not very good, was it?
> Q. Why do you say that?
> A. Well, because they, they – the organisers decided not to go to the Guildhall.[6]

MacLellan also explained that he was not aware of who the source was, or even what type of asset he was.

Assuming Eastwood knew about Observer B's information, is it possible to conceive of a rational explanation for his failure to impart the far more alarming details of it to the brigadier of 8 Brigade?

***

MacLellan drew up Order 2/72 in consultation with Lagan. It was an eighteen-page document the main object of which was to 'prevent any illegal march taking place from the Creggan and to contain it, with any accompanying rioting, within the Bogside and Creggan areas of the city'.

MacLellan wanted to deal with the march in as low key a fashion as possible while aware that nail and petrol bombers and possible IRA snipers might exploit the rioting, probably at the end of the march. MacLellan also appreciated the value of deterring the rioters with a heavy military presence. As far as he was concerned, the arrest of the rioters by troops from 1 Para was only to happen if he ordered them into action. He anticipated that if they were to be deployed, it would be on foot, not in vehicles. He said at Saville that the use of vehicles was not necessarily in contradiction of his orders as the intention could have been to use them to incarcerate rioters.

Observer B's intelligence would have stirred the combative impulses of the hard men of the army such as Ford, Kitson and Wilford. They had been itching for, and possibly planning since December, an open confrontation with the IRA in Derry. Observer B's intelligence provided them with what appeared to be a golden opportunity to take on forty gunmen, smash through into the no-go areas and bring about an end to 'Free Derry'. This was hardly a prospect they were willing to let slip through their fingers. By Ford's estimation, there were approximately 100 IRA volunteers in Derry, of whom forty were active gunmen, and they were able to rely on up to 300 hard-core hooligans to do their bidding.

If Ford, Kitson and Wilford – or any combination of this group acting with others – developed this type of plan, it is likely that Carver and Tuzo would have been kept in the loop. According to Carver's memoirs, London was closely monitoring what was going on. On Thursday, 27 January, he attended a meeting of the cabinet at Downing Street where it was agreed that a special magistrates' court would be set up on the Monday following the march. According to Carver, they also decided that: 'Maximum publicity would be secured for the arrests and court proceedings following the march. It is important to note that arrests were to be made for those rioting and not because they were marching. It was hoped that a number of the hooligan element would be arrested.'[7]

The Joint Security Committee at Stormont, chaired by Faulkner, also met on that day. The JSC resolved that the march would be stopped at William Street. Intriguingly, the JSC noted that the 'operation might well develop into rioting and even a shooting war.'[8] One thing is certain, Lagan was not responsible for the prediction that the soldiers could be facing a potential 'shooting war'.

On the night of Thursday, 27 January, the occupants of Palace Barracks where 1 Para was stationed suffered a public humiliation. Curiously, the event is rarely, if ever, mentioned in narratives about Bloody Sunday.

20

THE BOMBS AT PALACE BARRACKS

Byron Lewis, a member of 1 Para, wrote an account of his life as a paratrooper in Northern Ireland during which he recalled that:

> When in Palace Barracks [where 1 Para was stationed] we used to hold dances in the Naffi and bring in coach loads of local girls.[1] Again this only served to increase suspicion and dislike among the young male population. The girls sometimes took advantage of this, namely a group of them would bring in a stick of gelignite each in their handbags and assemble a bomb in the toilets. Fortunately we discovered them in time.[2]

One bomb had been found in one of the toilets at the base.

The solution to the gelignite smuggling was to search the handbags as guests entered the base. On Thursday 27 January, at around 11 p.m., two bombs exploded inside the transport pool, wrecking a personnel carrier and damaging a land rover. A third device was found outside the empty officers' mess and was defused. Around 130 women were admitted to a dance and all of them were searched on their way in. Nonetheless, it was suspected that some succeeded in smuggling the explosives through the security net.

The next day *The Evening Echo* reported that 'Security forces launched a full-scale investigation today' into the attack.[3] The report described the barracks as 'one of the most heavily guarded British Army bases in the Six Counties'.

The *Evening Herald* reported that during a search that

had taken place a '10 lb. bomb only a short distance away from the officer's mess' had been found. 'All visitors to the barracks, including the dancers, were then searched and given tests to see if they had been handling explosives. An army spokesman said: 'We are still trying to establish how the gelignite was brought in.' He said none of the girls who had attended the dance had been detained but investigations were still proceeding.[4] The military police officers or soldiers questioned all the female guests before they were let out of the base. Some of them were held until the early hours of the morning.

The Irish Press told its readers that there was 'no explanation last night as to how an explosion could have occurred in this extremely tightly guarded area.'[5]

The security checks at Palace Barracks had not failed. The bombs had been planted by Peter McMullen, a corporal in 1 Para. Born in 1947, he had been reared at a number of military bases in Britain while his father had served in the RAF. He was born in Magherafelt, County Derry and in 1962, aged fifteen, he had joined the British army reserves. Later, he married an Irishwoman, Eileen Loughran, who came from a Republican family. In 1968, he joined the Parachute Regiment and rose to become a corporal in 1 Para.

His battalion was sent to Belfast in October 1969 where he was assigned to a two-man foot patrol which took him along the Shankill Road. There, he experienced two minor altercations with Loyalists who enquired about his religion. 'I told them I was Irish and Catholic. Why deny it? I had nothing to hide, and besides I was there to protect them as well as the Catholics', he told Andrew Blake of the *Boston Globe* in 1979.[6]

The harassment, however, began to get to him and he went to his superiors requesting to be taken off the patrols. In addition, some of his wife's family had become active Republicans and he feared that he might have to fire on them one day. The solution reached was to send him to the army catering corps. After his graduation, he returned to his old regiment in Belfast. In September 1970, he was stationed in the married quarters at Palace Barracks with his pregnant wife and their three children. He worked in the officers' mess where he kept his eyes and ears open and picked up details about forthcoming operations but at that time did not betray any confidences.

A former officer who attended the officers mess at Palace Barracks and others like it in Northern Ireland on 'thousands of occasions' recalls how ample amounts of alcohol, especially gin, were consumed in the mess and that it was the job of people like McMullen to top up the drinks to keep the party atmosphere going. 'No one would ever think that the man in the white coat replenishing your glass was anything other than harmless. You would never be suspicious, especially back in those days'.[7]

In August 1971, McMullen overheard that internment swoops were about to start and informed members of his wife's family. The warnings must have been ignored as some of his in-laws were swept up. Elsewhere, senior IRA commanders had gone on the run. 'At this point my own personal feelings began to change drastically. Up to now it was a bit of a strain between me and the wife. I was defending the army and she was defending her people. But the army, sent in by the prime minister supposedly to keep peace and stop the murder of Catholics, now were going around arresting them and putting them in jail for nothing', he told Blake in 1979.

The one-sided nature of internment struck McMullen as unjust and anti-Nationalist. 'The British army sealed off and searched homes in sections of the Catholic Falls Road for days, but didn't touch the Protestant Shankill Road, where intelligence reports showed they had enough weapons to arm a battalion.'[8] McMullen became convinced the IRA offered the only protection for Nationalists from Loyalist extremists, not the British army.

The Provisionals began to appreciate his potential to them. Within a week of internment, he was approached by two IRA men who introduced him to some of their colleagues. 'I told them that my prime concern was for my wife and children and not for the Paras or the Provos. Still, they asked me to come up with a plan to do something at Palace Barracks, and in the meantime to gather whatever intelligence I could. I told them I'd see what I could do'.[9]

Martin Meehan was one of the Provisionals' most active members at this time. He was arrested and brutally beaten up during interrogations on a number of occasions. He was suspected by the army of being involved in the 1971 killing of three soldiers but was never charged. After the IRA in north Belfast killed six soldiers from the Green Howards regiment in September 1971, the finger of suspicion was pointed at him. He was captured and brought to Palace Barracks for questioning, requiring forty-seven stitches to the back of his head after his interrogation. McMullen was there when Meehan was being questioned. 'One night there was a party in the officers' mess. It was only about 50 feet from the interrogation centre. The doctor was called out of the mess. He asked me to keep his dinner warm for him. A little while later, he comes back and says "Gee, that's a tough guy they've got over there. They've split his head open, putting needles into his arms and fingers and scraping his bones and he still won't talk." The doctor took his hot meal and joined the party.'[10]

McMullen made a plan to smuggle twenty-two IRA volunteers into the base and conceal them in his house in the married quarters. Once inside, they would lie low for a while before creeping out to overpower the eight guards who were protecting the arsenal. According to McMullen, it housed over 1,000 weapons including machine guns, rocket launchers, semi-automatic rifles, handguns and mortars. 'The whole operation would have taken less than an hour. No one would have been hurt, because security was very lax in those days, and the IRA would have had a cache of weapons they sorely needed. We could have driven right out the gate with them in an army truck.'[11]

The IRA deliberated on the plan for two months without arriving at a decision. The hesitancy on the part of the Provisionals must have sprung – in part at least – from a concern that McMullen was an *agent provocateur* on a mission to trap them. The capture of twenty-two volunteers would have delivered a blow from which the Belfast Brigade would have taken a long time to recover.

In late January 1972 McMullen overheard officers talking in the mess about the forthcoming NICRA march in Derry. 'Some of the officers talked about showing these bastards what it's like to face a Para.' According to Blake:

> He also noticed that several brigadier generals had suddenly joined the officers' mess, and their general conversation was about flushing out the IRA in Derry, forcing them into a confrontation on Sunday and dealing them a heavy blow. Later that day, in the sergeants' mess, McMullen heard a sergeant-major say, 'We're going into Derry and these bastards are going to get their comeuppance.'

The reference to 'several brigadier generals' is intriguing. There was no one with the rank of 'brigadier general' in the army but there were two officers with the word 'general' in their title in Northern Ireland at the time, Tuzo and Ford and three brigadiers including Kitson and MacLellan. Tuzo, Ford and Kitson were based in Lisburn, some fourteen miles away. The other brigadiers, MacLellan and Lt-Col Ken Dodson, were stationed further away. MacLellan did not visit Palace Barracks at this time. If McMullen's story is accurate, it indicates that Kitson and Ford had travelled to Palace Barracks to review something that was afoot there.

According to McMullen, he was aghast that the regiment planned to use armed force against civilian demonstrators to provoke the IRA and draw them out into the open.[12] Like everyone else at Palace Barracks, McMullen must have been well aware of what happened in Ballymurphy, when paratroopers had run amok shooting innocent civilians.

McMullen immediately telephoned his IRA contacts

and relayed this information to them. He probably did this on the Monday or Tuesday before the march. Fearing a bloodbath, he asked them for explosives to destroy the parachute regiment's motor pool – all of it – consisting of 200 vehicles, including their armoured cars. The IRA decided to take him at his word and provided him with seventy pounds of gelignite and three timers. He had hoped for a lot more. The timers had been extracted from German washing machines. 'Still, I thought I could cripple the motor pool so they couldn't get to Derry,' he said.[13]

Ironically, 1 Para had taught McMullen how to prepare an incendiary device. Upon enlisting, he had received basic training for six weeks before a period of six months of intensive training in explosives, interrogation, riot control, unarmed hand-to-hand combat and the use of a wide range of modern military weapons.

McMullen prepared three bombs in the kitchen of his house: two 25-pounders and one 20-pounder. At 9 p.m. on Thursday night, 27 January, he placed two of them under the fuel tanks of trucks parked in the motor pool. He noted how they were parked on an incline and chose vehicles at the top hoping fuel would run down and ignite the other trucks. He placed the third bomb against an empty officers' barracks. All three washing machine timers were set for 10 p.m. 'There was a big dance on the base that night,' he told the *Boston Globe*. 'If I wanted to kill people, I could have killed about 600. But I wanted instead to embarrass the British. To show them that their elite units could be hurt by the IRA.'[14]

He maintained that his wife knew nothing about the

bombs. She and their children were in the house in the married quarters, a safe distance from the motor pool where the bombs exploded. At the time he was on his way across the border to Dundalk and listened to the late news on his car radio en route. The IRA was expecting him and he was hailed as a hero upon his arrival. Champagne was produced and he was later taken to Dublin to meet Sean MacStíofáin, the chief of staff of the Provisionals. The visit to Dublin probably took place on the Friday before Bloody Sunday. He warned the Dublin leadership about the plans for Derry. 'They still didn't grasp the significance of it, and I figured maybe they knew better than I, so all I could do was tell them and let it go at that. They partied for several days. Then came the news about the massacre of civil rights marchers. British paratroopers shot and killed 13 Catholic marchers.'[15]

The information McMullen gave to MacStíofáin may have informed the latter's analysis of what happened on Bloody Sunday. In his 1975 book, MacStíofáin said that the British army had learned that the only times the IRA 'would concentrate and emerge in open battle were for community defence'. He contended that 1 Para had been sent to Derry as part of a 'historically tested counter-revolutionary tactic' to 'brutalise the civilian population so as to trigger the revolutionaries into a suicidal open confrontation'.[16] He propounded that the Bloody Sunday march had provided the British army with an opportunity during which it was 'expected that the IRA would be drawn out and obliged to react in strength. Then the paratroopers would go in to smash the resistance in the Bogside'. He attributed the failure of the plot to the fact that the IRA had agreed to keep away from the march at the request of the organisers. Hence, the 'reason there were no IRA casualties that afternoon was simple. The IRA was not there':

> The aim was to bring about a spectacular defeat of the IRA which would destroy the morale of the no-go areas, enable Stormont to reassert its rule and leave the Nationalist people with no option but to accept whatever reforms the Loyalist right wing would let Faulkner get away with. To accomplish this, the IRA would have to be brought to battle in a situation that would be least advantageous for guerrillas and would offer conventional Army scope to exploit its superior numbers and equipment.[17]

The week after Bloody Sunday, Murray Sayle, Derek Humphrys and other journalists from *The Sunday Times* prepared a potentially explosive report about Bloody Sunday for their editor. It was never published. Part of it read as follows:

> Military Intelligence asserted that there were about 80 hardcore militants [in Derry]; if they were killed or locked up, the IRA problems would be, according to the reports, as good as over. But tactics were difficult. If one of these men was 'lifted' in a surprise dawn raid, the other 79 would flee over the border ... The Parachute Regiment staff planners believed they had the answer in the last weeks of the old year – a solution which in fact produced the massacre. 'The idea – worked out, we believe, by Lieutenant Colonel Derek Wilford on lines of thinking propounded by Brigadier Frank Kitson, British Army counter-insurgency expert, was based on the military principle that the way to bring your enemy to battle is to attack something that, for prestige reasons, he will have to defend – Germans attacking Verdun in the First World War or the same firm (*sic*) attacking Stalingrad in the second. Brought to battle, he will then be annihilated by superior strength.'[18]

The civil rights march, the Parachute Regiment planners believed, was just such an objective which the IRA would have to defend or lose its popular support in the Bogside – and either way the IRA would be finished:

> If the IRA gunmen could be induced to stand and fight while other demonstrators fled, a snatch squad but it would have to be a large one – would be able either to kill them or take them on. So, for some weeks the Paras have been drilling and rehearsing a company-size snatch squad – at about 100 men, the biggest one ever used in the present Ulster [*sic*] fighting.[19]

***

If McMullen was telling the truth about the conversations he overheard at Palace Barracks, the implications for the reputations of Carver, Tuzo, Ford, Kitson, Wilford and many others are immense. It implies they planned to provoke the IRA in a densely populated area at the culmination of a march comprising thousands of civilians.

The day after the bombing of Palace Barracks, Wilford flew by helicopter to Derry in preparation for the deployment of 1 Para to the city over the weekend. Many aspects of this trip raise questions about what he was really planning to do when he returned with his men the following Sunday, the day of the NICRA march.

21

THE SAND TABLE

On the Friday after Bloody Sunday, Murray Sayle, a veteran war correspondent who wrote for *The Sunday Times*, inveigled an invitation over the phone to visit Palace Barracks. There he was escorted on a tour by an army public relations officer. Astonishingly, he showed Sayle a 'sand table' representation of the Bogside, that is to say, a scaled model of the area. When he testified at the Saville Inquiry, Sayle explained that he asked the PR officer:

> ... 'Well, where did you plan this, where is the exam table,' fishing, if you like, and he said, 'it is in the next room'. What I do vividly remember is being taken into the room and seeing it. Now, I presumed there had to be one because that is how these operations are planned, but it was most interesting, indeed, to have it confirmed there was one and I remember thinking how detailed it was and I said, 'did you make this here', he showed me round it and he said, 'No, we made it in Germany'. He is the source of that information.
>
> I still have a vivid recollection of seeing, on something that looked like about the size of a billiard table, so it was maybe 6 feet long, 4 feet wide and it vividly sticks in my mind and is mentioned in the memo [to the editor of the *Sunday Times* shortly after Bloody Sunday], the detailed nature of this, this model ...
> Q. When you talk about 'a sand model', was it literally –
> A. No, these are collectively called 'sand tables' and the process is called 'sand tabling it'. No doubt – it is an ordinary military term – no doubt they were once made of sand, but they are usually called a sand table.
>
> Next, Sayle was shown a photograph of a model of the Bogside which had been used at the Widgery Tribunal and asked if it resembled the one he had seen at Palace Barracks.

A. Very much like that, very much like that.[1]

No one at Palace Barracks would have ordered a model of the Bogside in Germany and had it transported to Belfast without a reason. One use for it could have been to plan the most effective way to invade the Bogside.

Two modelling experts have examined the photograph of the model of Derry shown to Sayle. Both agree that it would have taken approximately two weeks to make in normal circumstances.[2] When asked about the representations of the Rossville flats, they agree that 'that would have been the easy part.' One of the modellers has said that there 'were probably architectural and engineers' plans in existence for them which could have been sourced from the planning authorities but probably 'not for the older buildings. The old church there is another example of where measurements would have had to be collected by an on-the-spot examination. A team of people could have gone in and photographed all of these buildings and the roads'. Once that was done, the data would have had to be matched to street maps before it was sent to Germany. 'A lot would depend on how many people were involved. A team could have done it in weeks'.[3] The other expert has pointed out that the lines of bricks could have been counted from photographs to reveal the height of buildings.[4]

If we are to believe Ford and Wilford, the first Wilford learned of his orders to go to Derry was the Monday preceding Bloody Sunday. In stark contrast to this, the existence of the sand table points to a plan to conduct some sort of an operation inside 'Free Derry' that was in gestation long before that date. It is inconceivable that Wilford would have hatched such a plan without the knowledge of Kitson and Ford.

When Wilford appeared in the witness box at Saville in 2003, he was not asked about the sand table and offered up nothing about it of his own volition. Any discussions he had around it with Ford and Kitson remain a secret to this day.

***

On the afternoon of Friday 28 January, Brig. MacLellan arranged a meeting at Ebrington Barracks with the officers designated to confront the marchers. They were joined by Lagan. MacLellan's overall objective was to divert the march into 'Free Derry' and separate the peaceful marchers from anyone who peeled away from it to riot.

Col Wilford flew by helicopter from Belfast to attend the Ebrington conference. In the witness box at the Saville Inquiry, he claimed to have driven to Derry. During his evidence, he was reminded that at the Widgery tribunal he had said he had reconnoitred the area in the helicopter. All of a sudden, his memory of the flight came flooding back in sufficient detail to raise questions about whether he had forgotten about it in the first place. He was asked:

Q. ... were you able to identify the Bogside?
A. Oh, yes.

The fact that he acknowledged flying over the Bogside – which he described as 'the enemy terrain' – is remarkable because his contrary orders did not contemplate sending 1 Para into it. He knew that it was expected by MacLellan to be no more than a 'scoop' operation, i.e., use the skills his troops had developed in Belfast to capture rioters. So, why did Wilford feel the need to reconnoitre an area beyond his operational terrain?

He was then questioned as to whether he had observed the Rossville Flats and Creggan from the air. His answer to both was, yes. After that, he was asked about two of the locations where his troops had shot civilians on 30 January 1972:

> Q. Did you check out Glenfada Park, Abbey Park?
> A. Well, I cannot recall that I did, now, but I was looking at *the whole area* [my emphasis].
> Q. And then you went down and you reconnoitred the area by car, not on foot?
> A. I did get out, I think, on a couple of occasions, yes.

Significantly, he added that he had informed his commanders at Palace Barracks the following morning that he would be going 'pretty far forward' with them:

> Q. When you did indicate to your order group [on Saturday 29 January at Palace Barracks] that you would give them further instructions at the forming-up place, you also indicated that it would be necessary for you to get pretty far forward in order to observe what was going on?
> A. Yes.[5]

Yet, his troops, if they were to be deployed at all, were meant to remain near the containment barriers at William Street, something that hardly equates with going 'pretty far forward'. The reconnoitre from the helicopter over the 'enemy territory' of Derry's no-go area, however, fits neatly with a plan to go 'pretty far forward'.

There are other clues suggesting that Wilford planned to go into the Bogside. An adjutant to 1 Para told the BBC in 1992 that:

> It was clear, to us, and I think very clear to Colonel Wilford that the formal, open, very public crossing of this line [into the Bogside] was going to be a very significant action by the security forces, it is not something that had been done for quite a long time.
> An invasion?
> Your words but, but – one might assume that the IRA would see it as such and react.[6]

***

At the conference at Ebrington Barracks that Friday, MacLellan brought the commanders, including Wilford, through Order 2/72 paragraph by paragraph. He stressed the importance of using the minimum amount of force. One of his primary concerns was to avoid endangering the lives of peaceful protesters in circumstances where it was anticipated the IRA might snipe at the troops during the arrest of rioters down at William Street. His concerns were rooted in common sense and experience, not any information provided by Observer B.

The recollection of others present at the meeting – as later relayed to a *Sunday Times* journalist – was that Wilford had remained silent during the briefing. At Saville, Wilford was asked about this:

> Q. Do you recollect that you were very quiet at this meeting?
> A. No, I do not.[7]

Whether Wilford was silent or not, he did not alert his fellow commanders to the information provided by Observer B. The spy had passed that information to his military intelligence handlers the previous Tuesday. Assuming Wilford knew about it by now – Friday – he may have assuaged his conscience by assuring himself that it was he and his men who were going to face a broadside if they ventured beyond the area where the stone throwing by rioters was expected to take place, not the troops of the other commanders at the Ebrington conference. Moreover, he knew that British army counter-snipers were going to be spread out along the walls of Derry overlooking the Rossville Flats. They were ideally placed to deal with any IRA gunmen who might take up positions in front of the blocks or appear on the balconies, behind windows or on the roof. There were also counter-snipers embedded in various vantage points who had the flat complex in their sights. One observation post, codenamed 'Echo', was located on the top of the Embassy Ballroom Building on the Strand Road and had a clear view of the balconies.

Could it be that there was an additional, even more compelling, reason for his silence? One plausible explanation is that he was treating Observer B's information as genuine and intending his troops to confront the formation of IRA gunmen of which the spy had spoken, and then invade 'Free Derry' reclaiming it for the crown. If this explanation is correct, his reticence about Observer B's information could be explained in terms of a desire on his part to conceal a plan to invade the Bogside from MacLellan. This would also account for his half a century silence about the sand table representation of Derry at Palace Barracks because that was where the plan was developed.

Wilford's behaviour became increasingly questionable as Sunday 30 January 1972 drew closer.

22

THE BOGUS GUNMEN

IN THE ROSSVILLE FLATS

Col Wilford assembled his commanders at Palace Barracks the following Saturday morning at 10.30 to give them their orders. Later, the instructions trickled down to the lower ranks. Significantly, Wilford was already contemplating defying MacLellan's edict that 1 Para was to confine its operations to the William Street area. According to his adjutant Michael Jackson:

> There was a sense that we might be heading for some sort of set-piece confrontation: it seemed unlikely that there wouldn't be at least some aggro. But it's worth stressing that the Battalion's mission was to capture rioters in the immediate vicinity of the barricades, which of course meant going over the containment line. The Colonel had *thought long and hard* about how to get in, how to get over the containment line into the area where the rioters would be. *The main difficulty was vehicle access.* [*My emphasis*] Of course we anticipated that the IRA might react when we 'invaded their turf'. *We had to be prepared to be attacked at any time* [*My emphasis*]. However, there was no sense in which we planned to use the arrest operation to 'teach the IRA a lesson'. This was not on the agenda.[1]

The use of the phrase 'long and hard' is intriguing since Wilford had allegedly only been told about the intention to send 1 Para to Derry the previous Monday, and had first visited the city the previous afternoon. Hence, Jackson's description implies a longer gestation period of whatever plan Wilford was contemplating.

At the Saturday morning briefing at Palace Barracks, Wilford warned his officers to expect sniper fire from the Rossville flats. One of those present was Major Edward Charles Loden who commanded Support Company. Born on 9 July 1940, Loden had been educated at Stonyhurst and commissioned in 1960. He joined the Parachute Regiment the following year. By 1967, he had become the Intelligence Officer of 1 Para which was then stationed in Aden. He won the Military Cross while serving there. He provided the following testimony at the Widgery tribunal:

Q: At the [Orders] Group was any consideration given to the possibility of your soldiers coming under fire if they were to go down Rossville Street?

A: It was not actually mentioned; going down Rossville Street was not actually mentioned specifically, but the Rossville flats were mentioned as a place where sniper fire might come from.

Q: Did you at some stage, whether it be that day or thereafterwards, give consideration to the question whether if you took soldiers down Rossville Street towards Rossville flats, you might not only come under sniper fire but might provoke young men to use pistols?

A: Well, I knew that Rossville Flats had been pointed out as the place where fire might come from, but my appreciation was – and I base this on my experiences in Belfast – that when a large body of troops appeared in armoured vehicles, any gunmen who might have been thinking of having a go would in fact not. So, I was surprised when the shooting started: I must say.

Q: I had assumed that when you spoke about the possibility of coming under sniper fire from Rossville flats, you were really referring to rifles and possibly IRA gunmen?

A: Yes, sir.

Q: Rather than to young boys with pistols?

A: Yes.[2]

In addition, the company's sergeant major told the BBC: 'I did expect when we went into the Rossville Flats to be fired at.'[3]

The platoon sergeant told the BBC: 'I was just told that there was a possibility that gunmen would be in the area and to keep our eyes out especially for high ground like the Rossville flats – obvious sniper position.'[4]

Yet, in his statement to Widgery in 1972, Wilford had described how he had warned commanders 'that we must look to our flanks and front particularly in the open area of Rossville and William Street where there has been so much sniping during previous rioting'.[5] While there was a reference to the 'open area' at Rossville Street, there was no specific mention of the flats themselves in Wilford's statement to Widgery. Why did he not state that he had provided a clear warning about the threat from the flats when he testified before Widgery? One possible explanation is that such an admission would have struck any of the soldiers attending Widgery from 8 Brigade as extremely odd. They had kept a log of all the occasions on which they had received sniper fire from the flats: in the previous three months 2,000 shots had been discharged in their direction, with only a tiny fraction from the structures themselves.

When he gave evidence at Saville decades later, Brig. MacLellan was reminded that when he had appeared at Widgery he had said that his command had 'no hard intelligence on the Rossville Flats'. Moreover, that he did not view the complex as a source of danger. 'I think in the three months prior to the 30th January, there were three confirmed shooting incidents from the Rossville Flats. To put it in perspective, I think there were 1,965 shots fired at us in those three months, and only nine shots from the Rossville flats in those three incidents.' At Saville, he added that:

> 5,000 people lived there ... and I would assume that the last thing they wanted was the IRA firing at the soldiers from there and the soldiers firing back and putting them at risk and no doubt they may – some of them may have supported the aims of the IRA, but I suspect they said 'go and do it from somewhere else'.[6]

Lt Col Ferguson, who commanded the city battalion responsible for Derry City, shared MacLellan's views, as did Lagan, that the complex was not a threat.[7]

Why did Wilford not repeat what he had learned from 8 Brigade to his commanders on the Saturday, namely that while there had been sniping near the blocks, only a tiny fraction had emanated from the windows or balconies of the complex?

Why did he advise them to the contrary?

One resolution to this puzzle is that although he knew that the blocks had never been a hotbed of IRA sniper activity, on this occasion he feared they were going to become a lethal threat based on the information provided by Observer B. Moreover, since he could not reveal the source of this intelligence as a British spy in 'Free Derry', he had to ensure his men remained on a high alert and wary of an attack from the balconies.

23

'We want some Kills Tomorrow'

The passage from Peter Taylor's book *Brits* which described how Support Company had become known as 'Kitson's Private Army' in Belfast was recited to Kitson at the Saville Inquiry after which he was asked if he had been aware of this at the time. In response, Kitson claimed he had 'no knowledge' of the nickname which might possibly be true as his reputation for being 'cold and aloof' might have insulated him from hearing of such a moniker. Implausibly, he added that he was 'completely convinced it would not have been used by any particular company of any particular battalion'.[1]

Kitson purported to know little or nothing about the Support Company's history, an odd fact, if true, for it had participated in Britain's counter-insurgency campaign in Aden in the 1960s. This is something that would have been of great interest to Kitson's studies and preparation for his 1971 book, *Low Intensity Operations*:

> Now, Aden is mentioned, for some reason. Aden was only four or five years back on this and quite likely, if 1 Para was in Aden, which I do not know, there would have been more – a higher proportion of that particular company than another company. But the fact that they had been in Aden would have, I would have said, no bearing on this whatsoever.[2]

He was asked if the Support Company was regarded as the battalion's hard edge.

> Not by me they were not.[3]

He was read a quotation from a platoon sergeant attached to Support Company quoted in Taylor:

> We were very experienced, and very highly motivated ... When barricades went up in Belfast, they came down very quickly. The whole training of the Parachute Regiment is built on aggression and speed and you can't afford to hang around. This gets through to the blokes and they get very hard-minded about their work. They know what they're doing and they're good at it. I don't think there was a better battalion at that time in the world, never mind the British Army, in terms of internal security. They'd seen it all in Belfast.[4]

Kitson was asked if this reflected the attitude of individual paratroopers:

> I would agree, and I certainly agree that there was no better battalion at the time, I do not say in the world, but they were an extremely good battalion. I would not say the best because there were probably others that would regard themselves as the best and I would not be saying 'you are better than you', but these people knew their job absolutely.[5]

When the barrister picked out the phrase 'built on aggression and speed' Kitson acknowledged 'speed' was a factor:

> Naturally if you are going to take down a barricade you want to do it forcefully and fast under circumstances -- if you are being resisted. If there is no resistance, you can do it at whatever speed you like.[6]

***

The briefing and orders Wilford gave to his officers, on Saturday 29 January, trickled down to the troops of Support Company during the rest of the day and night. One of the recipients was Byron Lewis, a radio operator with Support

Company. He appeared at the Saville Inquiry under the designation, 'Soldier 027'. By 1975, he had left the army. That same year he had put pen to paper resulting in an un-varnished account of what had really happened on Bloody Sunday. It did not surface until 1997 when Tom McGurk in *The Sunday Business Post* in Dublin published an account of it. It was the first substantial piece of new evidence to have emerged since the Widgery Report and was pivotal in the establishment of the Saville Inquiry.

The ex-para network became aware of Lewis' account after McGurk's article appeared. Back in 1975, Lewis had given his manuscript to an American writer called Seán Patrick McShane who was writing a book on Northern Ireland. The document was never used but was passed to others and made its way to McGurk. The journalist tried to trace Lewis but without success. In the *Sunday Business Post* article, McGurk referred to Lewis as 'Para A'.

An indication that Lewis was telling the truth can be gauged from the fact that his former colleagues realised he was the source of the information from the details outlined in McGurk's article. How could this have been otherwise if he was concocting a yarn?

In January 1998, a group of men acting on behalf of Lewis' former colleagues found out where he was living and beat up a man who was sharing the address with him. The assault took place on the 13 January. Lewis was lucky to escape with only a warning. The Saville Inquiry was told about it the following day and made a note about the incident which read as follows:

However, he has had to move out of his home. Last night 2 men attacked the person he has been sharing a bungalow with while he was outside the house in his car. First they attacked the car, then they dragged him [the other man living at the bungalow] out of the car and beat him up. They then threw him through the front door and dragged [redacted but undoubtedly Lewis] outside. They offered him a block of concrete and said, 'That's your one chance. Give it your best shot, because afterwards we're going to kill you.' They mentioned Bloody Sunday, blood money, the SAS, that friends of theirs had been killed, and people who dealt with the media. They were very violent and it was not possible to reason with them. [Lewis] did not resist them, was compliant, and they did not in fact harm him. His friend is in hospital and is seriously hurt. The assailants knew who [redacted but clearly Lewis] was but did not appear to be very well-informed about Bloody Sunday or his activities He did not know them.[7]

He was also branded a traitor on an ex-paratrooper website.

Lewis went on to testify at the Saville Inquiry. He has rarely been given credit for his courage. McGurk, however, described him as the 'brave' man, he undoubtedly was. He was eventually admitted to a witness protection scheme and his present whereabouts are unknown.

His earliest account – a statement for Widgery in 1972 – can be dismissed for what it was: a tissue of lies concocted for him to sign by manipulative Widgery Tribunal officials determined to cover-up the fact the paratroopers had shot at unarmed civilians.

Many elements of Lewis' 1975 account rang perfectly true: 1 Para was expecting trouble from the IRA. Michael Jackson the adjunct to Col Wilford who rose to the very pinnacle of the British army, confirmed as much when he stated in his memoirs that, 'of course we anticipated that the IRA might react when we "invaded their turf".'[8]

What really sets Lewis' 1975 account of Bloody Sunday apart was his revelation that a lieutenant – designated as 119 at the Widgery tribunal – had told him that 1 Para was expected to 'get some kills' in Derry the next day. The passage in Lewis' 1975 account of the Saturday night briefing is not long and is worth reproducing in full:

> One night in January 1972 I was sitting with the rest of my muckers of the Anti-Tank Platoon in the Barracks when our Lt [119] came in and informed us that we were due for an operation in Londonderry the following day.[9] He said that the heart of Derry had been bombed out. Several hundred soldiers had been hospitalised and that not one arrest had been made. We knew that the Creggan Estate was an I.R.A. fortress, conning towers, machine guns and barbed wire as well as land mines guarding its approaches. The people of the Creggan had not paid rent and had high-jacked all their food for several years. This was the symbol which led to the name 'no go area'.

The assertion that the IRA had conning towers and landmines is fanciful and absurd. Nonetheless, this is exactly the type of information that could have been fed to the paratroopers to rile them up and ensure they would expect a ferocious reaction when they went near the Bogside or the Creggan. Lewis proceeded to describe the impact this propaganda had on his colleagues:

> As I looked at my friends I could see that after all the abuse and nights without sleep, frustrations and tension, this is what they had been waiting for. We were all in high spirits and when our Lt. said 'let's teach these buggers a lesson – we want some kills tomorrow' to the mentality of the blokes to whom he was speaking, this was tantamount to an order (i.e., an exoneration of all responsibility). We set off in a convoy across Northern Ireland. It was a beautiful sunny day, patches of snow were still to be

seen. The shells of country mansions burnt out in bygone days. Winding rivers and greenery, an odd contrast to what was to follow. When we arrived at Derry we parked our vehicles in the back of town and debussed.[10]

The foregoing passage shows that the troops on their way to Derry were unable to distinguish the fundamental fact that the Civil Rights movement was different to the IRA. The protest scheduled for the following day was organised by people like Ivan Cooper MP, not the IRA. It was intended to be a peaceful event and the fact that the organisers of the march had asked the IRA to stay away from it underscores the chasm between them and the paramilitaries.

In his statement to Saville, Lewis also explained that, 'as squaddies, our perception was that probably all the people in Republican areas were IRA supporters.'[11]

***

Wilford's version of the briefing to his commanders on the eve of Bloody Sunday was that:

I do not recall any input from the company commanders, but they were a very vocal lot and there probably would have been comments. I do not recall any specific concerns. I had no involvement in the subsequent Order Groups given by the company commanders. Orders were then passed on by the platoon commanders, and then possibly by the section commanders. What I told my company commanders would have been passed down to the private soldiers in this way.[12]

As far as the accusation levelled at Lieutenant 119 was concerned, Wilford said that 'I do not believe that this is true.

Lieutenant 119 was a solid officer. I cannot imagine him or indeed any other of my officers saying such things'.[13]

Byron Lewis and Peter McMullen are not the only ex-paratroopers serving in Northern Ireland in 1972 who have provided information that can help us understand what took place on Bloody Sunday. There was another unnamed officer who attempted to write a book that was never published, but a chapter of it has survived.

24

'LONDONDERRY'S SHARPEVILLE'

A soldier who served with 1 Para wrote – or at least started – a book about his experiences in Northern Ireland. He submitted a chapter from it to his superiors in the early 1970s. It was passed to the Information Department at HQNI at Lisburn, where Col Tugwell and Colin Wallace read it. 'I think it is a work by a young officer – what is it the Americans say? – "with attitude"; and I do not think he is typical', Tugwell told the Saville Tribunal when asked about it.[1] Wallace, who thinks he was a captain, kept a copy of the chapter which he passed to the Saville Inquiry. 'It provides a perfect insight into the mind-set of 1 Para as Bloody Sunday loomed', Wallace believes. 'It should have been easy to have established who wrote it, yet Saville made no effort to trace the author. That was very disappointing'.[2]

Although the chapter was entitled 'Bloody Sunday', it dealt with the events leading up to the day of the march but not the actual day itself. In it, the author describes how he and his colleagues had been assigned to police a civil rights march from Dungannon to Coalisland on the day before Bloody Sunday. 'Our inner conscience hoped and prayed that if we had to deal with the crowd it would be a violent one – for this was what we were trained for, and not the thankless task of policemen,' he wrote. Ominously, he was under the misguided belief that the NICRA was a front for the IRA, a view he describes as having been shared by his fellow soldiers:

> The Dungannon to Coalisland march proved to be one of those
> ridiculous situations when the crowd remained consistently
> good-humoured and refused to be drawn by the elaborate
> military preparations, and the 'belligerent' stance struck by the
> soldiers, clad in their flak jackets, leggings, steel helmets, wielding
> clubs and rifles and standing defiantly behind the barricades. Led
> by Bernadette [Devlin] herself, the marchers paraded between
> the barricades, up and down the streets urgent queries as to
> the attitude of the crowd buzzed through the ionosphere ...
> remarkable significance was attributed to the most insignificant
> things; it was almost as though we were willing them to come
> out fighting, and bring the whole unreal business down to a level
> which we could at last understand and appreciate – violence.

Despite all its resources and manpower, the army lost the
trail of the march only to discover it was proceeding along an
old disused railway line. 'This was what we were all waiting
for – the battle in the countryside', the author recalls, but the
troops were to be denied a fight. When they caught up with
the marchers, they were 'huddled' in an old mill in Coalisland.
After some discussion, the protest broke up. As the soldiers
left Coalisland, 'abuse, catcalls, whistles and the occasional
brick accompanied us as we drove through the town on our
way to set up more roadblocks ... We sat, miserable, for an
hour, and not a soul came past us. Then came the welcome
call to return to the rest of the Battalion. Have we enough
petrol? What for? The journey to Londonderry of course'.

When they set off for Derry to re-join the rest of 1 Para,
it was in the hope 'as far as we were concerned, with any
luck' that the 'boys' would be there. The 'boys', of course, were
the IRA. The route they took was 'soon littered with broken
down "pigs"':

Morale, then, was high indeed. This was going to be no idiot chase of a few demonstrators across an Irish bog. This time the 'enemy' (they were inevitably thus categorised, for our military vocabulary – indeed whole training – did not allow of any other brand of belligerent) had promised us the biggest and best Civil Rights March ... The people would be there, the politicians would be there, the media would be there and (as far as we were concerned, with any luck) the 'boys' would be there. And we would be ready for them – indeed, this was an opportunity we had been waiting for. We, at last, had plans of our own ... The time had come to teach these young thugs – (and particularly those who had become known as the 'Derry Young Hooligans') a lesson.

During a 1998 Channel 4 interview, Col Wilford spoke of the operation that took place in Derry on Bloody Sunday as one which 'smacked' of 'it is time we taught these people a lesson'.[3]

Portentously, the author of the unpublished chapter recalls how, the previous Friday, a company commander had rushed 'excitedly into his office after the Commanding Officer's Orders group [meeting]. "We're really going to have a go at them this time".'

Significantly, the author pointed out that the 'intelligence part of the operational order predicted gunmen in the area of the Rossville flats'. Later that day, when the author explained to his wife what the weekend's operations would involve, she ominously predicted the headlines that would follow: 'Londonderry's Sharpeville'.[4]

***

None of this struck Saville as significant. He described the manuscript as one which 'does not appear to have been published, and no witness to this Inquiry has claimed responsibility for writing the piece in question. Although Colin Wallace retained the document, he could not assist further as to its origin or the identity of its author'.[5] The use of the word 'appear' raises the disquieting prospect that no inquiry, however superficial, was undertaken to see if it had reached a wider audience, for example, a literary agent or even submission to a magazine or as material for another writer.

Saville found that there were 'considerable doubts as to its provenance' and that it appeared unlikely that 1 Para, or any part of this battalion, was involved in policing the Dungannon to Coalisland march:

> *The Fusilier magazine* (volume 1 number 8, June 1972) recorded that the units employed in the operation came from 3 RRF, 1 KOB and 8 UDR. The first two of these were also deployed in Londonderry on Bloody Sunday. There is no evidence from any 1 PARA soldier that members of the battalion were present at this event, and several witnesses told this Inquiry that they did not recall the battalion being so deployed. In these circumstances, the authenticity and accuracy of the draft chapter cannot be verified, and we are unable to place any reliance on the information that is contained in this document.

The reasoning here is shallow. Why would someone who was not serving with 1 Para submit a book to his superiors claiming that he was a member, if he was lying? HQNI would have known precisely who he was and would have denounced him as a fraud immediately. If he was still serving in the army, it would have had a detrimental effect on his future career prospects. Crucially, when the book was passed to Tugwell for his consideration, he was not told there was any doubt about the fact the author had served with 1 Para.

Gilles Peress was one of the most important and respected witnesses to appear at the Saville Inquiry. His photographs were relied upon throughout it and he is mentioned over 150 times in the report. In *Hidden Truths*, Peress had described how he had driven from Paris to Belfast taking ferries en route before Bloody Sunday. 'I followed the Civil Rights marches.[6] The images I took were influenced by the images I had seen of Civil Rights movements in the United States; the two movements were very connected. I remember one march from Dungannon to Coalisland – it was just before Bloody Sunday. Bernadette Devlin was there. The British paratroopers were preventing the march from taking place so it was diverted across the fields.' *Hidden Truths* was published in 1998. Peress gave his evidence on 22 May 2002.

Why did Saville not ask Gilles Peress if he recalled the presence of paratroopers on the day of the Dungannon to Coalisland march? Why did he not ask to see the photographs taken by him – or any other photographer – that day? I have seen those pictures. They include clearly discernible images of paratroopers. If the award-winning photographer had been asked for them at the Saville Inquiry, he would have produced them. But he was not asked about the march at all.

***

Simon Winchester, *The Guardian* journalist, who is mentioned elsewhere in the unpublished chapter, could sense dark clouds gathering. He headed for Derry at about ten in the morning 'after reading the newspapers full of gloomy reports about the imminent dangers of the afternoon'.[7] He encountered a UDR road-block that generated a three mile traffic jam about ten miles outside Belfast. 'Every single car, every passenger on every bus, every sack on every lorry, was checked and rechecked by men clearly delighted to be delaying Belfast men on their way to the western counties. It was an infuriating delay, but reasonable army tactics in the circumstances.'

On the way he listened to John Taylor, the Stormont Unionist MP on the BBC's lunchtime news magazine as he predicted 'imminent civil war, and there were predictions of Loyalist hard men moving into the Bogside to rout the heavily armed Provisionals. It all sounded rather tense'.

When he joined his press colleagues in the city the consensus was that there would be 'a really big riot development during the day, a riot which would settle down during the night to a long exchange of gunfire, with perhaps the odd casualty on either side. And that was probably all'. This, Winchester learned was the 'basic view taken by the army and police back at headquarters: that after a serious riot, Londonderry would become a deadly battleground, with the IRA and the army fighting it out with their rifles long into the evening'.

At about 2 p.m. he joined a television reporter with whom he was friendly and together they 'ambled up into the Bogside, past the concrete slab and wooden and barbed-wire barricade that had been built at the bottom of William Street, and up to the Rossville Flats'. Here, Winchester spoke to some people he knew and received a different forecast about what was going to happen. The Bogsiders told him that they were not expecting serious trouble because the Provisional IRA commander in the city had ordered most of the organisation's 'arsenal to be removed from the Bogside "in case they use the opportunity to search the place" – the "they" referring to the massed British regiments on the outside'.[8]

25

STRAINING AT THE LEASH

Chief Inspector Lagan did not believe the IRA was planning to use the Civil Rights protest as a cover to attack British troops. When he drove up to Ebrington Barracks shortly before 2 p.m. to join MacLellan in the observation room, the marchers had assembled in the Bishop's Field in 'a cheerful mood'.[1] They finally moved off an hour later. Lagan arrived armed with news from his contacts inside the no-go area: the NICRA organisers had decided they would not attempt to breach the barrier at the containment area at the bottom of William Street. Instead, they would stop at 'Aggro Corner', turn right, proceed up along Rossville Street towards the flats, and rally for speeches at 'Free Derry' corner.

Simon Winchester recalls that most of the press walked ahead of the NICRA lorry as it 'trundled its way down the scruffy streets, and looking back the mood seemed almost ebullient, with mothers wheeling prams, children weaving here and there, laughing, joking, playing pranks on the television men and generally adding to an air of a Derry carnival'.[2]

Officially paragraph 9 of MacLellan's Order 2/72 made it clear that if the snatch squads from 1 Para were to be unleashed, they were to operate in the area of William Street–Little Diamond; a second assault would be directed towards those in the William Street–Little James Street area adjacent to it. These small streets had been turned into cul de sacs by the army's barriers. Meanwhile, the peaceful marchers could wheel away from them up Rossville Street and out of harm's way.

The marchers reached William Street at 3.30 p.m., and, just as Lagan predicted, the main body curled around onto Rossville Street in the direction of 'Free Derry Corner', where they were addressed by various speakers. Some marchers broke away to taunt the soldiers and began to fire objects at them but there were no nail or petrol bombs and no guns. In response, the troops kept them at bay with tear gas, rubber bullets and a cannon that sprayed purple water at them.

At approximately 3.50-55 p.m. a military sniper shot at the crowd in William Street and hit unarmed Damien Donaghy, aged fifteen, who fell to the ground. This was approximately twenty minutes before the heavy shooting by Support Company began. John Johnston also unarmed, fifty-nine, ran to the boy's aid and was shot.

If the IRA had had active service units ready to deploy, these shots might have incited them to confront the troops. The Officials, however, were also under instruction not to carry arms. Two Officials disobeyed their orders. The pair were ensconced on the top floor of a flat on Colmcille Court and fired at the paratroopers' Tactical HQ adjacent to the Presbyterian church near the end of Little James Street, and hit a drainpipe. Seán Keenan junior and other Provisionals raced to the flat to prevent any more firing. The Official IRA shooter and his colleague were on their way down the stairs when the Provisionals arrived. They discharged no more rounds that day.

Johnston died the following June from his injuries. Donaghy survived. 'I knew that the Official IRA had fired a shot even before the fella gave evidence [at the Saville Inquiry]', he explained.[3] 'He came to me and told me he fired a shot after I was shot. Everybody knew at that time. It was not hidden over the years. It was common knowledge in Derry. Saville and the barristers of the army tried to make it out far worse than it was. The Official IRA men admitting firing shots ... They were supposed to have [opened fire] before I was shot but the [Official IRA] man who fired it told me it was after I was shot [by the British soldier].'

An Official IRA Volunteer ('OIRA 4") fired two pistol shots from the gable end of a wall adjacent to Chamberlain Street, but without causing any significant impact on the course of events that were unfolding.

Col Wilford told Peter Taylor in 1992 that the significance of the 'drainpipe' shot was that 'there was at least one weapon on the other side, and if there was one weapon, then there were probably others. If someone starts shooting at you, you can behave in a variety of ways. You can run away – which of course on the whole soldiers do not – and certainly my battalion would never run away. You could take cover behind your shields and just sit in an area until it all passed over. You could do what of course my battalion were trained to do and that is to move forward and seek out the enemy.'[4]

Wilford had long been critical of the behaviour of the

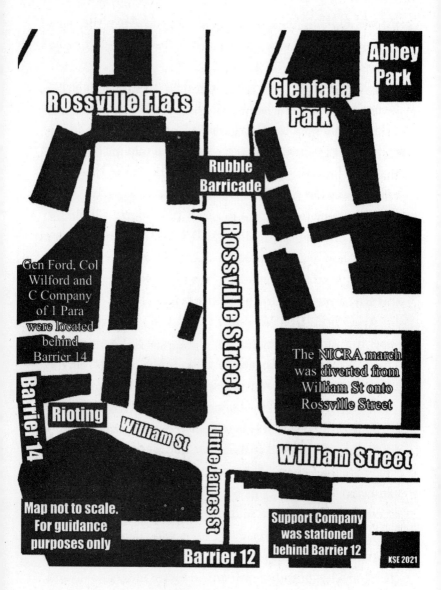

Bloody Sunday map

soldiers of 8 Brigade who did not engage physically with rioters: 'This to us was really quite horrifying because it was clear that the soldiers never went forward and just stood there like Aunt Sallies. I had actually said in public that my soldiers were not going to act as Aunt Sallies – ever.'[5] He also complained to Taylor that he kept 'using the word "innocent". There is no innocence in a riot'.[6] When reminded that Lord Widgery had used the word, he replied: 'Yes, of course he will, because you know that's a civilian word and riots actually sort of breed the idea that there is some innocence (*sic*) and some not so innocent'. To this Taylor countered: 'But you don't sign your death warrant by taking part in a demonstration' and he replied, 'some people do'.[7]

At 3.55 p.m. Wilford tried to entice MacLellan to unleash his men by telling him that he had deployed some of his troops 'slightly forward' in 'preparation for any orders which you may have' as he had been waiting almost half an hour and the number of rioters was becoming thin on the ground. As MacLellan hoped to de-escalate tension, he refused to issue the command. A few minutes later Wilford asked if he: 'would like to deploy a sub-unit through barricade 14 to pick up yobbos in William Street/Little James Street'. Again, MacLellan declined.

A military water cannon was aimed at the crowd and used to disperse the press photographers and TV cameramen who were congregating near the fighting.

As the minutes ticked by 1 Para became more impatient. By 4.02 p.m. the number of rioters had shrunk further. To Wilford, this increased the likelihood that the IRA would disappear too as the rioters provided them with cover for their sniping. One unit of the paratroopers now asked: 'Is there still a hooligan element in the area of William Street/Little James Street and around Barrier 14?' When they were told there was, they responded: 'Would you mind informing Zero [Brigade HQ] of this, as they don't seem to believe us on this point'. At about 4.03 p.m., Brigade HQ was told that the 'hooligans' were still present.

During 1983 and 1984, Desmond Hamill was researching a book he would publish in 1985 called *Pig in the Middle: The Army in Northern Ireland 1969–84* and secured an interview with the former CLF, Gen. Ford. The latter let something slip: Ford had called MacLellan and instructed him to send in the paratroopers. When Hamill spoke to MacLellan, he confirmed the call. Wilford had probably contacted Ford behind MacLellan's back to get him to apply pressure on MacLellan, something Ford could do as he was MacLellan's immediate superior.

According to the then Capt. Mike Jackson, his superior officer, Col. Wilford was impatient to deploy:

> Our main force was further back with the pigs [in a church yard], poised to go forward into the waste ground and scoop up the hooligans. We were kept waiting for what seemed a long time for the order to go – [8] Brigade Headquarters was concerned that there should be adequate separation between the violent and non-violent elements of the marchers. The Colonel became impatient. There were various communications over the radio, in which he expressed his desire to get a move on. He said something to the effect of 'They are all where we want them now.' Eventually, at 16:10 hours, we were given the order to go.[8]

It became clear that Wilford had divided his troops into at least two separate forces and they behaved as if on unrelated missions. C Company dealt with the rioters on foot while Support Company headed towards 'Free Derry' in a convoy of military vehicles.

Although the order was eventually given for the Paras to proceed at about 4.07 p.m., a time-limit was placed on their deployment. This was disregarded once they raced through the barriers.

26

'Rehearsed Blocking Positions'

Gen. Ford brought Col Maurice Tugwell, the officer in charge of military propaganda, along with him to Derry on 30 January 1972. He was also a seasoned counter-insurgency expert and his explanation for being there was that he wanted to see a civil rights march and had asked Ford for a lift in his helicopter. He was, he asserted, present as an interested observer only. This stretches credulity. Belying this, Colin Wallace, who worked for Tugwell on many psychological operations [often using disinformation and lies], says that he received a series of calls from him throughout the day indicating that he was there on an operational basis.

Tugwell swore on oath at the Saville Inquiry that he had not engaged in psychological operations while in Northern Ireland. This was untrue, so his word cannot be taken at face value. Tugwell was a trained dissembler and there must be more to his presence in the city that day than meets the eye. Ford may have brought him along because he knew that something more than the mere arrest of a few teenage hooligans was about to take place and wanted the top information specialist by his side to take care of what was about to unfold.

Ford too claimed he was a mere observer, yet he came with a driver, two military police officers armed with machine guns, a radio officer and radio equipment. Two hours before the massacre began, he and Tugwell went on a tour of the positions taken up by the soldiers. Ford was at barricade 14 on William Street as C Company was about to spring into action.

Inevitably, some people left the march to confront the British troops and a riot began.

Col Wilford released C Company from the traps first. 'Go on, 1 Para, go and get them and good luck', Ford urged them as they surged forward and descended upon the rioters on William Street with their boots, fists and batons flying.[1]

Three minutes later, Support Company, which had been concealed behind a wall in a Presbyterian churchyard, made their way through barrier 12 and sped along Little James' Street straight through the crossroads with William Street and into Rossville Street in a convoy consisting of a Ferret scout car, seven armoured Saracens and two four-tonne trucks. If the troops of Support Company were really intended to launch an arrest swoop on foot, Wilford had placed them in a disadvantageous location. What he did was the equivalent of the trainer of an athletics team handicapping his runners by placing them at a considerable distance behind the starting line. It would have made more sense to put them behind barrier 14 with C Company or close to the top of Little James Street, as near to the junction with William Street as possible. From there, they could have swept forward and trapped at least some of the rioters. Instead, he deposited them in the Presbyterian churchyard, which meant they would have to run all the way along Little James Street, losing any element of surprise they had and affording the rioters a significant time advantage in fleeing from them. The distance from the churchyard to the junction with William Street was more than half the length of Ross-ville Street. Even a slow runner could have managed to escape from them in those circumstances. The choice of the Presbyterian churchyard only makes sense if Wilford had planned all along to deploy his convoy of vehicles contrary to the orders issued by MacLellan.

Byron Lewis, acting as a radio operator for Support Company, was in one of the Saracens or 'pigs' which raced up Little James Street, then along Rossville Street. According to his 1975 account:[2]

> Looking around me our faces were blackened and we were wearing helmets. Adrenalin was running. There was excitement in the air. I know I speak for the majority when I say that the common feeling amongst us was, please let us be called in – we'll go nuts if we miss a chance like this ... Then I heard Major Loden's voice crackle on the radio 'machine guns and anti-tanks mount up and move in'. Coughing and spluttering [from the presence of CS gas], filled with all the emotions conceivable, we moved down to the Army barricade ... (I should mention that while we were in the church yard four or five yards away from me I saw a pall of dust and chips of concrete fly from the ground. It didn't occur to me until minutes later that we were under fire).[3] The scene that confronted us at Rossville Street were wooden and barbed wire barricades moved back to allow us through ... With visions of [Großdeutschland] on a wave of excitement to the point of shouting, we swept past them and on into Rossville Street.[4] In front and to the left was Rossville flats, to our right a complex of low flats and walk-ways, in between the two was an enormous wildly animated crowd with a frontage of about 150 yards.

James Chapman, a Welsh born ex-sergeant-major and civil servant who was now living in the Bogside, and described himself as 'a loyal subject to the crown', watched what was happening from the opposite direction. 'I then saw a fleet of seven Saracens preceded by a ferret scout car coming into Rossville at about forty mph from Little James' Street. Also, I saw a Bedford four-tonner follow the Saracens and pull up on the pavement at the mouth of Rossville Street. The ferret stopped in the middle of Rossville Street near the northern end of Rossville flats. Five of the Saracens took up positions at the northern entrance to the Rossville Flats. The other two Saracens took up positions at the northern end of Glenfada Park. The vehicles reached their positions by fanning out across the waste ground off Rossville Street. Between 50 and 100 paratroopers dismounted from the Saracens. Other paratroopers were running up Rossville Street and the waste ground in support of the Saracens. On disembarking from the Saracens the paratroopers assumed firing positions from the corner of the Rossville Flats and in Rossville Street itself and from the corner of Glenfada Park. They opened fire immediately on the crowd who were trying to flee through the rubble barricade near my house. I would estimate that about 20–30 shots were fired in the first burst and I saw three people fall, I believe, dead or dying. They fell over the barricade.'[5] According to Wilford's statement to Widgery, his men now 'came under fire [and] the whole arrest operation took on a different face: the soldiers were obliged to move tactically into cover and, engage the enemy gunmen'.[6]

Jackson, who was with him, has written that almost 'immediately it became apparent that they thought they had come under fire. They began zig-zagging from side to side and looking for cover'.[7] However, no one was shooting at them. If they were zig-zagging, they were probably doing so as they feared the presence of gunmen in the flats above them. Significantly, since there was no hostile fire directed at the soldiers, there was no need to have switched from an arrest mission to one involving shooting. A logical deduction is that the arrest operation was nothing more than a cover and the shooting was part of a hidden plan now unfolding into its operational phase.

The eyewitnesses in the Bogside have provided the only reliable reports about what happened. They saw troops who simply jumped out and started shooting. So, the claim by Wilford that his troops were engaged in an arrest operation is not true.

Film footage of what happened was taken but it was subsequently tampered with. According to Colin Wallace, his team at HQNI had been tasked with recording the operation on 16mm film from a helicopter 'overflying the Rossville Flats area':

> Having seen the film again it appears to have been edited. One sequence appears to be out of place and shows the crowd at Free Derry Corner staying calm at a period when I would have expected them to have scattered and the paratroopers had already deployed onto the waste ground in front of Rossville Flats. I do remember that the film was shown at the [1972 Widgery] Tribunal hearing, but I do not recall much else about it ... It is interesting, however, that the film was thought sufficiently important not to be processed in Northern Ireland, instead it was sent directly to the Ministry of Defence in London. I do not know who made that decision.[8]

The helicopter pilot, designated INQ 2030 at the Saville Inquiry, gave a statement describing how he recalled 'seeing lots and lots of people on the ground, perhaps as many as five or ten thousand. They appeared to be congregating in one particular spot. All of a sudden, there was a burst of activity. People began running in all directions and the crowd effectively scattered. I can think of no better way to describe it than the effect that dropping a stone on an ants' nest would have. It was almost as if the people on the ground had disappeared although I could see them hiding behind walls and buildings'.[9]

Murray Sayle, the veteran war correspondent, described the deployment of the troops as having been conducted according to a military attack plan. The extracts quoted next are from the article he wrote with Derek Humphrys for *The Sunday Times* but which were not published due to threats from the Widgery Tribunal. A copy was preserved in the archives of *The Sunday Times* and was handed over to the Saville Inquiry. His editor buckled and censored the story. Sayle resigned in protest. He pointed out that while civilian witnesses described a 'scene of horror', James Chapman, the former sergeant-major, recognised the execution of a military plan. According to Sayle and Humphrys:

> The Saracens took up rehearsed blocking positions along Rossville Street and next to Rossville Flats. Paratroopers wearing combat and not anti-riot gear jumped out and dropped into standard British Army firing positions in spots clearly selected in advance for the purpose of the operation.
>
> This clearly was to ambush the supposed concentration of IRA men in the Harvey Street/High Street/Eden Street/ Chamberlain Street area, pinning them against the Army defences in Waterloo Road. This area is usually a battleground between the Army and the stone-throwing demonstrators in 'normal' Derry riots. Another platoon ran through the narrow

alleys and walkways of the Little Diamond area, also a traditional battleground.

Executing the normal fire-and-movement tactic taught to British infantry (the trained and the untrained witnesses agree exactly on this, using different terms) the Paratroopers cleared the barricades in Rossville Street by shooting everyone on it or near it. Kelly, William Nash, Young and McDaid were killed here – ex-Sergeant-Major Chapman saw three people hit and slump on the barrier. Everyone at the barrier, considered by Bogside people to be their main line of defence, was either dead or wounded. Nash senior raised his arm to try and stop the shooting, was hit in the arm and lay shouting for an ambulance. A section of Paratroopers running through the Little Diamond to link up with their comrades at the barricade got behind it – there was no one left alive to stop them – and began laying down a field of fire behind Rossville Street flats. In this shooting Gilmour was killed; McGuigan who ran up to him was killed, and Doherty, crawling along at some distance to escape, was shot dead in the same line of fire.

Paratroopers leading the Little Diamond pincer movement ran into Glenfada courtyard, where a handful of demonstrators had taken refuge, and began shooting – a normal street-fighting tactic when entering a possible ambush area; in this shooting Wray was killed and Friel wounded. This section continued through to Abbey Park and repeated the clearing fire, killing Gerald Donaghy, Gerard McKinney and William McKinney.[10] The three bodies were piled up on top of a short flight of steps in Abbey Park. People under fire ran out from nearby houses and dragged the bodies in and Dr [Raymond] McClean, who was present, at once pronounced them dead.[11]

27

Disobeying the Major

Byron Lewis has provided a visceral account of the movements of Soldier F and his 'EFGH' unit. Soldier F was the man 'mentioned in despatches' for his alleged gallantry during internment the previous August in Belfast.

Lewis described how his vehicle swerved to a halt, the men pulled off their gas masks as they leapt out. Two platoons were involved in this leg of the operation:

> The machine-guns on the left hand side advanced leap-frog fashion to the base of Rossville flats. I was in the Anti-tanks which scurmished [*sic*] through broken bottles and bricks down the right hand side of the road. As we moved along the wall towards the crowd I noticed several strikes in the roadway beside us. I was with the leading group of half a dozen as we reached a small garden at the corner of Kells Walk. At this point approximately 100 yards short of the crowd lance corporal F went into the kneeling position and fired at the centre of the crowd from behind a low wall some 2 feet high which ran around the garden. Soldier G immediately jumped down beside him and also opened fire. Just beyond the wall on the pavement INQ 635 also commenced firing. Looking at the centre of the barricade I saw two bodies fall.[1]

At this point, Lewis raised his rifle but 'on tracking across the people in front' of him, he could see a crowd which included 'women and children although the majority were men ... [but] no one with a weapon'. He lowered his rifle. Members of the crowd were shouting 'wildly':

> I remember thinking looking at my friends who had now grown to half a dozen in a line side-by-side, do they know something

I don't know? What are they firing at? Opposite us I could see members of the machine-guns *(sic)* helmeted and black faced in a standing position also pumping off rounds at quite a rapid rate. In the initial 30 seconds I would say that 100 rounds were fired at the crowd ... Several people had dropped, bodies were being dragged away, men were lying on their faces crawling along the pavement in front of Rossville flats in an effort to get away. After an eternity of timeless moments and sights [Major] Loden's voice came on the radio and ordered a ceasefire. I knew the blokes were getting in while the going was good as people with gleeful expressions were running up from the rear and elbowing their way through to get into the firing line.[2]

TV footage exists during which Loden can be heard shouting: 'Do not fire back for the moment unless you identify a quality target.'[3]

Lewis relayed Loden's order to 'cease-fire' by running along the line of soldiers tapping them on their shoulders. The firing slacked and died as the crowd dispersed. Then, in defiance of Loden, Soldier F and others moved into Glenfada Park where they would continue the murder spree. According to Lewis:

[Soldiers] E, H, G and F and myself then leapt the wall, turned right and ran down Kells Walk into Glenfada Park, a small triangular car park within the complex of flats. A group of some 40 civilians were there running in an effort to get away. H fired from the hip at a range of 20 yards. The bullet passed through one man and into another and they both fell, one dead and one wounded. He then moved forward and fired again, killing the wounded man. They lay sprawled together, half on the pavement and half in the gutter. E shot another man at the entrance of the park who also fell on the pavement. A fourth man was killed by either G or F. I must point out that this whole incident in Glenfada Park occurred in fleeting seconds.[4]

Lewis recalled that when the soldiers first appeared in

Glenfada Park, the people had 'turned to face us and raised their hands'. That was the way they were standing 'when they were shot'. Moments later a 'Catholic priest ran across to the bodies shouting about giving the last rites, he was clubbed down with rifle butts. A hysterical woman, short, fat, about 50 years old dressed in black was crying uncontrollably about one of her sons being shot. She too was beaten and I recall soldiers kicking her when she was on the ground.'[5]

Why did the EFGH unit disobey the orders of their major? Unfortunately the best-case scenario is that they were psychopaths consumed by a lust to kill unarmed civilians who posed no threat to them. The worst-case scenario is that they were in receipt of secret orders from Wilford to provoke a reaction from the IRA, if the local gunmen looked like they were not going to defend the Bogside. Such a mendacious plot could have been conceived as an insurance policy to hand 1 Para the excuse it needed to invade 'Free Derry', i.e. a street battle with the IRA. In this respect, it should be recalled that neither wing of the IRA had taken the bait during *Operation Hailstone* the previous July. On that occasion, 1 Para had done little more than conduct a few searches to provoke the DYH and the IRA and had elicited no response from either group. Shooting civilians was, however, a far more serious provocation. If there were forty IRA men or Auxiliaries, as Observer B had claimed, the chance that one or two of them would have responded was enormous. But, Observer B was a deceitful fraud and there were no gunmen lurking about Glenfada Park or the Rossville flats.

Soldier F has revealed that shortly before he and his

colleagues went into action on Bloody Sunday, Wilford visited them at their temporary base. Wilford spoke to him and Soldier G. Soldier F added that 'it was a bit unusual for [Wilford] to come around like this'.[6] Wilford may have discussed the intelligence from Observer B. Soldier F is one of those who alleged that gunfire emanated from the direction of the Rossville Flats.[7]

Maj. Loden could not have been a party to the intrigue to provoke the IRA as outlined above, as he was urging his men to exercise caution in choosing targets

Lewis' account reveals other strange occurrences that were taking place around him: he was about to come upon a man in civilian clothes who identified himself as an 'officer'.

28

THE MEN IN CIVILIAN CLOTHES

After Byron Lewis lowered his rifle to let a group of local men in donkey jackets remove two bodies, he realised he was alone and moved 'back down Kells Walk expecting to be shot any second'. He became 'filled with an overwhelming desire that the truth should be known' about what had happened and when he reached the area where 'the prisoners were spread-eagled against the walls I grabbed one of a large group of pressmen who was standing there and said as accurately as I can remember "there are a lot of bodies down here – you've got to come and see them".' As he was 'dragging my pressman off a plainclothes character approached us, informed me that he was an officer and asked me what I was doing. This brought me to my senses, remembering I had a black face and there was still a lot of commotion going on. I broke off and rejoined my Platoon'.[1]

Lewis' description of the presence of a man in civilian attire was corroborated at the Saville Inquiry when a soldier who was not wearing a uniform testified that he had been present in his capacity as a public relations officer. He may or may not have been the individual Lewis described. There could have been a number of them. If he was a PR man, it is a mystery why he was placing himself in such danger. Whoever he was, the fact he was present and 'behind the lines' at such an early stage is perplexing.

A video, which survived the atrocity, showed the scene

after the shooting had stopped. In it, a group of civilians are being herded towards the junction between William Street and Rossville Street. A man in civilian clothes walks nonchalantly across the screen. The solders are not bothered by him, or he by them. When Gen. Ford was in the witness box, he was shown the footage.[2] Saville commented: 'You will then, I think, see why we are quite interested in this particular piece of video.' It was slowed down to a frame-by-frame sequence:

SAVILLE: ... we see this person coming from the left to the right. There are soldiers on the left. There, do you see immediately to the left of the screen?
A. I do, sir.
SAVILLE: ... You can see why we are somewhat interested in who he might be.
A. I understand, sir.
SAVILLE: Can you help at all?
A. I cannot help at all, sir. I certainly did not send anyone in civilian clothes into Londonderry that day. I do not, from that photograph, recognise this man and I think that is all I can say, sir ...
SAVILLE: Can I put it like this, Gen. Ford: would it entirely surprise you if in fact there had been some undercover soldiers out of uniform in the city on that day?
A. It would surprise me if any undercover soldiers were operating on that day; it would surprise me, yes, sir.
SAVILLE: Or take out the word 'undercover'; soldiers in civilian uniform?
A. I suppose it is possible that a soldier was there on his own decision on that day, but I think it is extremely unlikely, sir. I am trying to think of circumstances.
SAVILLE: Is it so unlikely, I mean, if you want people to be there, to observe and so on?
A. Well, I did not send any there –[3]

When MacLellan appeared in the box, on 19 November

2002, he was shown the footage and asked if he recognised the man:

> A. No. I have no idea, sir. Could it be a journalist? Certainly the media were given total freedom, and they may have known it, but to me it means nothing.

Whoever these elusive characters were, they were present in the Bogside very shortly after, if not during, the shooting. It would certainly appear that they were not reporting to 8 Brigade. Perhaps they were MRF soldiers assigned to keep an eye on figures such as Martin McGuinness, the IRA leader, who took part in the march. Certainly, one of the tactics of the MRF was to infiltrate marches to gather intelligence. From a counter-insurgency point of view, it would have made perfect sense to infiltrate the march with armed and trained soldiers as they could get in behind the lines of the IRA and take out any snipers that emerged if a gun battle erupted.

Since the MRF was based at Palace Barracks and shared facilities with 1 Para, the soldiers of Support Company could have known them. This might explain the non-reaction of the soldiers in the film footage to the man in civilian attire. A further possibility is that part of their mission may have been to take photographs of people who might manage to escape during the anticipated confrontation with the IRA. Yet a further possibility is that they were assigned to plant evidence – four nail bombs were planted on the body of a seventeen-year-old called Gerald Donaghy.

The Home Office withheld evidence from both Widgery and Saville. It recently emerged that a spy operating under the *nom de guerre* 'Sean Lynch', was an agent of the National Public Order Intelligence Unit – part of the Metropolitan Police – and infiltrated the ranks of the people organising the march in Derry on 30 January 1972. Evidence at the Mitting Inquiry revealed that 'Lynch' had infiltrated Irish political groups in London in the late 1960s and subsequently became involved with NICRA.[4] He travelled between Britain and Northern Ireland in the months leading up to Bloody Sunday and his reports probably reached David Eastwood. However, they were not furnished to either the Widgery or Saville Inquiries. What, if anything, did he say about the likely presence of the IRA on the march? Was he one of a team who had infiltrated NICRA? Did he report that no one had fired at the soldiers before the massacre began? It emerged at the Mitting Inquiry that 'Lynch' was later promoted to the role of a 'manager' within the Special Demonstration Squad, between 1982 and 1984. 'Lynch' has since died.

29

Dum-dum Bullets

Another soldier at the Saville Inquiry corroborated yet a further aspect of Byron Lewis' account: the presence of a paratrooper firing from the hip. This was a reckless manner in which to discharge bullets as it is difficult to control their trajectory and was contrary to training. The witness was overlooking the activities from the Essex factory in Bligh's Lane and had binoculars. He saw one of the soldiers move into Rossville Street and run across the waste ground firing his rifle from the hip. A photograph taken by the RUC confirmed that the soldier had a clear line of sight to the incident. There were plenty of eyewitnesses, including Joe Mahon, who saw a soldier fire from the hip.[1]

Lewis also claimed that some of his colleagues had fired dum-dum bullets, a particularly devastating type of projectile. Efforts were made to undermine his credibility for making this claim, on the basis that no official evidence was found that any of the deceased or wounded had been struck by dum-dums on the day. This was yet another weak point in light of the fact that the forensic examinations after Bloody Sunday were unreliable. The results were used to show that some of the victims had discharged weapons or had been in possession of nail bombs. All of this was subsequently discredited. The use of dum-dum bullets could easily have been concealed as part of the cover-up.

Dr Raymond McClean, who treated victims on Bloody

Sunday, certainly suspected that dum-dums had been discharged. He took a phone call asking him to represent Cardinal Conway at the post-mortems being held at Altnagelvin Hospital. 'When I arrived in the post-mortem room the awful task had already begun. I took up my position as an observer and made my own independent hurried notes as the clinical work went on and on and on.' Regarding Michael Kelly, Gerald Donaghy, William McKinney, Hugh Gilmour, Kevin McElhinney and Bernard McGuigan, he said:

> My understanding is that normal entry wounds in these cases should not be more than 7mm to 8mm diameter. In all cases the entry wounds are larger and I would like the reasons to be examined. It is possible that the bullets involved were tumbling or softened. Dum dum bullets, which are apparently softened to create more tissue damage, were banned in 1933 by the Geneva Convention. If these bullets were used on Bloody Sunday, they would not have been part of the official supply of ammunition. I am aware it is possible to make nicks in a bullet which will cause it to tumble in the air, and therefore cause more damage upon impact.[2]

A company sergeant major (CSM) serving with 1 Para confirmed what Byron Lewis said about some of the soldiers having their own supply of bullets. The CSM, also called Lewis, discovered that Soldier H had fired two more rounds than had been issued to him. When interviewed by Peter Taylor for the programme *Remembering Bloody Sunday* about his reaction to this, he responded:

> **CSM:** I said, 'What the hell were you doing?' and he said, 'I was firing at the enemy,' he said (*sic*), 'I was firing at gunmen.'
> **Taylor:** Did you believe him?
> **CSM:** I did not know what to think at the time.
> **Taylor:** Did you believe him?

CSM: No. Knowing the soldier – as I do know him, I do not believe he was firing at gunmen.
Taylor: Did you see any gunmen?
CSM: No.
Taylor: Did you see any weapons?
CSM: No.
Taylor: Did you see any nail bomber?
CSM: No.[3]

Overall, Byron Lewis' account tallied with the evidence of the local witnesses present that day in a great many respects. Yet, despite this, Saville was disparaging of him.

30

SOLDIER F'S MURDEROUS PLATOON

Saville determined that none of the deceased nor wounded on Bloody Sunday were gunmen or presented any sort of a threat to anyone in Support Company. Soldier F's 16-man platoon committed the majority of the murders on Bloody Sunday. It was led by Lt 119 and included soldiers E, F, G, H, J, 1581, 147 and UUK 355.

From the moment the soldiers began to fire, their prey turned out to be male and predominantly young men. Only one woman, Margaret 'Peggy' Deery, was wounded by gunfire.

Jackie Duddy, seventeen, was the first to fall during this phase of the turmoil. He was moving across the Rossville car park with Fr Daly (later Bishop Daly). Saville determined that 'Soldier R' had 'probably' aimed at and shot him.

Michael Kelly, seventeen, was picked off by Soldier F's rounds at the rubble barricade. Saville concluded that he had not done so in panic or out of fear for his life and that he knew that Kelly did not pose a threat to him. Kelly was carried to the safety of a house and died in an ambulance on the way to hospital.

It could have been one of three soldiers who shot Michael McDaid – E, P, or J. Mary Friel witnessed his death:

> I was in the doorway of Rossville flats. There were two young fellas and another [woman]. The three Saracens pulled up alongside the

doorway. The minute they stepped out, they opened up at the fleeing crowd. The young fellow McDaid and two other young fellas were running across the car park. The paratroopers called at them to halt. They did so and they were arrested and put into the Saracen. They threw gas in on top of them. The three of them jumped out. They put McDaid up against the wall beside Chamberlain Street. He had his hands on his head and they shot him. I went berserk and a fellow carried me up to the second floor of the flat and [I] was taken in. It was an execution.[1]

John Young, seventeen, was struck by a single round to his head discharged by one of the same group, Soldiers E, P, or J. One of them probably shot William Nash, nineteen, who was struck in the chest at the rubble barricade.

Kevin McElhinney's short life was terminated by either 'Soldier L' or 'M' as he sought the shelter of the rubble barricade in Rossville Street. He was struck in the back as he crawled away from them towards Rossville Flats. Like many of the other victims, he was only seventeen.

Soldier F was a cruel, cynical and clinical killer. He shot Patrick Doherty in the buttock while he was on the ground crawling away from him. As Doherty lay crying out in pain, his life draining away from him, Barney McGuigan, an exceptionally brave and humane man, stepped forward with a white handkerchief looking to help Doherty. F dropped to one knee, aimed his rifle and shot McGuigan in the head.

While F, the most prolific of the killers, admitted at the Saville Inquiry that he was responsible for the death of a string of people, he was unrepentant and clung to his fiction that they presented a danger to him. When it was put to him in October 2003 that he had shot at unarmed people without justification, he responded that 'the people I shot are the petrol bombers or a person who had a weapon'.

The shooting party moved next to Glenfada Park. Saville determined that it was 'more likely than not' that either F or Private H discharged the round that mortally wounded William McKinney, twenty-six, here. Decades later, a PSNI investigation resulted in F being charged with McKinney's murder, but those charges were dropped in July of 2021.

Jim Wray, twenty-two, was also murdered by the EFGH unit in Glenfada Park. He was struck twice in the back. The PSNI investigation also resulted in F being charged with his murder. Those charges were also dropped.

Joe Mahon was shot by a bullet in Glenfada Park that went through his hip bone, into his stomach and finally lodged in his other hipbone, but he survived. Jim Wray was lying in front of him. Mahon tried to get up until he was urged to stay on the ground by a woman who told him to play dead, which he did. Wray, who was still alive, was moving his shoulders. One of the soldiers walked over to him and fired an additional two bullets into his body. Mahon has described how the shooter went through an alleyway and probably killed Gerard McKinney and Gerald Donaghy before he returned to where he was. When he did, he removed his helmet to reveal a head of tightly cropped fair hair. He also heard a soldier with a Scottish accident boast, 'I have got another one'. Another paratrooper called from behind, 'Okay Dave [i.e. Soldier F], we're pulling out.'[2] Mahon listened as the soldiers withdrew and waited for what seemed like an eternity to be sure that the paratroopers had fully retreated from Glenfada Park. He then made a mistake that nearly cost him his life, he looked up and let F see he was alive. When the soldier was half to three-quarters way across the square from where Mahon lay, he got down on one knee and readied to fire at Mahon. Just then a woman, who was administering first aid, walked into his shot. The bullet went through the cloth of her trousers and missed Mahon. 'He just walked away and I saw him looking back.'[3]

Gerard McKinney was shot as he fled from Glenfada Park to Abbey Park at a range of only a few yards. The projectile that passed through his body maintained a velocity sufficient to also mortally wound Gerald Donaghy, aged seventeen. Saville decided there was 'no doubt' that Private G had taken this shot. Donaghy had been orphaned at the age of ten after his parents had died within four weeks of each other. He was a member of Na Fianna Éireann. He did not die immediately and was being taken to hospital by Hugh Leo Young and Raymond Rogan, when soldiers took Young and Rogan out of the vehicle and drove it away with Donaghy still inside. A blanket that had been placed around him was removed and nail bombs were planted on him. This incident led to a clash of evidence at the Saville Inquiry with one soldier saying that he had not seen any device, while one of his colleagues claimed to have seen four. Geraldine Doherty, a niece of Donaghy, attended the Saville Inquiry in London when it investigated this killing. A sandy-haired and 'very skinny' former soldier testified that he would not have sat into the car and driven it away, if he had thought there were nail bombs in it.[4]

Saville made no finding of foul play instead concluding

that the objects were probably on Donaghy when he was shot, but that he had not been preparing or attempting to throw one at that time; moreover, that he was not targeted because of the alleged nail bombs. On the contrary, he determined Donaghy was taken down while trying to escape from the paratroopers. This finding by Saville is strongly contested.

Gerard McKinney, the man who shared the impact of the same round as Donaghy was a thirty-five-year-old father of seven children. Seven days after his death, his wife gave birth to another child. His daughter Regina recalls how:

> Mammy never got over it. It took twenty-five years for her to even start to come to terms with it. We all went to hear the evidence at certain times. Those particular soldiers who were in Glenfada, we all went to hear their evidence. It was hard on mammy, and hard on us all because she was there. You are watching her reactions and seeing it all over again. These men took away everything we had. We can discuss it now as adults. Getting married, having children – my brother had to give every one of us girls away. Five girls in the house. Things like that. Knowing that your children have no granda.[5]

Hugh Gilmour, seventeen, was slain by one of 'Soldier U's' bullets as he raced away from the troops. He fell just yards from the safety of the Rossville flats where he lived.

***

Those wounded included: *Damien Donaghy*, fifteen, who was shot in William Street.

Peggy Deery, thirty-eight, was shot in the leg. One of the paratroopers snarled that she 'deserved it' and added, 'let the whore bleed to death', as she was being treated for her wounds. The same soldier refused to move an army vehicle to allow an ambulance get nearer to her. She had lost her husband to cancer the previous October and was raising fourteen children aged between eight months and sixteen years old. She spent four months in hospital, developed a chronic kidney disease and became effectively housebound for the rest of her life. Her older daughters had to assume responsibility for her care and of the rest of the family.

Patrick McDaid, twenty-five, who helped carry Peggy Deery to safety was also wounded.

Patrick Campbell, fifty-one; was shot as he sought shelter in Joseph's Place.

Daniel McGowan, thirty-eight, was shot while carrying the wounded Patrick Campbell to safety.

Alex Nash, fifty-one, father of William Nash, was shot while trying to help his son.

Joseph Friel, twenty-six, was shot in Glenfada Park.

Daniel Gillespie, thirty-two, was wounded in Glenfada Park and lay unconscious as the shooting continued.

Michael Bradley, twenty-two, was shot in the car park of Rossville Flats having seen the murder of Jackie Duddy.

Michael Bridge, twenty-five, was shot in the car park of Rossville Flats when he confronted paratroopers after the murder of Jackie Duddy.

Michael Quinn, a seventeen-year-old schoolboy, was shot as he tried to escape in Glenfada Park.

Joseph Mahon, sixteen, was shot in Glenfada Park.

Patrick O'Donnell, forty-one, was wounded in Glenfada Park. He was then arrested and ill-treated before being released to receive medical attention.

Alana Burke, aged eighteen, was crushed and badly injured by an armoured personnel carrier in the courtyard of Rossville Flats.

A large number of people were also beaten up, including a Knights of Malta paramedic, an outrage that also constituted a flagrant violation of the Geneva Convention. A photograph of the man crumpled on the ground was taken within seconds of his beating.[6]

***

Soldier J told the inquiry he fired at but missed a man who had been in the process of hurling a nail bomb from behind a barricade on Rossville Street. He added that he had discharged a round at another individual who had hurled a smoking object from the corner of the Rossville Flats in his direction. Earlier, he had spoken to Toby Harnden of the *Daily Telegraph* during which he had disgorged a pack of lies about his actions. When asked about the interview later by the inquiry, he lied again. After his deceit was exposed, he apologised, acknowledging that he had 'hammed up' the account he had given the journalist.

Another shooter, 'Soldier P', who killed two people, sought shelter behind the ruse of forgetfulness. He told Saville he could not even recall discharging his rifle. 'I don't see anyone from the Army and I don't go to reunions – I have just got on with my life and work. Accordingly, I recollect very little about the 30 January 1972.' Yet, when pressed, he accepted that he had shot someone who he had claimed had been a nail bomber and a man carrying a pistol.

'Soldier S' maintained he had been justified in firing twelve shots at an alleged gunman in the flats who was trying to kill him. He strove to appear contrite. Had he felt genuine remorse, he could have told the truth.

One of the most disturbing shooting incidents of Bloody Sunday was yet to happen. The Saville Report dismissed it as a 'false memory'. There are, however, many reasons to believe that it was genuine.

31

Killing 'Fenian Bastards'

Antoinette Coyle, a volunteer paramedic with the Knights of Malta, spotted Jack Duddy lying on the ground beneath the flats and dashed across the balcony in her uniform to get downstairs. 'As I ran along the balcony, I was conscious of chips of concrete flying out of the concrete ledge by my feet,' she testified. 'I saw three or four pieces of concrete being chipped away in quick succession. The splintering concrete was about two feet away from my feet. The chips seemed to follow me as I went across the balcony.'[1]

This attack may have taken place to eliminate the supposed IRA gunmen Observer B had pretended he had seen practising ambush tactics on the balconies.

Two other Knights of Malta volunteers, Leo Day and Alice Long, were going towards the flats when they reached a Saracen. When Day looked inside the rear of the vehicle, he saw bodies and blood on the floor. Long recalls how:

> I met Leo Day, our superior officer. Someone told us that there were three young fellows shot and put into a Saracen tank in Rossville Street. We could hear shooting as we went over with our hands up and asked if we could see who was inside. Fr Mulvey was there and he said, 'They'll not let me in to give the last rites.' The door was ajar. Leo Day and I looked in. There were three fellows piled on top of each other, all face downwards with their coats pulled over their heads. We heard a slight moan. I went to open the door of the Saracen but the soldier standing

there kicked it shut. He was very wee and had on a different uniform from the rest of the Paras – no markings or insignia, and a different scarf too. Leo and I saw a foot twitch, so I tried once more, and he kicked it shut again.

The paratrooper kicked the door shut again and ordered the paramedics not to look inside:

There was a bit of an argument with him and he pulled up his gun and poked it into a small side flap on the Saracen – he had to reach right up – and he said, 'When we do this, we do it right. The Parachute Regiment doesn't make mistakes.' Then he fired into the tank and said, 'Well that's the end of them Fenian bastards'.

He fired three rapid shots.[2] The man seemed very pleased with himself, said something like, 'They'll not make any more noise now.'

Day told her there was no point in remaining any longer, but as they went to move on, she noticed two discarded bullet cases on the ground:[3]

I lifted two bullet cases off the ground. Fr Mulvey was saying they were shooting dum-dum bullets – if you get a chance pick them up. They were cut wide open at one end like a flower with petals. I put [the cases] in my pocket but the soldiers saw and cocked his gun at me, so I had to leave them.[4]

The soldier ordered Long to give him the cases. He warned her she would be the next casualty if she did not comply and Day told her to hand them over. As they left, the soldier shouted some sort of a threat and:

a shot came out of the blue, I do not know in what direction. I do not think it was meant for me because it just skimmed my coat and left a burn mark.[5]

There are similarities between Soldier F and the assassin at the Saracen described by Alice Long. Soldier F was a small man, a description which matches Long's description of the mysterious figure as a 'very wee' individual. By his own account, he has stated that after the shooting the 'next thing I recall is standing by Pigs [i.e. Saracens], watching the Rossville Flats. How long we were there I do not know'.[5]

Long testified before the Saville Inquiry. Her account was rejected by Saville on a number of grounds including the inconclusive nature of some of the forensic evidence relating to the interior of the vehicle. This assumes that the vehicle was not sanitised or manipulated before the Widgery tribunal in 1972; moreover, that the correct records for the actual Saracen were supplied.

Saville was also persuaded by the fact that 'senior soldiers' were present nearby yet had not heard gunfire at this time at the vehicle.[6]

Saville concluded that Long had suffered a 'false memory' because she had been in 'a very distressed state' which had 'led her to believe things that did not happen'.[7] Yet, this analysis fails to explain how she also had a strong memory of having discussed the matter with Leo Day on at least one other occasion. Is it plausible that she also imagined what Day said to her on this and other occasions about the issue? Saville did not comment on this aspect of her account in his conclusions.

If Saville had extended this form of reasoning to other witnesses who had found themselves in a 'very distressed state', it is doubtful if anyone from the Bogside could have testified in a credible manner, unless there was corroboration by others, e.g. 'senior soldiers'.

There are other problems with Saville's conclusion about Alice Long. If she had suffered a 'false memory', how is it that she was able to describe an assassin who matched the description of a known killer who was in the vicinity of the vehicle and flat complex, Soldier F? She described the assassin as being approximately five foot and four inches in height. Those who saw Soldier F during Bloody Sunday and in his appearances at the Widgery and Saville tribunals, described him as a small man. When he appeared at the Saville Inquiry, he was described as a 'stocky'. Long had described the assassin as 'stout'.

Readers can make up their own minds whether these similarities deserved closer attention from Saville or not.

32

SOLDIER F BEATS AND TORTURES PRISONERS

There were other victims of Bloody Sunday, people who were beaten up by the paratroopers.

While the shooting was taking place, the people who had been on the march fled in a variety of directions. One of them, James Doherty, ran towards the car park of the flat complex but fell. As he tried to get back to his feet, a paratrooper struck him on the back of his head with the baton, while another kicked him in the back, arms and head. He lost consciousness for a short while from the blows. When he regained consciousness, he realised he was being:

> dragged by the hair, and by the coat by these two soldiers. Each time I tried to get to my feet, I was kicked as they shouted, 'Come on, you pig, it is the paratroopers you are dealing with now.' I was dragged into a Saracen – there were five soldiers there as well as the two who brought me in. They kept shouting, 'Just you wait, you pig, we're going to kick you to death.' They kept striking me with batons and mouthing obscene remarks. Another man, about my age, was dragged in with his face covered with blood. A soldier kept hitting him across the face, butting him with his helmet – and bruising and cutting his mouth and nose. I saw through the open door a line of teenagers and men – all prisoners of soldiers – go past, with their hands on their heads.[1]

Fr Terence O'Keeffe, a local parish priest, was one of those swept up by the Paras in the chaos. Like the other prisoners, he was put onto a lorry and taken to Fort George, a fourteen-acre military base on the banks of the River Foyle, where he was forced to stand in various stress positions. Some of the prisoners were made to hold barbed wire. The room was cold with a floor of exposed concrete. Their ordeal lasted for three hours. The stress positions they were forced to adopt were rotated with one short five-minute break for a cup of tea.

Fr O'Keeffe was made to stand for an excessive amount of time with his arms above his head, which he found extremely difficult because his left arm had been battered so badly – he had sustained radial nerve damage.

At approximately 8 o'clock, a British officer arrived and issued orders that the prisoners were to be seated on chairs and electric heaters were to be provided. This was only a temporary respite. 1 Para had returned to its temporary base at Drumahoe after the shootings.[2] Soldiers E, F, G, J, O, and U were brought to Fort George at about 9.30 to identify alleged rioters so the RUC could charge them.

Soldier F seized the opportunity to assault the prisoners. According to O'Keeffe:

> About 12 to 15 Paras came into the room and chose three or four apiece. I was not chosen at this time. Along with six others I remained on the chairs. During approximately 1 to 1½ hours, I witnessed many acts of brutality committed on the prisoners. The Paras kicked shins, stamped on feet, kneed groins, and struck the prisoners with fists. In one incident one youth of about 15 was severely struck twice by a paratrooper. I could not see whether it was with his fist or his knee but the youth was struck both times in the groin. He fell backwards and struck his head on the concrete. He was kicked on the ground and then hauled to his feet. He was unable to stand and had to be propped against the wall.

Two youths were forced to put their heads back in an unnaturally strange position to bring their faces close to the electric heater which were overhead heaters on stands. The smaller youth was forced to stand on the larger youth's feet to bring his face closer. They had to keep this position for 20 minutes to half an hour. During this time one paratrooper asked the young fellow whether he wanted a drink. When he said yes, he was ordered to open his mouth and a paratrooper spat into it. Eventually another paratrooper arrived to identify the seven or so of us who were still sitting on chairs. We were then brought up to the wall also and Lance Corporal F [Soldier F] kneed me several times in the groin when accusing me of throwing stones. We were photographed and Lance Corporal F made a statement accusing me of throwing stones. I was then brought into another room where the RUC were interviewing the prisoners.[3]

Fr O'Keeffe was not released until 11.40 p.m.

Once the bullets stopped flying, the lying began with Wilford in the vanguard of a ham-fisted attempt to twist the truth.

33

LYING LIKE TROOPERS

As things stood that afternoon, the Provisional IRA was nowhere to be seen and only a small number of Official IRA gunmen had shown themselves. A pitched battle had not materialised and Support Company found the ground around them was strewn with corpses and dying civilians. It was time to concoct lies and excuses.

Interviewed shortly after the massacre by a news reporter, Wilford provided an account from which it is difficult to winnow even a shred of truth:

> **Wilford:** It is unfortunate but when we got up there past William Street – here where we're here standing – and up towards Rossville flats – we came under fire. We came under fire from the bottom of the flats. We were also petrol bombed and some acid in fact was poured on us from the top of the flats.
> **Reporter:** Local people are saying that you used excessive force when you went in there.
> **Wilford:** Well, what is force? If you are being fired at you return fire and they know that perfectly well.
> **Reporter:** How many gunmen do you feel you've hit in the Bogside?
> **Wilford:** Well, I am told from my quick sit rep [situation report] – you must understand it's a very quick sit rep – that three gunmen were hit. We have not got the weapons but this is the usual thing. We saw people come forward. I am not going to say that I saw weapons taken away because I don't know yet. I have not spoken to the men on the ground although I was forward when the shooting was going on.
> **Reporter:** You have no worries about this action?
> **Wilford:** None at all.

Reporter: Local people have also said that you were disrespectful – your troops were disrespectful and flung around the bodies of dead Bogsiders.

Wilford: Well, I am sure we did not. In fact, I was there when those bodies were recovered and I ordered in fact the vehicle to go forward to pick them up. We did not know at that stage whether they were dead or whether they were wounded and a vehicle went forward under the very real threat of fire because we were still being fired at, at that stage.

Reporter: How do you feel about today's operation in the Bogside?

Wilford: Well, I think any of these sort of operations are un-fortunate – we shouldn't have to do it but they put us in a position where we can do no other – when we are fired at, we must protect ourselves.[1]

***

That night, Mike Jackson drew up a handwritten record of the shots fired by the soldiers. It was later shown to be at odds with the accounts they presented to Widgery. Furthermore, none of the shots recorded by Jackson corresponded to the forensic and eyewitness evidence. After the discovery of what became known as the 'shot list', Jackson, who had already testified before the Saville Inquiry, was recalled. Michael Mansfield, QC, who acted for some of the families of the victims, contended that the purpose of the list was to justify the killings and hence some of the victims were described as 'nail bombers', 'pistol firers', and 'carrying rifles'. Mansfield put it to Jackson that: 'None of the 13 were carrying nail bombs, none of the 13 were carrying pistols, none of the 13 were carrying rifles, do you follow that?' Jackson replied: 'I hear what you are telling me, but this is surely a matter for the tribunal'. The general said he could not explain discrepancies between his list and a typed document later sent to the Widgery tribunal, based on what soldiers who fired shots later told him. He added: 'If it is to be suggested that there was an attempt by anyone to sanitise ... a true version of events, for whatever reason, I would emphatically reject such a suggestion.'

There were other problems facing the army. Many photographs were taken during the shooting. Gilles Peress who smuggled his rolls of film out of the Bogside with the help of locals, stated:

> There was a full moon that night and a snowstorm; I remember the car skating down to Dublin on the ice. I arrived at the airport in Dublin – it must have been two or three in the morning. It was late; I went to the cargo department and I woke some guys and I said, 'Here's what happened. You've got to help me get this film out.' They really worked hard to find a route to get that film out to Paris without going via London. They fed me sandwiches, gave me some tea. I took a nap on one of their wooden benches and then I drove back to Belfast. I was in Belfast by eight or nine the next morning.[2]

News about what had happened in Derry spread rapidly. Lord Carver was contacted at his home by Maj.-Gen. Coaker, the director of Military Operations in the MoD. Coaker gave him the 'bare outlines and told me that a fairly hostile description of events, making accusations of firing without being fired on, had been given on the BBC TV news'. He was told that HQNI had been in contact with Heath and Carrington. According to Carver, his initial reaction gravely under-estimated the furore that was erupting:

> Bearing in mind the rather lurid picture that had been painted

beforehand of what might happen, 13 dead (and I am not sure that at that stage this figure had been clearly established) did not seem out of line with the sort of casualties that a head-on confrontation between troops and the IRA in the Bogside could have been expected to lead to. As far as I can recall, I rang up Carrington and confirmed that he had received the news and discussed it with Heath. His reaction was, if I remember aright, his normal, phlegmatic and resigned one.[3]

This quote, taken from Carver's 1989 memoirs, reads almost as if he had expected 1 Para to encroach upon, if not invade, the Bogside. Where else was it possible they might have become involved in a 'head-on confrontation' with the IRA?

Yet, after the Saville Inquiry was set up, nearly a decade following on from the publication of these memoirs, Carver began to distance himself from this position. By the time he provided a statement to the Inquiry, there was no hint of an anticipated 'confrontation' with the IRA. Instead, he laid the blame on his subordinates alleging that he did not know why the 'paratroopers were in Glenfada Park. The role of Support Company was to protect the rear of those carrying out the arrests'. He now put Wilford in the cross hairs saying: 'The vehicles went into the area even though the order stated that the arrest operation should take place on foot'.[4]

The Paras returned to Palace Barracks on Monday 31 January. Meanwhile, the British establishment had switched into full cover-up mode.

34

'A Powerful Reaction Against the Irish

On the Conservative Backbenches'

The dirty tricksters were busy influencing receptive British reporters. John Chartres, the lead reporter for *The Times of London*, was taken to see the body of someone alleged to have been carrying nail bombs. Chartres subsequently spoke to Simon Winchester. 'The single fact had convinced [Chartres] that the day's military operation had been, in his words, "a jolly good show". I was to remember this phrase for some long while'.[1]

Dr McClean, who had come face to face with the consequences of the shooting, told a different story:

> Despite the endless litany of precise measurements and details of horrific internal destruction of tissues, I found it difficult to avoid an emotional involvement with the bodies on those slabs. I remember most vividly the contents of several opened young stomachs: partially digested meat, peas and potatoes – the same lunch I had eaten before I went out on that march yesterday. This thought, more than anything, brought it clearly home to me that only for the grace of God, I could have been lying on one of those slabs. My faith in mankind was at a very low ebb that day.[2]

Edward Heath had been at Chequers, the country estate of the prime minister, when, at approximately 7 p.m. on the day of the shooting, he received an urgent and confidential signal transmitted by way of teleprinter from 10 Downing Street by Lord Bridges, his private secretary. He was informed that at least five civilians had been shot dead in Derry and that the media was claiming a higher figure. Bridges told him he would be kept up to date as further information came to hand.

Shortly after this, Heath received another message saying the MoD was now advising it was believed that at least twelve people had been killed and another fourteen wounded. The army, he was told, was adamant that snipers had fired at them as they set about trying to arrest rioters. Bridges told Heath that one of the deceased was a wanted terrorist and another was carrying nail bombs.

Later that night Jack Lynch rang Heath. He began by apologising for ringing so late, 'but you will probably have heard', he explained, 'the unfortunate news about Derry this afternoon'.[3] Heath's response was that: 'It is very bad news, yes'.

Lynch explained that 'from reactions received around the country it looks as if a very serious point has now been reached and the situation could escalate beyond what any of us would anticipate at this stage. I am told that, according to reports I received and checked on the spot, the British troops reacted rather beyond what a disciplined force might be expected to, and, as you know, there were 13 killed and as many again injured'.[4]

'Well, now, as far as any accusations are concerned, I obviously cannot accept that', Heath replied. 'But I must also point out that this arose out of a march which was against the law, which was banned ... Now the people therefore who deliberately organised this march in circumstances which we all know, in which the IRA were bound to intervene, carry a heavy responsibility for any damage which ensued.'[5] His comment that 'the IRA were bound to intervene' raises the possibility that he had been expecting a gun battle with the IRA.

A moment later Lynch pointed out: 'There is no indication at all that the IRA intervened before shots were fired from the British side.' Heath responded: 'I am not going to prejudge that.'

Lynch blamed Faulkner's administration saying, 'the whole thing arises as a result of the Stormont regime', to which Heath responded: 'If you had dealt with them (the IRA) this would have been over long ago'.

Lynch urged Heath to take control of security measures away from Stormont. Heath dismissed this on the basis that those responsible for the conflict were '... the people who are challenging the law' and '... the IRA trying to take over the country'. Lynch held his ground saying, 'well, we have no intention of letting them do that'.

Lynch reiterated his concern about the future saying 'and as I have said to you already, if this kind of thing is going to have its repercussions south of the border ... I can assure you that my role is becoming more and more difficult and I am very, very fearful of what is likely to happen... I just want to tell you how gravely apprehensive I am ...'[6]

***

Meanwhile, Carver was beginning to appreciate the full extent of the unfolding catastrophe: 'By Monday morning I was left in no doubt that the public and political reaction to the events of the previous day was extremely sharp and critical of the way in which the operation had been executed. As always, it was difficult to get at the truth of what had happened.'[7]

Shock registered across the spectrum of Irish politics, even among parliamentarians normally favourably disposed towards Britain, such as Garret FitzGerald, Conor Cruise O'Brien and Erskine Childers. Reluctant to believe news reports from Irish sources, FitzGerald contacted a British journalist who had been in Derry to ask if the paratroopers had been provoked, only to be told they had not. He visited Derry for the funerals. Afterwards, he had lunch at a house that he considered to belong to 'moderate' Nationalists and was shocked to hear one of the women present express her support for people who were queuing up to join the IRA.

Tánaiste Erskine Childers became the target of derision by members of the public for his criticisms of Republicans.[8]

The Minister for Foreign Affairs, Patrick Hillery, flew to New York for meetings at the UN with the US Secretary of State, William Rogers. Hillary described 'capital punishment' as the price of protest in Northern Ireland and suggested that there had been either the release of very undisciplined troops in Derry or a cold decision taken in London to kill people. 'Whichever it is, the situation has been totally changed,' he said.[9] He went on to say that if the help he was now seeking to bring pressure on Britain did not come from 'friendly' countries of the west, he would turn elsewhere. Asked if he would turn to the east he responded: 'My orders are to seek help wherever I can get it.' He added that feelings in Ireland had never been so hostile. People regarded what had happened as an act of war against innocent people. 'Relations between the Irish and the British governments had never been worse', he declared.[10]

The Irish ambassador was withdrawn from London and the government announced that Wednesday 2 February, when the funerals of the dead in Derry were due to take place, would be a national day of mourning. Protest marches took place all over Ireland. A crowd in excess of 20,000 people descended upon the British embassy on Merrion Square in the centre of Dublin and besieged it until 2 February when it was set on fire. One of the protesters, Billy Doolan, ran a family pub close to the embassy which like all of the pubs in the city, was closed for business. Doolan recalls the bedlam of the night after the shooting:

> The square was packed solid. I was standing at the railings outside Holles Street Hospital. You couldn't get near the embassy. I remember a man in a black anorak stood up on a box at an early stage and gave a speech about pushing the Brits out of Northern Ireland, and then lit the fuse of a device and threw it at the building. It arched through the air and landed on the granite steps behind the police. They had their backs to it. There was a loud explosion – much louder than a large firework. The police pushed into the crowd to get away from it. The crowd hunched down. I don't think there was much explosive in it. People started throwing rocks at the building and that never stopped. There was some respite in the early morning but crowds returned again. This went on for a few days. I felt for the guards; they were only doing their job. Some of them had a hard time of it. The embassy had reinforced bullet-proof glass and no matter how many rocks were

hurled, the building remained intact. Some people went into the park. It was owned by the Bishop in those days and the public did not have access to it. People climbed in and dug up the ground with their hands to get rocks. There might have been 100 in there at one time. The dockers came up with trucks followed by a line of people. The trucks were full of bricks and rocks which they poured out onto the road. People were throwing petrol bombs too. After a few days, one of the windows cracked. After that it was possible to set fire to the building. The guards were worn out. I think they were relieved after they lost the battle. I even saw one smirking when the building went up in flames. Bloody Sunday was the biggest mistake the Brits ever made. Everyone wanted to be in the IRA at the time. That all changed later of course but at that time they had huge support.[11]

When the Fire Brigade tried to put the fire out, someone cut their hose pipe. The culmination of the attack took place on the same day as the funerals of the victims.

Embassy staff living in Dublin also came under pressure. One of them, a first secretary, whose wife was expecting a baby, was living in rented accommodation and their landlord was threatened with violence if he did not eject the couple.

An array of British owned properties in Dublin were attacked as well.

Ambassador Peck was in London while the siege took place. When he returned, he was 'horrified to find my embassy in flames'.[12] Heath was so alarmed that he suggested the 'special aircraft' which had brought Peck back to Dublin remain on the tarmac to evacuate the staff and their families. Peck hoped that it would not be necessary to take 'such a drastic decision for at least 24-hours' and it was unnecessary.[13]

Peck called on the Taoiseach at noon on Thursday, 3 February only to find a 'grey and ghastly' looking Lynch who was 'much put out at my arrival as he had apparently sent a message, which never reached me, to say that he had to open an emergency debate in the Dáil at 2 p.m. and could not see me until after that. However, as I was there he could hear what I had to say, but could I please make it quick as he had to prepare his speech'.

Peck began by noting that Lynch had promised to 'make full recompense' for the burning and went on to say that he was 'even more mortified by the news in this morning's papers of the insane hooliganism throughout Dublin later last night which had apparently included the aimless damage to British-owned business property and the petrol bombing of a maternity home. I could only conclude that there was a total breakdown in law and order'.

Peck expressed no remorse for what the soldiers of his country had done in Derry. On the contrary, he asserted that after the burning of the embassy, the British government was going to face opposition to new political initiatives on Northern Ireland. Heath 'now had to contend with a powerful reaction against the Irish on the Conservative backbenches, due, unfairly, no doubt, but understandably, to a belief that the Irish government were (*sic*) incapable of standing up to the IRA'.

***

In retirement, Frank Steele of MI6, who had been stationed at Laneside, County Down, claimed that he had been shocked at what had happened in Derry. He and UKREP Howard Smith had been monitoring events that day from Belfast. Steele spoke to Peter Taylor, author of *Brits*, thus:

'We just found it very difficult to believe when three, then five and then seven deaths came in,' [Steele] told me. 'I think when we got to seven, Howard [Smith] and I looked at each other and said, "Right. That means Direct Rule [from London]." Of course, when it got to 13, Direct Rule was inevitable'.[14]

What was the logic in this remark? Was Direct Rule inevitable because Northern Ireland had spun out of control? Because Britain was not to blame for it, rather Stormont? Why, since *Operation Forecast* was a British army initiative, should it cost the Unionists control of Northern Ireland? One consequence of Direct Rule would be an end to Faulkner's influence over the British Army via the Joint Security Committee (JSC). It also meant that London would have more control over the flow of RUC intelligence.

Steele found some positive aspects in the disaster telling Taylor that immediately after Bloody Sunday many Loyalists:

were 'cock-a-hoop, that the "Brits" had finally got tough. I know it's a horrible thing to say,' Frank Steele remarked, 'but although it did us the most enormous harm with the Catholic community, it did us quite a lot of good with the more bloody-minded of the Protestant community. The good thing that came out of it was that it enabled Direct Rule to be brought in.'[15]

One of the 'bloody-minded' of the Protestant community was John McKeague of the Red Hand Commando, which was allied to the UVF. McKeague, a one-time bodyguard to Ian Paisley, was a notorious serial killer, sadist and paedophile – he was one of the Kincora Boys Home child abusers. In early 1972, he appeared on television and described Bloody Sunday as 'Good Sunday'. His newspaper, *Loyalist News*, pronounced that: 'What we need are one, two, three, many more Bloody Sundays.'

On the ground, some of the paratroopers were rejoicing at what had happened. Some of their colleagues in 2 Para, also stationed in Belfast, were envious of what they had achieved. One of these was 'Spider', a paratrooper described by Michael Asher in his memoirs, *Shoot to Kill*. Spider took Asher and a couple of others to a Loyalist drinking club in the Shankill:

> Our battalion is a lot of crap!' Spider announced after two or three pints. 'Now, 1 Para, they had the right idea! They shot all those Taigs down Londonderry! They reckoned there was only 13 dead. There was only 13 found, is what there was. All the real IRA men were carried across the border and buried in shaller (*sic*) graves!'[16]

The Loyalist audience cheered. Someone passed Spider another pint. 'Ay, that's the spurut!' someone said.

'We know who the enemy are,' he went on. 'We should get 'em against the wall and top the lot! That's the only thing those bastards understand!'[17]

Byron Lewis described how:

> After Bloody Sunday our reputation for cruel efficiency was established. The mere mention of our approach was sufficient for hard line I.R.A. supporters to move their own barricades.[18]

Heath abolished Stormont in March 1972 and introduced Direct Rule. Henceforth, a secretary of state, based at Stormont Castle, would govern Northern Ireland, a building he would share with a high-powered team of intelligence officers. This ended Faulkner's control over the British army through Stormont's JSC.

Comments Jackson made about the first meeting between Kitson and Wilford after Bloody Sunday bring Kitson back into the picture.

35

Kitson's Secret Debrief

In the witness box at the Saville Inquiry, Col Wilford was asked about his discussions with Kitson:[1]

> Q. It is likely, is it not, that you had discussions with Gen. Kitson about the forthcoming operation that your men were to take part in [in] Derry?
> A. Not whatsoever.
> Q. None at all?
> A. None at all.
> Q. He gave you no opinion, no view?
> A. No opinion.
> Q. No guidance?
> A. No guidance.
> Q. No instruction?
> A. No instruction.
> Q. And nor, you have said, did Gen. Ford?
> A. And neither did Gen. Ford.[2]

Kitson went on to testify that he had 'no recollection of the days leading up to 30 January 1972' when plans for *Operation Forecast* were being made and little interest afterwards in what had happened in Derry. He said towards the end of January he went on leave to England:

> I have no record of the dates, but I think that I was away from Northern Ireland for about a week up to [Thursday] 3 February. While in England I heard on the wireless or read in the newspaper that there had been a serious disturbance in Londonderry.[3]

His concerns after the massacre were bureaucratic:

> I realised that members of 1 Para would be required to give

evidence in court in the normal way regarding those who had been arrested and that they would have to participate in the routine inquiries that were always carried out by the military and RUC when shooting incidents occurred. Soon afterwards I heard that there was to be a judicial inquiry under Lord Widgery. My concern was that the absence of officers and men involved in these proceedings would reduce the effectiveness of the battalion for some weeks.[4]

The reference to 'routine' inquiries being 'carried out' by the RUC was misleading. As Judge O'Hara pointed out in 2021 during the trial of two paratroopers accused of murdering Official IRA volunteer Joe McCann in April 1972, an 'understanding was in place between the RUC and the Army' which ensured the police did not arrest and question soldiers who had been involved in shooting incidents.[5]

There are other problems with Kitson's testimony. According to Jackson, Kitson descended upon Wilford 'shortly' after the massacre to ascertain what had happened. Jackson, describes how, although Kitson was a 'brusque commander', he would have appreciated that Wilford:

was feeling bruised and battered and worried about what had happened that Sunday in Londonderry. Shortly after we got back to Belfast, Kitson came to see the Colonel. To reach the office of the commanding officer [of 1 Para] one had to pass through that of the adjutant, so I greeted the Brigadier and ushered him in, before leaving the two of them alone together. Kitson has a very distinct nasal voice, so it would have been difficult not to overhear what he was saying even if I had been trying not to. 'Well, Derek,' Kitson began, 'You'd better tell me what happened.' So I heard the Colonel describe the snatch operation across the containment line into 'Free Derry'. Kitson was generally supportive, but when Wilford had finished, he offered a trenchant comment. 'What I don't understand is why, having got that far in, you didn't go on and sort the whole bloody mess out.'

Kitson expressed himself pretty brutally, but he had a point. There was no doubt that we could have gone on to retake the 'no-go' area, though this would almost certainly have resulted in more deaths.[6]

This raises the possibility that there had all along been an understanding, if not a plan, of which Kitson and Wilford were aware 'to sort the whole bloody mess out'. The 'mess' was the no-go area and the presence within it of the IRA.

Kitson was confronted at the Saville Inquiry with the unpublished *Sunday Times* story, described earlier, which claimed that Wilford had been acting in accordance with a plan to provoke the Derry IRA into an open confrontation. It had reported that the 'idea – worked out, we believe, by Lieutenant Colonel Derek Wilford on lines of thinking propounded by Brigadier Frank Kitson, British Army counter-insurgency expert was based on the military principle that the way to bring your enemy to battle is to attack something that, for prestige reasons he will have to defend ...'[7] Kitson dismissed this as 'rubbish'. Unfortunately, he played so many games with Saville that nothing he said can be taken at face value. His response was:

If I may just say so, this is total rubbish. I mean, I can quite understand why [*The Sunday Times*] did not publish it. When you see all that, me the great expert looking at Verdun and Stalingrad, that is not counter-insurgency at all, these were huge battles. None of this would have worked in any counter-insurgency sense and the Parachute Regiment planners that come into this, again, he is not talking about the Parachute Regiment's plan but 8 Brigade's overall plan and it is about as totally contrary to anything could have been thought of by 8 Brigade or any other Brigade.

Yet, it was perfectly possible such a plan could have been prepared behind MacLellan's back and overseen on the day by Gen. Ford in conjunction with Wilford. Such a plan could have borne fruit if the IRA had taken the bait. *Operation Hailstone*, which had involved 1 Para the previous July, had attempted to provoke the IRA to emerge into the open in a similar fashion.

Kitson did not tell the Inquiry what he had said to Wilford – that he could not understand why, 'having got that far in, you didn't go on and sort the whole bloody mess out.'

Kitson was asked, however, if there was anything in any of his books which 'represents this sort' of plan? 'No, mercifully not', he replied. Kitson did not disclose that he had once considered a similar 'sort of plan' while he and Carver had been on their peacekeeping mission to Cyprus in the late 1960s. Their task had been to keep militant Greek-Cypriots and Turkish-Cypriots apart. An officer suggested provoking a situation whereby the British army could intervene and shoot at the warring parties. Kitson considered and rejected the plan while acknowledging that it could have been used, but only 'as a last resort'. A moral objection was notably absent from his considerations:

> Some of the braver spirits [in the British army in Cyprus] were of the opinion that we should try and push our men between the two sides in such a way that they would automatically be shot at unless the contestants ceased firing. We would then be entitled to shoot back in self-defence! Although prepared to admit that such a course might be justified, if it was the only way of averting a massacre, I felt that it should only be adopted as a last resort.[8]

It is not possible to pin point the date of the visit by Kitson to Wilford after Bloody Sunday. On 24 September 2002, one of the barristers asked him: 'Should we understand, by the reference to your having no record of the dates, that no diary of yours for the time survives?':

> Well, I did not keep a personal diary. There would have been a desk diary-type thing, but because of security that was kept by the PA.
>
> 'You no longer have it?' the barrister continued, to which Kitson replied:
>
> And I do not have it, but I do not know what happened to it. I mean, that was the Brigade Commander's appointments book, as you may say.

There was another document Kitson did not mention, his 'Commanders Diary'. This author has obtained a copy of one for the period 1 January 1971 to 31 January 1971. The entry for 15 January shows that Kitson sent a message at 2.06 p.m. to the 2nd Royal Anglian regiment telling them: 'No holds barred, Any (*sic*) action taken, I will back. If they shoot we shoot back.'

A cloud of doubt must hang over Kitson's denial that he kept a personal diary because his books are immensely rich in detail, especially in their description of his foreign escapades. Unless he was blessed with picture-perfect recollection, he must have kept a comprehensive personal journal or diary. His book *Bunch of Five* was written in 1977 and sparkled with details about Kenya, Malaya, Oman and Cyprus that were undoubtedly based on diaries or journals. If he kept a record of any sort while in Northern Ireland, he did not surrender it to either the Widgery or Saville Inquiries.

36

HER MAJESTY'S CHARACTER ASSASSINS

Frank Kitson believed that there were two ways of administering law during a counter-insurgency. The first was that the law should be used as:

> just another weapon in the government's arsenal, and in this case it becomes little more than a propaganda cover for the disposal of unwanted members of the public. For this to happen efficiently, the activities of the legal services have to be tied into the war effort in as discreet a way as possible ... The other alternative is that the law should remain impartial and administer the laws of the country without any direction from the government.[1]

The Widgery tribunal is a good example of how the law was used as 'just another weapon in the government's arsenal'. The manipulation of evidence in the course of its proceedings was carried out on an industrial scale. For a start, there were substantial material discrepancies between the accounts provided by the soldiers of 1 Para and what appeared in their statements. Another Widgery wile was to exclude witnesses. Dr McClean, who attended to many of the dying and wounded, decided to offer himself as a witness to Widgery, but was spurned. By excluding McClean, the doctor's observations about the use of dum-dum bullets were suppressed.[2]

Widgery sat for a mere seventeen days between 21 February and 14 March 1972 during which he heard 114 witnesses. Only thirty of them were Derry civilians. Some of the most important eyewitnesses were not called to testify.

Soldier F and his colleagues received coaching in how to present their testimony. On the day he gave his evidence, he was provided with a green jacket and a pair of dark glasses with an instruction from his minders to march into the hearing with them, to ignore the public gallery and not remove the eyewear until he addressed Widgery. Like the rest of his colleagues, he proceeded to claim that the people at whom he had shot had posed a threat to him.

Widgery reported on 19 April 1972.[3] He pointed a finger of blame at NICRA for the tragedy because they had – in his view – created a dangerous situation where a confrontation had become inevitable. He proceeded to argue that there was no reason to suppose that the soldiers would have opened fire if they had not been fired on first.

Widgery argued that the soldiers had not only been fired on by gunmen but had returned fired in accordance with the standing orders in the Yellow Card. He proceeded to say that their training made them aggressive and quick in decision, and some showed more restraint in opening fire than others.

Insofar as he had any criticism, he opined that while some soldiers had displayed a high degree of responsibility others, particularly in Glenfada Park, had fired in a way that bordered on the reckless.

While it has long since been established that not a single one of those killed on Bloody Sunday was a gunman, terrorist, nail bomber or troublemaker, Widgery carelessly stole many of their good names, all they had left in this world. According to him, although some of the deceased and wounded were acquitted of complicity in wrongdoing, there was a 'strong suspicion' that others 'had been firing weapons or handling bombs' and that the Support Company troops had returned fire, but only at threats.

Carver, who knew that Widgery was a former brigadier, felt that the army had been 'fortunate to have, in Lord Widgery, a President of the Tribunal who understood soldiers well and sympathised with them in difficult situations in which they were placed'.[4]

***

Despite the publication of the Widgery Report, international, and some domestic, opinion remained aghast. The journalist T.E. Utley, who knew Hugh Mooney of the Information Research Department (IRD), held up one possible light at the end of the tunnel for the British army. The two often met when Utley visited Northern Ireland. At the time of the Bloody Sunday atrocity, Utley was working for the *Daily* and *Sunday Telegraph*, both pro-Tory papers popular with middle and upper class Britain. Mooney and the journalist discussed the Bloody Sunday problem together. It was ultimately resolved that Utley would write a paperback about it. According to a confidential letter dated 24 March 1972, the Foreign Office reported to the MoD that Utley hoped to 'complete the writing in about six weeks, though this may be a little over-ambitious.'[5] Utley was what was known in the intelligence community as an 'agent of influence'. According to the letter, he was 'obviously' going to 'need a certain amount of help from Army PR, particularly on the propaganda aspect'.

While Utley failed to produce the book, in 1975 he published the rather grandiosely titled *Lessons of Ulster* which took a broader look at Northern Ireland and a litany of developments that had occurred in the meantime. Bloody Sunday merited a few pages wherein he outlined his thesis that the British army had been the real victim because it had fallen for a trap sprung for them by the IRA. According to Utley, the IRA lured the paratroopers from behind their barricades to arrest the rioters and then fired on them in the expectation they would make mistakes under pressure. Utley's dark fantasy described how 'the Army proved to have walked straight into an IRA trap … The most familiar of terrorist techniques – the use of an apparently innocent protest demonstration as a shield for a gun attack on security forces, designed not primarily to injure them but to tempt them to action which could be misrepresented as the deliberate slaughter of the innocent – had worked to perfection'.

At one point, he argued that some of those killed were 'fresh-faced boys who might otherwise have lived to swell the ranks of patriotic militancy'. The damage occasioned by the snake oil Utley fed his credulous readers should not be under-estimated: Margaret Thatcher later described him as 'the most distinguished Tory thinker of our time'.

***

Long before Utley's book appeared, an Australian, Brian Crozier, published a paperback called *Ulster Debate* which pushed the IRD line on Bloody Sunday and much more besides. According to Crozier's autobiography, *Free Agent*, in 1964 he had been approached by 'a long-time IRD friend, H. H. ('Tommy') Tucker. I had already turned down a full-time job proposal from him, but he now made me an offer which I accepted immediately: a part-time consultancy for the IRD'. Later again, Crozier was asked to head the Institute for the Study of Conflict (ISC) which produced propaganda on behalf of the IRD and MI6.

Crozier produced another bombastically titled publication, the *Annual of Power and Conflict 1971, A Survey of Political Violence and International Influence* for the ISC, published in early 1972. It was little more than IRD-MI6 propaganda and was able to build on earlier proselytising materials Crozier had published. It put Fianna Fáil in the cross hairs, alleging that the 'support given by the Irish Republic to the IRA was much more serious ... The supervision by the Irish Army of their side of the border was perfunctory. The Prime Minister of the Republic, Mr Jack Lynch, whose own position is precarious and his party Fionna Fial [*sic*], has historic links with the IRA'. The implication of this smear was that Lynch and his Minister for Justice, Des O'Malley, did not have the courage to stand up to the IRA.

Perhaps the most risible claim in the 1971 *Annual* was that Catholics at the Harland and Wolff shipyard had marched to demand internment in March 1971. If there were any Catholics on such a march, they can only have been present due to intimidation. When internment was introduced in August, it was certainly not the product of a clamour from Belfast's Catholics. While Crozier's claim will strike Irish readers as preposterous, it is worth recalling that the propaganda themes in the book were aimed at a less well-informed international audience.

***

One of the greatest MI6-IRD coups of this era was to inveigle Garret FitzGerald to become a member of Crozier's ISC Study Group (ISCSG) on Ireland. FitzGerald became Minister for Foreign Affairs in February 1973 and served as Taoiseach twice in the 1980s. As a member of the ISCSG, FitzGerald contributed a chapter to Crozier's 1972 book, *Ulster Debate*. It formed yet another part of the IRD's propaganda offensive to exculpate the Parachute Regiment after Bloody Sunday.

FitzGerald was friendly and often indiscreet while in British diplomatic company. He was a regular visitor to the British embassy in Dublin, where he once supplied information – since declassified by the UK's National Archives – about Charles Haughey and the Dáil's Public Accounts Committee to British diplomats.[6] He was also a source of information about Jack Lynch. Ambassador Robin Haydon drew up a secret profile in 1980 of Lynch's successor as Taoiseach, Charles Haughey, for the British government. It contained a passage speculating about the cause of Lynch's resignation the previous year, based on information supplied by 'Garret FitzGerald and many others'.

While FitzGerald was happy to disclose his involvement with the Bilderberg Group, the Trilateral Commission, British-Irish Association and his support for Irish membership of NATO in both of his autobiographies, there is no mention of Crozier or the ISCSG anywhere in either of them; nor indeed in any of his writings. Hence, we do not have FitzGerald's account of his relationship with Crozier or how long the relationship lasted.[7] Crozier died in 2012.

In his autobiography, Crozier also revealed his close friendship with Sir Maurice Oldfield, who was Deputy Chief of MI6, 1968–73, and Chief, 1973–78. It is inconceivable that Crozier did not report to Oldfield about what FitzGerald did, said and thought at the meetings of the ISCSG and on its fringes. Crozier's insights into FitzGerald may have informed British negotiations in the run up to the Sunningdale Agreement. Oldfield was central to the process leading up to the conclusion of the agreement, even flying to Dublin on at least one occasion. In addition, the Crozier-FitzGerald link may help to explain what Oldfield's friend and biographer Richard Deacon had in mind when he described the 'comprehensiveness of certain of [MI6's] intelligence reports' which Oldfield was able to furnish to Whitehall after he became MI6 chief in 1973.

The introduction to Crozier's *Ulster Debate*, explained that 'the Institute commissioned four of the five studies that appear in this book and convened a Study Group with the object of considering each of the papers and producing constructive suggestions'. Like all skilful propagandists, Crozier spun a good yarn: 'The guiding principle of the Study Group was realism. The outcome is a guide to the Irish problem and proposals that respect the facts and possibilities of a dangerous and delicate situation. Each paper is a separate contribution. It does not necessarily reflect the views of the other members of the Study Group'.[8]

Unfortunately, the 'guiding principle of the Study Group' was not 'realism'. Some of the more risible allegations in the book included:

* That on 13 December 1971 the IRA 'hi-jacked a Canadian aircraft but were apprehended';
* That Catholics in Belfast had marched in favour of internment on 13 March 1971;
* That on 10 March 1971 a 'feud between the Officials and the Provisionals broke out into open violence. There were murderous street battles in which it was estimated that 40 to 50 members lost lives'. However, not a single soul died on 10 March. Six people in total died during March 1971 of whom four were British soldiers;
* That Cathal Goulding was leader of the Provisional IRA. Goulding in fact led their bitter rivals, the Official IRA;
* Lord Chalfont, a former FCO minister, referred to the 'Mini-Manual of the Irish Guerrilla'[9] which contained 'a characteristic attack on the Catholic priesthood' by the IRA which described the Church as 'the enemy in our midst, the vipers nourished by the fruits of our sweat, the black beetles eating away at our very sustenance'.[10] This absurd quote can only have been included to undermine the IRA in the eyes of Catholic Irish-America.
* That Fianna Fáil (i.e., Lynch and O'Malley) had rendered the Republic a safe haven for the IRA.

FitzGerald was not the only high-profile dignitary to lend

his name to the publication. Professor J.C. Beckett of Queens University and Prof F.S.L. Lyons of Trinity College did so too, alongside Lord Chalfont. The real purpose of *Ulster Debate* was to portray Britain in the best light possible in America and elsewhere. It was distributed throughout the world by British embassy and consulate staff.

One group that emerged well out of *Ulster Debate* was the Parachute Regiment. According to it, on 2 October 1971 a 'paratrooper gave his life in an effort to save some children'. No one died on 2 October 1971, let alone a paratrooper, although a soldier did save a child in similar circumstances on another occasion. An allegedly 'clear' account of Bloody Sunday, one that could be relied upon 'beyond doubt', was tendered by Lord Chalfont: the IRA had been responsible for starting the violence of that dark day and the soldiers were the victims of unwarranted IRA propaganda. Chalfont argued that, 'when the IRA used the mobs as shelter for ambushes and snipers, sooner or later a tragedy of that sort is inevitable. When this happens another weapon in the armoury of terrorism comes into its own – the weapon of propaganda. The action of the security forces in London was the subject of unceasing IRA propaganda … and much of it was swallowed whole in sections of the British press'.

For his part Garret FitzGerald described Bloody Sunday as an 'aberration' that had caused an 'astonishing' rift between the UK and Ireland which had traditionally been 'basically friendly'.[11] Clearly, FitzGerald had not taken much heed of the Ballymurphy massacre of August 1971.

FitzGerald argued that, 'against this long-term background

the present unhappy state of Anglo-Irish relations can be seen as an aberration. An almost total – and unprecedented – failure of communications between the two countries, especially after the Derry shootings, created a momentary mutual hostility that is uncharacteristic of the normal complex but friendly relationship with each other. That this could have happened in the face of the means of mass communications now available is astonishing and indeed deeply worrying. Past experience suggests, however, that in time the misunderstandings caused by such communications blockages will be dissipated'.[12] Strangely, in *Ulster Debate* FitzGerald referred to 'the events of Londonderry' on p. 78, whereas on p. 73 he described the city as 'Derry'.

FitzGerald also used *Ulster Debate* as a platform to attack the Republic's failure to contribute to the defence of Western Europe by refusing to join NATO.

On 31 August 1972, *This Week* magazine in Dublin published a nine-page extract from *Ulster Debate*.[13] The front page ran with the title: 'The Options for Peace'.

***

John Hume, an opponent of internment, was also smeared in Crozier's *Ulster Debate*. An entry in the chronology section for 16 February 1972 contains a reference to an arrest warrant issued for him. The entry is silent as to what alleged offence it related. It merely stated that a 'summons was served on Mr John Hume in the Bogside, by police escorted by armoured cars'. The anti-Hume smear was not the only time the Derry man was targeted by British black propaganda.[14] Hugh

Mooney and his IRD colleagues also created links between the IRA, KGB and Arab terrorists to spark paranoia among Irish-American politicians.[15]

**

A little repetition is necessary to draw together the strands of these fabrications and smears, so as to reconstruct the type of argument that British diplomats might have circulated in Washington and elsewhere around the globe. They might have contended that:

* John Hume, a critic of internment and Bloody Sunday, was corrupt, self-serving and a thief; and there were bank statements and newspaper reports to prove it;
* Catholics had marched demanding the internment of the IRA in 1971;
* Bloody Sunday had been a trap set by the IRA during a march they had organised against internment;
* Paratroopers were in fact prepared to sacrifice their lives to save Irish children;
* The KGB were pulling the strings behind the scenes and supplying the IRA with arms they were smuggling to Donegal on-board Soviet submarines, and there were photographs and news reports to prove it;
* Arab terrorists were also arming the IRA;
* Jack Lynch, his Justice Minister Des O'Malley and others in the Fianna Fáil government of 1969–73 had rendered the Republic a safe haven for the IRA in a craven attempt to appease the backwoodsmen in their party:
* Garret FitzGerald of Fine Gael, the party which had won the 1973 general election, was now Minister for Foreign Affairs and was a far more reliable figure who not only supported NATO against the Soviets but also felt that it had been 'deeply worrying' that Bloody Sunday had ever created a rift between Ireland and the UK.

Looming large over all of these sleazy machinations and perpetuating them into the future was Sir John Leahy, whose father was Irish. Leahy was 'Head of News' at the FCO 1971–73, and Undersecretary to the NIO, 1975–77. According to one of his obituaries, Leahy was full of admiration for 'the discipline and self-control of the "squaddies" in Northern Ireland as they coped, for example, with foul-mouthed harpies spitting in their faces or shrieking abuse from street corners'.[16] Margaret Thatcher later made him ambassador to South Africa. He died in December 2015.

The combined deceit of Wilford, Mooney, Crozier and Widgery created a noxious atmosphere that allowed all sorts of mouldy nonsense about Bloody Sunday to fester for decades. Various authors, sympathetic to the Paras, including Charles Allen, author of *The Savage Wars of Peace* (1990), and Peter Harclerode, *Para!* (1992) sought to exculpate the regiment for its actions on Bloody Sunday. Harclerode argued that Support Company had inflicted a heavy blow on the Provisionals. On his account the troops had come under heavy fire from the Creggan Estate:

> Support Company's commander and his company headquarters had established themselves at the foot of Rossville Flats, out of the line of fire from the Creggan Estate, which by then had become heavy ... Firing had also come from a barricade which had been erected across Rossville Street and a nail bomb had exploded nearby. Another bomb had been thrown from an alleyway which led into Glenfada Park. Three members of the Anti-Tank Platoon, who were sent into the park to protect the platoon's flank, saw three armed men running. As the three terrorists turned to face the troops, they were engaged.[17]

He argued that the alleged slur that the troops had 'opened fire indiscriminately' could be refuted by:

> the fact that those killed were all males aged between 18 and 26 years old. Anything other than aimed shots would in all likelihood have resulted in women and children, of whom there were many in the crowd, being among the dead.

The Saville Report dismissed this type of nonsense as erroneous. Moreover, Harclerode does not seem to have considered the possibility that the firing was not 'indiscriminate' as most of the targets were in the same age bracket as the Derry Young Hooligans and the fresh wave of IRA recruits. His research overlooked the fact that Peggy Deery was shot and so severely wounded by the paratroopers that she never recovered.

He also propounded an allegation that there had been:

> unconfirmed reports that the total of those killed was between 20 and 30, and that the missing bodies had been spirited away across the border, where they were buried. If this was indeed the case, the motive for their concealment can only have been that forensic examination would have revealed that the individuals concerned had been handling and firing weapons.[18]

John Parker published *The Paras: The Inside Story of Britain's Toughest Regiment* in 2000. He maintained there was:

> little doubt that the IRA themselves 'doctored' the scene by whisking away incriminating materials and, it was speculated, several other bodies or wounded personnel.[19]

Parker also portrayed the soldiers of Support Company as a group of 'frightened young men' who had panicked:

The soldiers involved in the shootings were themselves pawns. They may have fired the shots; but who was it that placed them in that position, gave them live ammunition and a little yellow card explaining under what circumstances they might open fire, which was utterly useless in such a dramatic, nerve-racking, fast-moving crisis? Why was that decision, in the end, left to a bunch of frightened young men confronted by a mob?[20]

37

Getting Away with Murder

In January 1998, Tony Blair announced a fresh inquiry into Bloody Sunday to be led by Lord Saville of Newdigate.[1] Blair stated that Widgery had rushed his work, had failed to take evidence from the wounded and had not personally read the eyewitness accounts.

Saville made his introductory statement at Derry Guildhall on 3 April 1999. Oral hearings began on 27 March 2000, with an opening speech by Christopher Clarke, QC, counsel to the inquiry. The first witness took the stand on 28 November 2000. In the end, he held that the paratroopers had lost their self-control and fired at unarmed civilians, either forgetting or ignoring their orders and training; furthermore, they had failed to satisfy themselves that they had identified targets who were threatening to cause death or serious injury.

He also decided that Republican gunmen had fired some shots. However, these were not in the circumstances the paratroopers put forward; nor were they in circumstances which justified the shootings.

Col Wilford gave a number of interviews in the 1990s to the media, in which he hinted that he had participated in a secret plan on Bloody Sunday and that people above his rank were really to blame for what happened. When he appeared at the Saville Inquiry in 2003, he stuck to the cover-up story even if that meant jeopardising Soldier F who ultimately faced criminal charges, which were dropped in 2021. Wilford's evidence has been dismissed as a tissue of lies by virtually every commentator on the massacre.

Jimmy Duddy noted that: 'At times from across the room, you could see [Saville] was exasperated by the lying. I watched his body language especially with Colonel Wilford. He never looked at him. If he asked him questions, he looked away. You could see Saville's exasperation that this man, even after all these years, who made a mistake which caused 27 people to be shot, still wouldn't admit doing anything wrong. Saville asked Wilford very hard questions. You could see he just didn't like the man and did not like his attitude and lack of remorse.'[2]

Despite justification, Saville displayed no such distaste for either Ford or Kitson.

***

Wilford had the benefit of knowing that Ford had given little away when he had testified at the Saville Inquiry a year before him. Ford had refused to accept any blame for what had happened, although he purported to be 'extremely sad' about the deaths. Belying this, as late as 2013, he was making excuses for the killings, telling members of his old regiment, the 4/7 Royal Dragoon Guards, that Bloody Sunday had been blown out of proportion and was 'political.' He claimed to have no recollection of writing the memo of 7 January 1972, which discussed shooting 'selected ringleaders' of the Derry Young Hooligans.

When asked if he had communicated with 1 Para in the days leading up to Bloody Sunday, he answered:

A. On the day, no.

Q. On or before, Gen. Ford?

A. Not before either. I am talking between the time we started to think about this operation. I cannot remember when I last spoke to Colonel Wilford, it was probably weeks before.[3]

Ford did say that he had spoken to Wilford twice after the shooting had taken place.

Saville concluded that Ford's 'decision to use 1 Para as the arrest force is open to criticism but he did not know his decision would result in soldiers firing unjustifiably'.

Ford's disclosure that Kitson 'used to say to me why can't you sort out Londonderry?' came under the spotlight momentarily. The use of language here indicates that this was something about which Kitson pressed Ford repeatedly. Yet, at Saville, he attempted to play it down as a casual once-off remark of no consequence: 'Perhaps my words are not terribly carefully chosen there. Gen. Kitson and I used to meet occasionally socially, because we happened to live very close to each other. And I suspect that – I do not remember the exact occasion, over a drink or something – he said, you know, "Why is Londonderry ... you know, I have sorted out Belfast and no one seems to sort out Londonderry". And that is what I think it really came to. It was a social remark.'[4]

***

Kitson had long since retired, but he donned the same uniform as the army of witnesses who went to Saville to cover up what had happened, that of the thick skin. He only had to endure a few hours in the box. Yet, during that time he denied that his colleagues appreciated his counter-insurgency experience, let alone that they viewed him as any sort of an expert. He portrayed himself as a 'comparatively junior officer', almost as if he was directed by remote control via his superiors. He even went as far as to say that he doubted they had any interest in his books on the issue.

'It has been suggested,' he asserted, 'that I might have had some special influence in Northern Ireland because of my earlier experiences of counter-insurgency and peace-keeping and because I had recently prepared a report for the army on these matters which was published as a book called *Low Intensity Operations* in November 1971. I had also written an account of my personal experiences during the Kenya Emergency published in 1960. I do not consider that either my experiences or my books would have been of much interest to my superiors at the time, most of whom had been involved in these sorts of operations themselves. Furthermore, *Low Intensity Operations* was only published towards the end of my time in Northern Ireland and did not become very well known until some months after I left ... I very much doubt whether the GOC or the CLF had read it by January 1972; indeed, they may never have read it'.[5]

There are many problems with these assertions. Kitson left Northern Ireland at the end of April 1972. By his calculation, his book would not have become well known until July or August 1972. Contradicting his assertion, on 6 January 1972 the MoD issued a document entitled, *Preparation Training Arrangements for Units Going to Northern Ireland*. It recommended *Low Intensity Operations* as 'Background

Reading' because it 'provides a very valuable summary of the art of intelligence duties in an [insurgency] situation'.[6] This document was not put to him at the Saville Inquiry. In addition, the book was obviously known to Carver who had written the introduction to it.

During another phase of the questioning, Kitson sought to give the impression that his superiors would not have been interested in his views on anything beyond 39 Brigade area:

> I have no recollections now of discussions with Maj.-Gen. Ford about the general situation in Northern Ireland. As we were both based in Lisburn, I expect that we would have chatted about things generally from time to time, but he never asked me for a considered view of the situation outside my area ...[7]

He added that he knew nothing about the 'political decisions which governed security policy and very little about the situation elsewhere ...'

When he was asked about his interest in Derry, he said that it was under the command of 8 Brigade and hence not a part of his domain and he had no interest in it. Aside from a 'lunch party' to bid farewell to Brig. Cowan in his house, he could not recall ever having visited Derry.

When asked about Ford's remark about the comments he – Kitson – had made to him about Derry, Kitson decided not to dispute what Ford had said but to massage it with banalities:

> I have no specific recollection of asking Gen. Ford this question, although it would have been a natural topic of conversation bearing in mind that some procedures in force in other parts of the Province [*sic.*] such as removing all illegal road blocks as soon

as erected did not seem to apply in Londonderry. As I explained in paragraph 12 of my first statement to the Inquiry, we were both based in Lisburn and our houses were close to each other. We therefore met informally quite often. Had I asked him the question mentioned he would no doubt have pointed out the political and military factors bearing on the problem, but what was going on in Londonderry did not feature greatly in my mind as I had plenty to keep me occupied in Belfast. In any case such a question to Gen. Ford would not have been concerned with the 'subjugation' of Londonderry and I do not understand why such a suggestion should have been made. The Army's task in Northern Ireland was to assist in maintaining law and order, not to subjugate the Province (*sic.*) or any part of it.[8]

Lieut Col (later Gen.) Sir David Ramsbotham, who was Carver's military assistant, gave evidence a few weeks later. He said that he knew Kitson 'well' and that he was the 'master' of Belfast 'as one knew when you went there, and he would always say he did not know anything about Londonderry and he only concentrated on the area where he was based'.[9]

Kitson denied having any knowledge of Ford's 7 January 1972 memo about shooting the young hooligans in Derry. Yet, it is difficult to imagine that Kitson was not keenly interested in 'Free Derry', especially as it presented a different sort of challenge to the British compared to that which prevailed in Belfast. In Derry, the IRA operated in a large 'no-go' area with relative freedom. They were also very close to the border with the Republic. Belfast was about an hour's drive from the border and when mini 'no-go' areas emerged in the city, they were soon reopened by the troops.

The notion that Kitson would have passed on an opportunity to monitor in detail the entire infrastructure to understand the relationship between the Derry wings of the IRA and Belfast is absurd. He was a man fascinated by such interplay. What the paramilitaries did in Derry had repercussions for the rest of the island.

When the tribunal asked Kitson if he had been a party to any discussion 'with anyone for and against the proposition about using 1 Para in Londonderry prior to the operation on 30 January 1972?' his response was that, '... My input, if any, would have been limited to discussing the danger to stability in Belfast of removing 1 Para'.[10]

Contradicting this alleged disinterest, in his memoirs Mike Jackson revealed how Kitson had gone to Palace Barracks after his return from leave to quiz Wilford about what had happened in the Bogside on Bloody Sunday. This meant that he either interrupted his journey from the airport to Lisburn to divert to Palace Barracks, or travelled the fourteen miles from Lisburn for the encounter. In either case, it displays a strong level of interest in what had happened.

Jackson's 2007 memoirs revealed that Kitson had made a comment to Wilford about the latter's failure to 'go on and sort the whole bloody mess out'. The Saville Report did not arrive for another three years. Kitson, Wilford, and Jackson were not recalled by Saville to elaborate on this revelation. Curiously, this contrasted sharply with Saville's reaction to the discovery of Jackson's 'shot list'. It was found after Jackson had testified on 7 April 2003 and he was recalled the following October. Jackson then faced questions about the contradictions between the list and the statements provided by the Support Company troops to Widgery.

Kitson did not refer to the MRF when engaging with Saville. By throwing a cloak of silence and secrecy around the MRF, Kitson did not have to acknowledge that he was the sponsor of an assassination unit to an arena packed with lawyers eager to find out why another elite group under his command, Support Company, had shot dead unarmed civilians on Bloody Sunday.

The nearest Kitson came to having his feet held to the fire was when he was asked about some passages in yet another of his books, *Directing Operations*, published in 1989. It contained a chapter written as a follow-up to his book *Low Intensity Operations* called 'Directing Low Intensity Operations'.[11] In it he vented his frustration at what he perceived was a western society that had become 'soft and gullible' after an extended period of comparative peace, something which he felt only served to prolong insurgency campaigns. The west, he argued, had become a place where it seemed politically impossible for strong government measures to be taken against insurgents for any length of time, before being assailed by popular outcry at home or abroad. He felt the answer to this problem was to attack the sources of adverse opinion. This could be achieved, he believed, by using the public relations machinery of the state together with such legal sanctions as may be available.

There is a disturbing passage where he argued that 'anyone who is prepared to use illegal force against his own country has no right to expect anything other than total extermination, as fast as possible, by any legal means, regardless of how much force he is using'.[12] When Kitson was asked if he regretted that he had not been able to exterminate the IRA 'within the law' because the west had become soft and gullible, he replied: 'No, I am not talking about the IRA.' He then proceeded to argue that 'extermination' did not 'necessarily mean killing. They can be put away in some way, such as the Americans have put away a large number of Taliban in prison'.[13]

Another organisation set out to mislead, misdirect and misinform the inquiry, this time about Martin McGuinness.

38

MI5 TAKES AIM AT McGUINNESS

The Officer in Command (OC) of the Derry Brigade of the Provisional IRA on 30 January 1972 was Robbie Griffin. 'He was only there for a short while', recalls Des Long.[1] Griffin was a man who was 'uncomfortable with violence and armed struggle' according to Shane O'Doherty.[2] Martin McGuinness was Griffin's adjutant.

The Saville Inquiry was provided with a debriefing of an informant codenamed Infliction who claimed that: 'one thing that bothers [Martin] McGuinness about the Bloody Sunday thing was that he fired the first shot, and no one knows this. This seems to be on McGuinness's conscience. He has spoken to "Infliction" about it several times.' However, a tape of Infliction's debriefing was not disclosed.

David Shayler, a former MI5 officer who worked for the organisation's counter-IRA section T8 branch, had come across Infliction and said he was known in the organisation as a 'bullshitter'.[3] McGuinness described him as 'an informer who may or may not exist, the claims that I told "Infliction" that I fired the first shot on Bloody Sunday is a concoction, rubbish and a blatant lie'.

MI5 was acting in a devious manner in furnishing the 'Infliction' material about McGuinness to Saville. They knew better from a far more reliable agent called Willie Carlin, a Sinn Féin activist who spied on Republicans for MI5, and who told them a story that contradicted 'Infliction'. Carlin realised that the relevant information had been withheld from the Saville Inquiry. He believed that it must have been 'sitting somewhere on my files in the MoD. I am sure that my handler would have collated the information and passed it on'.[4] He decided to make a statement to the tribunal and went public about what he had done, which severely undermined MI5's attempt to blame McGuinness for precipitating Bloody Sunday.

Carlin published a book in 2019 which tallies with the statement he made to the inquiry.[5] According to his book, in 1984 he had been in a car with McGuinness. He explained that some people in Derry wanted to know what a Sinn Féin led council would do about raising the issue of Bloody Sunday. McGuinness responded by agreeing 'it was an issue but didn't think there would ever be another enquiry'. Carlin reminded him that the Bishop of Derry, Edward Daly, 'had said there were guns in the Bogside' on the day of the atrocity:

> 'There was, but the situation was very confusing and hectic,' Martin said.
>
> 'So we did nothing to defend the marchers?' I asked him.
>
> 'At the time I wished we had but I suppose it was a good job we didn't, or there would have been a lot more dead, mostly us, and we would have got the blame for all of it.'
>
> 'So who owned the guns?' I asked. Martin was getting a bit fidgety, he clearly didn't like this line of questioning but answered all the same.
>
> 'The Stickies [Official IRA]. They had issued two revolvers in Creggan after the shooting started but we managed to step in and get them off-side. We gave word to John Hume and Ivan Cooper the day before that we would move all weapons out of the Bogside, which wasn't much in them days.' Martin stopped talking as we travelled on. Bloody Sunday was a turning point in his life and obviously still had an effect on him.[6]

McGuinness provided a statement to the Saville Inquiry and testimony in person at the Guildhall in Derry in November 2003. He confirmed that the organisers of the march had asked the Provisionals not to intervene and that they had removed their arms.

Griffin arrived on the scene after the paratroopers had begun shooting and issued an order not to retaliate. McGuinness believed that the British army had attempted to lure the Provisionals into a trap. 'Having weighed it up,' he said in his statement, 'it was my personal view that we should not react. I decided that it was better to let the world see what the British army had done.'

McGuinness relayed this command to the leaders 'of the various units of active service volunteers':

> The IRA orders were, simply put, that no offensive action should be taken against the British military/RUC during the course of the march on Bloody Sunday. I can never recall a civil rights march where the IRA had taken advantage of people on the street to attack the British army. It was unthinkable.
>
> There were no IRA armaments in the Bogside area of any description. There were no explosive devices there. There were no explosions that day, none at all. The nail bombs were in a number of dumps. It would have been lunacy of the worst kind for anyone to have had nail bombs about them when 30,000 people were on the streets.
>
> We were very angry and emotional. A critical and difficult decision had to be made.
>
> It was concluded that any military engagement with the British army then would see us fall into a trap. We felt that we should let the world see what we know to be fact: that the British army had shot innocent civil rights marchers.
>
> There was no maverick action by IRA volunteers that day. No one tried to overturn or flout the decision [not to fire on the army] once it was taken.

McGuinness stressed that no member of the IRA was either killed or injured on Bloody Sunday. 'Had this happened,' he said, 'I would have known. Indeed, the entire community in Derry would have known'.

Regarding Gerald Donaghy, he stated, 'my understanding is that following Bloody Sunday the youth wing, Fianna Éireann, claimed he was a member. I did not know Gerald Donaghy. I never met him. He was not a member of the IRA.' Membership of the Youth Movement did not signify membership of the IRA, he stressed.

In the end, Saville concluded that neither McGuinness nor anyone else in the IRA had provoked the massacre. When he reported on 15 June 2010, he overturned Widgery's findings. He accused the paratroopers of having made false claims that they had been attacked. None of the victims, he stated, had posed any kind of threat to Support Company.

After the publication of the Saville Report, Tory Prime Minister David Cameron formally apologised on behalf of the British government for the 'unjustified and unjustifiable' events of Bloody Sunday.

Infliction may have wasted a lot of MI5's time but he does not appear to have caused much damage with those lies. The same cannot be said about Observer B.

39

THE DECEIT AND AVARICE OF OBSERVER B

MI5 must have realised that Observer B was a liar at some stage. Yet, if their testimony to Saville is to be believed, he was a credible and selfless agent. Julian, one of his MI5 handlers, referred to files from 1970 to 1973 that described him as 'a reliable agent ... His reports are essentially detailed'.[1] Julian stressed that the greater the detail an agent provided, the easier it was to confirm his reliability. He added that others had corroborated Observer B's information.

While Observer B provided Saville with a statement, he never gave evidence in person and was not cross-examined as he was suffering from ill health. Hence, the falsehoods he peddled in 1972 about Bloody Sunday were not challenged. Observer B was certainly alive in June 2001 as he spoke to Greg O'Neill, a lawyer working for the campaign for justice for the families of the Dublin and Monaghan bombings. That conversation took place on 31 October 2001.

After Bloody Sunday Observer B decided to smother the fact he had been lying with a fresh snowstorm of deceit. His statement to Saville was heavily redacted but this hardly matters as what is missing is probably just more fiction:

> On 31.1.72 **[REDACTION]** I talked to two men **[RE-DACTION]** and who had been in Londonderry on Bloody Sunday. Their names were A and B **[REDACTION]**. They told me that after the march they had made their way to Free

Derry Comer. When they got there they were surprised to hear shooting start. They then described that after the shooting had gone on for a couple of minutes they observed several men run from the Rossville Flats to a Mark II Ford Cortina parked ... **[REDACTION]** A said that they saw two men open the boot of the car and throw in two Thompson sub-machine guns, a rifle and pistol before getting into the car and driving off. **[REDACTION]** B said that the back of the car was full of Thompsons. I telephoned [Intelligence Officer 1] with this information shortly afterwards. Document 1 of the attached Annex A details the conversation, save that I did not say anything to the best of my recollection about weapons being distributed from the car and nor was I told that weapons had been distributed from the car.

This must have been music to MI5 and senior military ears for he was telling them that IRA gunmen had been present in the Bogside after all:

On Tuesday the 1 February I met 'Julian' **[REDACTION]** Julian wanted to know if there was a passageway between Glenfada Park North and Glenfada Park South. I told him that there was and drew a sketch. He also asked if there was anywhere where it would be possible to witness someone being shot in that passageway other than the passageway itself. I told him that you could have seen it from a window on one of the corner houses in Abbey Park. Finally, he asked me if someone could have fired on British soldiers in Glenfada Park and then escaped from any return fire. I said that someone could have escaped through the passageway. I then told 'Julian' what A and B had told me the previous day. Document 3 of Annex A attached to this statement details this conversation.

Observer B sought to rely on a corroborative source called 'X'. Unfortunately, since 'X' alleged he saw Auxiliaries [i.e. those who assisted the IRA], the report that emanated from him cannot be accurate either. Observer B probably fabricated his conversation with 'X'. According to Observer B's statement:

[REDACTION] On about the 12th, 13th or 14th [REDAC-TION] I met X and C [REDACTION] I asked both of them what had happened on Bloody Sunday and [REDACTION] C said that he did not know as he had shut his door and stayed inside

[REDACTION] X's account was that when the shooting started he saw the Auxiliaries firing from the balconies. He did not see how many guns were used but said that there were a wide variety of firearms used and that not all of the Auxiliaries had a weapon. He said that 'it was pandemonium – absolute bedlam'. He said that the Paratroopers had made it to the Flats faster than that section of the crowd that had been rioting had anticipated. This had caused panic among the rioters and their response was to run. He said that the Auxiliaries also panicked when the Paras reached the Flats and they [REDACTION] stashed their weapons in small rooms off the landings where water mains were housed. X said that the first shot he heard was the thud of a Thompson and was convinced that the IRA had fired first that day. I reported this information to IO1.

I told X to keep quiet about what he had told me. He said 'Why? – it was their fault the Army are being blamed'. I told him that if he carried on saying that that he would get himself into trouble but he was adamant. I got the impression that he had told a number of people what he had told me.

I only saw X once or twice after the conversation referred to in paragraphs 22 and 23.

Curiously, MI5 did not reveal any contemporaneous reports from Observer B describing the alleged 'drilling' by the auxiliaries in Glenfada Park in the week before Bloody Sunday. When asked about this, Julian speculated (or pretended to speculate) at Saville that it was a 'possibility' that Observer B had confused this occasion with another. This is highly un-likely considering other documents and accounts which have come to light, in particular one from the very pinnacle of the intelligence community, the Joint Intelligence Committee in London, which reported that 'the IRA had planned to 'organise disturbances in Londonderry designed to draw the security forces into the Bogside and there attack them'.[2]

Observer B was not named at Saville. Observer B was James Miller, an Englishman born in 1932 who had served in the Parachute Regiment as a sergeant major and, in later life, became a lift engineer. This occupation afforded him access to places within the borders of the 'no-go' areas of Derry such as Rossville Flats, that had elevators serving the nine floors of the complex, and to the Divis Flats in Belfast. According to 'Julian' of MI5, Miller was originally introduced to British military intelligence through 'officers in the Parachute Regiment'.[3]

Miller had settled down in Ireland after he had married an Irish woman. At one stage in the early 1970s, members of the IRA denounced him as a spy but he managed to convince Ivor Bell, a senior Belfast Provisional IRA member, that he had been wrongly accused and was exactly what he presented himself as: a straightforward working-class man. At the time the accusation was made, Bell took him to his home and protected him.

Having settled in Ireland, Miller had moved to Monkstown in County Antrim. In the late 1980s, when he was in financial difficulty, he made contact with Barry Penrose of *The Sunday Times* and told him he had been recruited by military intelligence in 1970. Penrose had written a series of articles based on information furnished by Colin

Wallace and Fred Holroyd relating to a slew of dirty tricks which had been perpetrated in Northern Ireland. One of the things Miller told Penrose was that he had come across Wallace's name during his time working for MI5. Penrose was sceptical. Miller gave him the phone number of his MI5 handler, to whom Penrose placed a call. At first, the MI5 officer on the other end of the line did not realise Penrose was a journalist, assuming instead he was another MI5 officer and asked: 'What's the problem with him, now', before proceeding to complain that Miller was never satisfied. The phone went dead when the MI5 officer realised Penrose was a journalist.

Subsequent to this, MI5's legal advisers confirmed to Penrose that Miller had worked for the security forces in Northern Ireland. Further confirmation came through the intervention of the D-Notice Committee, a body that intervenes to preserve state secrets. Admiral William Higgins, secretary to the committee at the MoD, requested Penrose's editor not to identify the names of Miller's case officers or his current whereabouts.

In 1970 or 1971, Miller infiltrated the Loyalist paramilitary organisation Tara and became aware of William McGrath's sexual abuse of boys. McGrath was the housefather at the infamous Kincora Boys' Home in Belfast. Miller informed his handlers about this, although they already knew all about McGrath. Children as young as eight were being abused by members of the vice ring, which included McGrath. Miller spoke about some of this to Penrose, who reported in 1987 that he had said 'that McGrath's sexual tendencies were common knowledge inside Tara' and that 'my MI5 case officer later told me to leave McGrath to them and I understand they used the information to recruit him as an informer.' Penrose contacted McGrath who 'confirmed that he knew Miller' but would not elaborate any further.[4]

Liam Clarke, who worked on the story with Penrose, revealed that Miller and Observer B were the same man.[5] Clarke revealed that he spoke to Miller in 1987 'about his efforts to alert the authorities to Kincora, before his handlers made his financial problems disappear to shut him up'.

Roy Garland, once second-in-command of Tara, recalls that Miller 'was never a Tara member but appeared at a meeting at the Clifton Street Orange Hall. I am pretty sure it was in 1970 but possibly early 1971. I think he was of medium build. The UVF people recognised him as having worked on lifts in the Falls Road and said he was MI5 – they may have said British Intelligence. I passed this information on to McGrath and was asked by him to see Miller out, which I did. Miller said nothing – not a word from what I remember as he left. That was the last I saw of him. He walked back towards Belfast centre. I knew little about him before this and since, apart from what I have read. I suspect McGrath had invited him'.[6]

Garland's suspicion that McGrath invited Miller makes sense, as the latter had been both an MI5 and MI6 agent at various stages in his paramilitary career. After this, Miller was instructed by MI5 to join the UDA, which he did. It is interesting to note that they allowed him join, despite the fact the UVF believed he was an informer. Miller rose to become the UDA's Director of Intelligence. In 1987, he told Barrie Penrose that his MI5 handlers had encouraged him to generate opposition in Northern Ireland to the British government, then led by Harold Wilson of the Labour Party. 'My case officers told me to do it. M15 wanted to get at Wilson. They said he was a Soviet agent.'[7] Penrose quoted him in *The Sunday Times* as having said to him that:

> 'I did a dangerous job over there for nearly five years and many UDA and IRA men went to prison as a result,' Miller said last night. 'But I could never understand why my case officers, Lt Col Brian X and George X, wanted the UDA to start a [Loyalist] strike [against the Northern Ireland Power-Sharing Executive] in the first place. But they specifically said I should get UDA men at grass-roots level to 'start pushing' for a strike. So I did.
>
> ... [He] said that in early 1974 his case officers instructed him to promote the idea within the UDA of mounting a general strike which would paralyse Northern Ireland. The result, says Miller, was the Ulster Workers' Strike in May 1974 which severely embarrassed Wilson's government and helped to torpedo the Sunningdale Power-Sharing Executive of Catholics and Protestants, which had included an 'Irish dimension' by allowing the Irish government a consultative role in Ulster (*sic*).[8]

Author and journalist Paul Foot later revealed that 'Brian X' was Lt Col Dixon.[9]

Members of the UDA pointed the finger of suspicion at Miller in 1974. With that, his career ended and he was spirited to England where he was provided with a house and a small business in Devon.

In later years, his position came to be occupied by Brian Nelson, another British intelligence agent.[10]

***

In disclosing details about his career as an agent for MI5 (but notably nothing about his role in Bloody Sunday) Miller was able to blackmail MI5. In the first instance, he applied pressure by telling Penrose that he was going to hand over information to Merlyn Rees, who had served as both Secretary of State for Northern Ireland in the 1970s and as Home Secretary. In addition, he threatened to tell other former Labour ministers what he knew about anti-Labour plotting. All of this was happening at a time when senior figures inside the Labour Party were pressing for an inquiry into a range of unlawful activities perpetrated by MI5. The former British prime minister, James Callaghan, was one of those supporting Rees.

After a series of disclosures made about Kincora that cast doubt on the 1983 Terry Report, which exonerated the intelligence services and the RUC of wrongdoing, Rees wanted the scandal re-examined. Although Rees professed no direct knowledge of Kincora from his time in Northern Ireland, or as Home Secretary, on reflection he felt that it fitted 'in with conversations I heard at the time. This whole affair must be investigated.'[11] The pressure on MI5 was immense. Then suddenly Miller disappeared. According to Paul Foot, he moved to another address and changed his phone number.

***

At Saville, Julian claimed that Miller, was 'a very valuable agent'; someone who had initially refused a salary and was a courageous man who performed 'very dangerous' work.

'He didn't have anything to gain by lying to us. I believe his motivation to have been a desire for peace'. Miller, however, had accepted expenses. In August 1972, he began to accept a monthly payment of £50 along with a once-off bonus of £500, which made up for some of the work he had performed in the past. By the standards of other agents, this was generous.

What we know about Miller, therefore, includes the fact that he lied to his handlers about the IRA making plans to attack British troops in Derry on 30 January 1972; participated in treason in 1974; knew about the Kincora scandal yet did nothing to prevent the on-going abuse of children; failed to come forward during any of the Kincora inquiries held during his life time, i.e., 1982 and 1984 (when he spoke out to *The Sunday Times* in 1987, it was only to blackmail MI5 into paying off his debts) and that he stood over the lies in the statement he prepared for the Saville Inquiry. As Director of Intelligence for the UDA, he was also privy to most, if not all, of the torture, intimidation and assassinations that it undertook.

Despite all this, Julian portrayed him as a hero, an individual whose files established he had become tired from his strenuous clandestine work. By February 1973, his handlers were contacting him 'too frequently for his own good'. The file for 1974 noted that he had given 'four years valuable service under very hazardous conditions'. The deceit he pedalled to his handlers in January 1972 must have reached Ford and Tuzo, and may have travelled onwards to Carver in London. Since the Saville Inquiry did not probe this issue deeply, the full significance of the spy's actions remain a mystery. It is reasonable to suggest that when the officers who stood around the sand table at Palace Barracks, heard the alarming news that emanated from him, it encouraged their plan to invade the Bogside.

Incredibly, Miller merited only a fleeting mention in the Saville Report. Saville's conclusion was that despite the 'absence of a record, it is possible that Observer B's recollections are accurate and that he did pass to IO1 the information to which he referred in his evidence to us, though there is nothing to suggest that the information played any part in the planning by the Army for the march'. This is a baffling analysis, one that is almost incomprehensible. Saville seems to be saying that a large group of IRA men could have been drilling in and around Glenfada Park and the Rossville flats, and that this information did not have any impact on military intelligence, the wider British army and MI5.

Saville must have realised that Miller was a deceiver, for there had been no drilling near the flats, yet he did not denounce him.

The most untruthful of the Bloody Sunday liars, however, was not a secret agent of MI5, rather an officer of the British army. From time to time, however, he grappled with the notion of telling the truth, but never quite summoned the courage to open up fully. Still, some of the glimpses he has afforded us are quite illuminating.

40

THE COLONEL'S CLUES

But for Bloody Sunday, Col Wilford would have continued his ascent on the military ladder. Instead, he was assigned a number of desk jobs where he was hidden from public scrutiny. Finally, it dawned on him that there would be no rehabilitation and he retired. He ended his career teaching art in Belgium. He has spoken out on a number of occasions about Bloody Sunday, sometimes intimating that there are people above his rank who have questions to answer – Kitson was directly above him. He has even hinted that questions should have been asked of Gen. Ford and the former British prime minister, Edward Heath.

He informed Peter Taylor in the 1990s:

> There has to be a scapegoat and I was the one. I'm not bitter about it. The only good thing about being a scapegoat is that you protect other people. I adored my soldiers and I protected them because I believed they were right.[1]

When asked by Taylor if he was still 'protecting them twenty years later?' he replied: 'I suppose so.'

Some of his comments reinforce the possibility that he and Ford had planned all along to go behind MacLellan's back and invade the Bogside. Strings of possibilities arise for Wilford's bewildering behaviour. One is that he can sometimes become so frustrated with his plight that he will reveal the truth only to calm down later and revert to full cover-up mode.

During a 1998 Channel 4 News broadcast, reporter Alex Thomson raised the issue of a 'secret plan' saying: 'and all these years Derek Wilford's wondered if the secret plan that day was to take over the Bogside and end the no-go area; if so, it never quite happened'. If anyone knew whether there was a hidden scheme, it was Wilford. As the commander on the ground, it is inconceivable he would not have been a party to it, so his pretence at suspicion was probably a ruse to put the notion before the public and warn off those in power who were thinking about calling a fresh tribunal at that time. If there was any class of a plan to provoke the IRA and retake the no-go area, it is inconceivable that Wilford was acting behind the backs of Ford and Kitson. Wilford is still alive. He may yet clarify exactly what he has meant when he has dropped these hints.

What other clues has he provided?

On another occasion he stated that the politicians bore the ultimate responsibility because the plan 'has to come from higher than the brigade commander [i.e., Kitson]. The germ of it must have started in London.'[2] When it was mooted that the victims should get an apology, Wilford was aghast and suggested: 'Well I think the Prime Minster of the time [Edward Heath] ... should be the person who's discussing it frankly ... perhaps with the ... aid of some of the senior cabinet officials or people responsible for Northern Ireland at the time and ... the senior army officers.'[3]

Other insights about secret planning emerged during his Channel 4 interview. They indicate that the purpose of the covert action was to retake the Bogside. Wilford was quoted as saying, 'I ended up in the situation where ... I really controlled the Bogside ... You know I had my battalion in there and no troops had been in there for months it was a no-go area ... We occupied it and I stood there ... Wondering what to do next. I said here I am, I control this block.'[4]

He has dropped other hints about secret planning that took place before he went to Ebrington Barracks. He has said that during a briefing before Bloody Sunday, he had 'asked that um – the question which in fact for a long time has – has worried me. I said, "What happens if there is shooting?" To which I got really a very er – very sparse reply to the effect that: "Oh, well, we'll deal with that when it comes. I asked that um – the question. It's my greatest regret that I didn't actually pursue that question and say: "Right, you know, what do you want us to do if we are shot at?"'[5]

The casual advice that if the troops were fired at, 'we' could 'deal with that when it comes', implies that shooting was deemed likely by the planners and that Wilford's superiors took it for granted that the troops of Support Company would be well able to handle themselves.

This conversation can hardly have taken place at Ebrington Barracks. If this assumption is correct, it means that Wilford was in receipt of orders from other quarters. This is contrary to the official narrative, which attributes all of the planning to 8 Brigade.

The reasons for doubting that he raised the issue of how Support Company was to respond if fired at, while he was at the Ebrington briefing include the following. First, he could have said, but did not, that Ebrington was where these concerns occurred to him. Second, he attended that conference on the Friday afternoon before the Sunday march. Hence, any questions arising from it could not have been troubling him 'for a long time'. Third, no one at Ebrington had said anything along the lines of: 'Oh, well, we'll deal with that when it comes.' Fourth, he had remained silent at Ebrington. All of this implies strongly that he discussed what Support Company was going to do, sometime before he went to Derry on Friday 28 January.

Ford is a good fit for a partner in these machinations as he was present on Bloody Sunday. It was he and Tuzo who were responsible for having secured the presence of eight regiments consisting of 2,000 troops in Derry that day. That was an army sufficient to retake the Bogside and soak it with soldiers capable of holding it indefinitely. Furthermore, Wilford spoke to Ford after the massacre had become apparent and the issue of withdrawing from the Bogside had sprung to the top of the agenda. 'I said to Ford, Gen. Ford, when he asked me what I was going to do next and I said in the absence of any orders I am going to pull back and that's what I did ten minutes later; I pulled my troops out ... and I did not pull them out ... because they had been shooting, I pulled them out because I just could not leave my troops on the ground ... with no orders. What was I supposed to do? Just sort of sit around there ... you know twiddle my thumbs, I had to be there – [there] had to some kind of er constructive er decision made ... and there were not'.[6]

Wilford believes that after the shooting, his superiors wasted an opportunity to retake the Bogside. This can hardly be a reference to MacLellan, as he had had no desire to retake the Bogside. Furthermore, MacLellan had not wanted Wilford to go anywhere near the no-go area. In fact, he had ordered 1 Para to remain near the William Street barricades and not to use vehicles. So, who was Wilford talking about when he said, 'They were offered an opportunity to take over the Bogside and regain proper control of it'? Again, Ford is a good fit. He was on the spot and could have, but did not, order him to proceed. Instead, as Wilford added, 'they decided not to take that opportunity because there had been the shooting. I think they lost their nerve, frankly.'[7] This cannot have been a reference to MacLellan, as he had never proposed an invasion of the Bogside, so the notion of him having lost his nerve because of the shootings does not arise.

There was a consistency to the comments Wilford made to Channel 4 News in 1997. Six years earlier, he had made similar remarks to the BBC: 'Quite honestly I owned the Bogside in military terms. I occupied it.'[8]

Having implicated his military superiors, in 1998 he went further saying that the 'germ' of the plan that unfolded on Bloody Sunday 'must have started in London'.[9] This implicates Lord Carver and Edward Heath.

When the issue of making an apology to the victims of Bloody Sunday emerged, Wilford complained that:

> if people start talking about apologising then I think one has actually got to look at who was responsible for the decision to carry out that particular type of operation and to use the only troops capable of doing it who, if you like, were battle hardened troops who would take no nonsense.[10]

The comment that only the troops of 1 Para – most likely those of Support Company – were the only soldiers 'capable' of carrying out a 'particular type of operation' cannot have been a reference to a snatch operation. The suggestion that only Support Company could have chased and arrested young rioters is absurd. This comment, however, fits neatly if it is a reference to an invasion of a no-go area such as the Bogside. Invasions were, after all, precisely what paratroopers did. That was why the regiment was established during the Second World War.

On occasion, he shone a little more light on some of the discussions he had with his co-conspirators. In 1998 he told Channel 4 News that: 'We were put into an arrest operation which I do not think had been thought out ... erm fully ... the implications of which had not been ... thoroughly thought out – it is implications of ... It smacked of its time we taught these people a lesson ...'[11]

It is difficult to conceive that anyone above Wilford could have felt that the mere arrest of a group of teenage hooligans was really going to teach those opposed to the crown a 'lesson'.

When asked about his Channel 4 interview at the Saville Inquiry, he tried to distance himself from what he had said on camera:

> This is talking, what, 25 years after the event. I think the remarks that I made were – and I said this before in this room – were the result of frustration and angry – anger, perhaps a certain amount of bitterness, all those sort of things. I think many of those remarks I made were foolish, insupportable, inadvisable, and I was certainly doing what I deplore in others, becoming an armchair general.[12]

Wilford is one of a tiny number of people who still maintain that Support Company was fired at first by the IRA on Bloody Sunday and that some of those shot dead by his troops were gunmen or nail bombers.

During his 1992 interview with the BBC Wilford declared: 'I do not believe my soldiers were wrong'. Asked whether the victims could be considered innocent, he had replied: 'Oh no. I cannot believe that. That would be to believe that my soldiers were wrong.'[13]

He would also insist that his troops had not run amok, claiming that 'if my troops had run amok there [would have] been far more than thirteen people killed ... you would have been counting the dead and dozens ... many dozens.'[14] This was tantamount to saying that Support Company had remained in a disciplined mode and under his control throughout the shootings. Since we know they were not fired upon, there must have been some reason for what they did. The most malign interpretation of this quote from Wilford is that a unit within Support Company was acting on orders to provoke the IRA. In this scenario, Wilford might consider that they had not run amok, for they had stopped shooting when it became abundantly clear that the IRA was not present in the Bogside.

By the time he came to testify at the Saville Inquiry in March 2003, Col Wilford had returned to full cover-up mode and tried to brush aside the hints he had dropped to the media previously. Now, there was no more to Bloody Sunday than an arrest operation that had gone wrong and there had been no plan to invade the Bogside.

There is no doubt that Wilford is capable of telling dark

falsehoods, but he is a poor liar. He once gave an interview to *The Daily Mail* during which he said that he had seen 'Soldier H', a member of the Support Company killing unit that attacked the Bogside on Bloody Sunday, firing at an alleged sniper inside the Rossville flats. This contradicted other statements he made. When he was confronted with this at the Saville Inquiry, the best he could say was, 'Yes, I got it wrong'. When it was put to him, 'You did not see any of that?' he was forced to acknowledge that he had not.[15]

Despite all of this evidence, Lord Saville concluded, in 2010, that Wilford had failed to appreciate what he had been authorised to do by 8 Brigade HQ but he did not offer an explanation for this momentous lapse. This hardly passes muster.

Wilford has never displayed remorse for what he did. He gave an interview to James Naughtie of the BBC's Radio 4 programme *Today* in 1999, during which he refused to accept the word of Michael McKinney, the brother of William McKinney who had been shot on Bloody Sunday, that he was not a Republican. 'No, of course I do not accept it', he said. When asked, why not, he replied: 'Well, because they will all say that, won't they? I mean, every Republican, every, every, I regret to say, almost every Ulster (*sic.*) Catholic will say that'.[16] In other words, all Catholics in Northern Ireland were IRA supporters and liars.

Unfortunately, despite the passage of half a century, he has lacked the courage to do more than drop a few hints and then recoil from them. During that time, he has sought to portray himself to the world as a man who has remained loyal to his soldiers. If he truly knows more than he has disclosed, it renders this self-portrait a sham. If Wilford had information that could have assisted Soldier F, why did he cower beneath the table before the charges against his former subordinate were dropped?

And what of Kitson? From the moment it became apparent that the Bloody Sunday massacre was a calamity, Kitson remained tight-lipped. While he was the man in overall charge of 1 Para, Bloody Sunday had occurred in Derry which was not part of his brigade area. He has made the point that he was on leave at the time of the shooting. But, at the very least, he set the tone for the troops under his control. His influence over many aspects of how they operated was enormous. After the Saville Report was published, a number of the Support Company soldiers faced the prospect of criminal proceedings; Soldier F would actually be charged with murder. As ever, Kitson made no comment – and washed his hands of the men he once led.

41

KITSON, RECRUITMENT SERGEANT FOR THE IRA

The storm that had been gathering over Northern Ireland truly broke after Bloody Sunday. A wave of unprecedented anger swept away much of the soil around the feet of the moderates in the Nationalist community. The Official and Provisional IRA benefited from a swell in support, which manifested itself in a wave of new recruits. A group of young men from Derry who had joined the Provisional IRA before Bloody Sunday were 'up a mountain' in the Republic at a training camp on the day of the massacre. When news began to filter through to them about what had happened, they told their instructors they wanted to leave, return home and take weapons with them. Des Long, the OC of the Munster Brigade, who was in command of the camp, was having none of it and ordered them to stay put despite their pleas. 'They weren't trained and it would have been dangerous to have let them anywhere near the city. Some of them were insistent and I nearly had to load a pistol to keep them in place. Some even tried to break out. I can understand how upset they were. Their town had been attacked but I couldn't let them go.'[1]

The combination of bloodbath, victim vilification, cover-up and the blind eye that had been turned to Loyalist terror injected a venom into the Troubles which would blight the island for decades to come. These events shattered a prediction Kitson had made in *Low Intensity Operations*. 'In practice,' he had written 'the fact that the army is so heavily engaged in Ireland now makes it unlikely that it will be involved in exactly this task between 1975 and 1980 because it is reasonable to hope that the present emergency will be resolved within five years'.[2]

To Nationalists, Kitson became the personification of evil, Britain's counter-insurgency bogeyman driving many young men into the ranks of the paramilitaries. Had he set out to become a recruitment sergeant for the IRA, he could not have done a better job. Paddy Devlin MP wrote that Kitson 'probably did more than any other individual to sour relations between the Catholic community and the security forces'.[3]

On 15 February 1972, he was awarded a CBE at Buckingham Palace.

On 22 February, the Official IRA attacked the HQ of the British army's 16th Parachute Regiment Brigade at Aldershot, Hampshire in revenge for Bloody Sunday. Five kitchen staff were killed by the devastating shrapnel shredding explosive wave of a car bomb. Not a single soldier died. In a grotesque variation on the lies pumped out by the British black propagandists after Bloody Sunday, an Official IRA spokesman declared that 'initial reports confirmed that several high-ranking officers had been killed [at Aldershot]. British propaganda units then moved into action, and miraculously the dead officers disappeared'.[4] The statement added that the

Official IRA's intelligence department had ascertained that twelve officers of the Parachute Regiment had been killed in the attack. Nothing of the sort had happened.

The following day the Official IRA added that the Aldershot attack had been perpetrated in revenge for Bloody Sunday: 'Any civilian casualties would be very much regretted as our target was the officers responsible for the Derry outrages.' Stripped of the crocodile tears, the Officials were saying that it was acceptable to slaughter a handful of kitchen staff, a gardener and a priest, wound others and turn children into orphans in a botched attack because their motives had been pure – revenge. The Officials promised that the bombing would be the first of many such attacks on buildings occupied by British army regiments serving in Northern Ireland.

Kitson and his wife Elizabeth lived in the married quarters at Thiepval Barracks, a place where she was safe. Joe McCann, a leading Official IRA volunteer, however, had placed her and her husband under a surveillance net. He was directly involved in shadowing them. As part of his operation, McCann may have followed her as she rode a horse around isolated tracks beyond the precincts of the complex. Perhaps he was hoping she might be joined by her husband, perhaps he intended to kidnap her. He also followed Kitson at this time as he moved about in his black limousine.

McCann was a serious threat. He was behind the attack on the car of John Taylor MP in February 1972. Taylor was badly injured but survived. McCann and his team may have killed more than a dozen soldiers in Belfast. He did not get to complete the Kitson mission because he was killed by paratroopers in Belfast on 15 April 1972. They shot him three times in the back as he fled from them. He was unarmed at the time. Aged 24, he left a wife and four young children behind.

***

Having taken up the cudgels in September 1970, for what should have been a two-year term, Kitson was informed that he was being stood down as brigadier of 39 Brigade. A party was held in his honour at Thiepval Barracks before he left. He was flown out of Belfast in a helicopter on 22 April 1972. The perceived wisdom is that he was deposed due to pressure from Nationalist politicians, but a number of factors were responsible for his removal. The new Secretary of State for Northern Ireland, William Whitelaw, was not an admirer and wanted to appease Nationalist politicians who, like Paddy Devlin, saw Kitson as a menace. Kitson had at least one champion at cabinet, Peter Carrington, but Whitelaw's will prevailed. Heath and Whitelaw also needed the support of the SDLP and other Nationalist politicians in their negotiations for the Nationalist-Unionist power-sharing agreement that was concluded the following year at Sunningdale.

Kitson's departure made little difference to the behaviour of the British army. No sooner was he gone than his MRF soldiers took to the streets of Belfast and began shooting at unarmed civilians.

On 2 May, while the bullets were flying in Belfast, Kitson assumed his next role, as commandant of the School of Infantry at Warminster, Wiltshire in England. Some commentators felt he was sent there to pass on the urban counter-insurgency skills he had developed in Ireland to the next generation of officers. The advocates of this theory opine that the British establishment was afraid that the breakdown of law and order in Belfast and Derry was a harbinger of strife in British cities and that Kitson's tactics would be required to quell the forthcoming unrest. They pointed, for example, to Wolverhampton where race riots had taken place. Unions, especially the miners, were in a militant phase too. In *Low Intensity Operations,* Kitson had warned of 'other potential trouble spots within the United Kingdom which might involve the Army in operations of a sort against political extremists.'

In a six-page profile of Kitson in *This Week* magazine, the investigative journalist and author Sean Boyne wrote that 'while in the North he was involved in the re-organisation of the RUC and that he is continuing this work from England. Part of the plan, apparently, was to replace the present structure of the RUC by a county constabulary system based on the English model'.[5]

In May 1972, the Official IRA announced a unilateral ceasefire. Henceforth their arms would lie dormant except for self-defence. There was a sting in the tail: the cessation of hostilities did not extend to Kitson who remained a target.

Sir Basil Eugster, the commander in chief of the UK's land forces, arranged protection for the brigadier, who was living in Wiltshire. Eugster did so in conjunction with the under-secretary of state for the army at the MoD. It was decided that 'as a temporary measure' he was to be provided with a 'guard armed with ammunition at [his home] and for the Brigadier to carry a personal weapon'.[6] The protection was withdrawn at the end of 1973 after the Special Branch had re-assessed the threat to him concluding that he was no longer at risk.

No doubt Kitson observed the collapse of 'Free Derry' with satisfaction from Wiltshire. The enclave fell in the early hours of 31 July 1972 when an army of bulldozers and Centurion tanks smashed through the barricades with troops following behind in lighter armoured vehicles, as part of *Operation Motorman*. The Provisional and Official IRA did not confront the troops on this occasion.

After this, the army constructed a series of fortified military bases in Derry and Belfast in the centre of the most ardent of Republican areas. These corrugated fortresses permitted them to carry out 24-hour surveillance with mounted cameras. Later these strongholds were stocked with highly sophisticated, powerful microphones and laser-detection devices. All of this allowed the troops to monitor the movements of countless people.

Kitson's spirit lingered in other ways. One of his protégés was Lt Col Robin Evelegh. He commanded the 3rd Battalion of the Royal Green Jackets in an emergency tour of duty in the Upper Falls area of Belfast in 1972. He later led the battalion in the same area in 1973–1974. In his 'End of Tour Report' for 1972, he recommended returning fire even where there was a risk of striking passers-by. This, he argued, 'will discourage the gunmen from opening fire at all':

While complying in every way with the Yellow Card, I believe it is important to fire back an adequate number of rounds at the enemy whenever they fire at us, even if only in a neutralising role. There is no doubt that return fire puts the IRA off their aim even if it does not hit them. The chances of hitting innocent civilians at this stage are fairly small as most of them will have taken cover as soon the shooting started. Moreover if fire is always returned at gunmen, the local population will discourage the gunmen from opening fire at all.[7]

Evelegh published a book called *Peace-Keeping in a Democratic Society - The Lessons of Northern Ireland*, in 1978. In it he said: 'to have been able to say, as the Riot Act would have allowed, "Disperse in one hour or be shot dead", would have quickly put an end to all rioting in Northern Ireland'.[8] After, Daniel Rooney, the eighteen-year old unarmed civilian, was shot by the MRF, Evelegh said that he had got 'his just desserts'.[9]

By the time Evelegh was completing his report, Northern Ireland had descended into a murderous abyss. 1972 proved to be the worst year of the 'Troubles'.

On 9 July 1972, another mass shooting perpetrated by British soldiers took place in Belfast. It has become known as the Springhill/Westrock massacre. Five unarmed civilians were shot dead. Three were teenagers, one a thirteen-year old girl. The fallen included a priest who had been waving a white flag when he was struck down. 'Two of the dead were in the Fianna, the junior wing of the IRA', wrote Kevin Myers, 'but this was not why they were shot: they were, like Father Fitzpatrick, killed gallantly trying to help other victims of the para killfest. One of these was thirteen-year-old Margaret Gargan. Many years later, a former member of the Paras told me that an NCO involved in his training had boasted of shooting her. The killer – by his own account – positively identified Margaret as a young girl in a dress – he even remembered the colour – and then he deliberately shot her. Nearly a decade later, this cold-blooded murderer was actually boasting to trainee paras how he'd got away with killing an innocent girl, even describing in detail and with relish how she went down like a sack when he shot her.'[10]

***

Kitson returned to soldiering on 22 January 1976 when he became general officer commanding 2 Division of the British army, with the acting rank of major general. The division was re-designated as an armoured division in Germany before he stepped down on 28 February 1978 and returned to military academia as commandant of the Staff College, Camberley, 5 March 1978 to 18 January 1980. During that time, he wrote and published *Bunch of Five* about his experiences in Kenya, Malaya, Oman and Cyprus but not Ireland.

Gen. James Glover, commander of British forces in Northern Ireland, produced a report, *Northern Ireland: Future Terrorist Trends* in 1979 which set out the British army's analysis of the IRA's re-emergence.[11] This report was meant to be top secret but leaked out. It hardly made for comfortable reading by Kitson when it appeared in the Irish press. According to Glover, the IRA gained momentum after 1969 against a background of decades of Loyalist oppression. 'Republican fears of a Protestant ascendancy being re-established would enable the PIRA to pose as defenders of the minority interest', Glover reasoned, and that the 'fear of a possible return to Protestant repression will underpin this kind of support for the Provisionals for many years to come.' He also cautioned that an 'isolated incident, such as "Bloody Sunday", could radically alter support for violence.'[12] On 27 August 1979, the Provisional IRA's South Armagh Brigade detonated two roadside bombs outside Warrenpoint killing eighteen soldiers, of whom sixteen were paratroopers. It would prove to be the IRA's most deadly attack of the 'Troubles' and the Parachute Regiment's biggest loss since the Second World War. Glover described it later as 'arguably the most successful and certainly one of the best planned IRA attacks of the whole campaign'. Lord Mountbatten was killed on the same day by a bomb planted on his boat in Sligo. Martin McGuinness from Derry was involved in, if not the mastermind behind, both attacks.[13] Graffiti appeared in Republican areas that would have been unimaginable in August 1969 bragging: '13 gone and not forgotten, we got 18 and Mountbatten'.

Kitson continued to ascend the military ladder and received another award, Knight Commander of the Order of the Bath (KCB) in the 1980 New Year Honours list. On 17 March 1980, he became the deputy commander-in-chief UK Land Forces and inspector general of the Territorial Army and was promoted to lieutenant-general. On 30 May 1982, he became commander-in-chief, UK Land Forces and a general on 1 July. In parallel, he served as aide-de-camp to Elizabeth II from 1983 to 1985.

He retired from the army in 1985 but held many honorary military positions. He lived in the countryside in Devon, remained a keen horseman, indulged his passion for gardening and enjoyed his library, the contents of which were used as source material for some of the books he wrote in retirement.

The threat of assassination from Ireland – real or imagined – clung to him for decades. Kitson was an enthusiastic fan of horse-racing and was often to be seen at race meetings in Britain. On one occasion, a TV pundit mentioned him by name on air and he had to be rushed away for his safety. If he ever came to Ireland for a race meeting, he did so without the knowledge of Garda Special Branch. The odds are, unlike so many horse-racing enthusiasts from Britain, he never had the pleasure of watching the sport in the Republic of Ireland.

The ghosts from Derry came back to trouble him in the late 1990s as pressure for a fresh inquiry into Bloody Sunday grew. The publication by Tom McGurk of Byron Lewis' account of Bloody Sunday in the *Sunday Business Post* was considered the vital 'new' evidence that was required. In 1998 Tony Blair announced a fresh inquiry to be led by Lord Widgery of Newdigate.

After the Saville Inquiry commenced, Kitson had to engage with it both through correspondence and later by testifying in person. In the years before his eventual appearance at it on 24 September 2002, he published two books about Prince Rupert of the Rhine, the royalist general of the English civil war and nephew of the ill-fated King Charles 1st of England. The first appeared in 1994, *Prince Rupert Portrait of a Soldier*[14] and the second, *Prince Rupert: Admiral and General-at-Sea,* in 1997.[15] Clearly, his mind was firing on all cylinders. Yet, when he appeared briefly as a witness at the Saville Inquiry on 24

September 2002, he would suffer purported memory lapses.

When the US-UK coalition forces were planning the so-called 'surge' in Iraq in 2006, Gen. David Petraeus of the US army, who served as the commander of the United States Central Command and Coalition Forces in Iraq and Afghanistan, visited Kitson for guidance and advice. Petraeus was a great believer in the use of counter-insurgency techniques. The surge involved an increase in the number of American troops to provide security to Baghdad and Al Anbar Governorate.

The Saville Inquiry issued its report in 2010. Kitson was mentioned on ten occasions. Aside from a single fleeting reference to having asked Ford about sorting out Derry, his name otherwise merely cropped up when army command structures were being described. Put simply, Saville found him irrelevant to Bloody Sunday. Saville, however, did say that Bloody Sunday had played a part in the success of the IRA. In his 2010 report, he stated that:

> What happened on Bloody Sunday strengthened the Provisional IRA, increased Nationalist resentment and hostility towards the Army and exacerbated the violent conflict of the years that followed. Bloody Sunday was a tragedy for the bereaved and the wounded, and a catastrophe for the people of Northern Ireland.

Kitson undoubtedly wrote an end of tour report after his departure from Lisburn in 1972, if not a multiplicity of papers about his time in Ireland. They will be sealed for decades, if not centuries, to come. As a prolific writer and military educationalist, Kitson must have been tempted to record his Irish counter-insurgency experiences for the public. His 1977 book addressed many of his endeavours in Kenya, Malaya, Oman and Cyprus but nothing of substance about Ireland. He gave the occasional private interview, such as the one to Jonathan Riley while the latter was writing his biography of Farrar-Hockley. Kitson spoke to Riley in 2014 and had many interesting things to say. No doubt, this was only the tip of an iceberg.

It is possible that Kitson wrote a few chapters about Ireland for *Bunch of Five* but was not able to include them. There is little chance we will ever get to hear his side of the story now because, if he attempted to publish anything at this juncture, it would make a mockery of his performance at Saville and open a can of legacy worms horrific to behold.

Instead, he published *Old Ironsides: the Military Biography of Oliver Cromwell* in 2004.[16] *When Britannia Ruled the Waves* followed this in 2007.[17]

If Kitson hoped the spectre of the heavy-handed side of his time in Northern Ireland was drifting over the horizon as the Saville Report faded into history, he was to be sorely mistaken. Events that took place the year after Riley interviewed him shone a spotlight on him yet again. On 27 April 2015, he was cited as a co-defendant along with the MoD in the action taken by Mary Heenan, the widow of Eugene 'Paddy' Heenan who had been killed by Albert 'Ginger' Baker's UDA gang.

The Ballymurphy inquest finally commenced in 2018. Whether he was asked to attend or not, he did not turn up to testify.

In November 2019, Gen. Petraeus, by now a former director of the CIA, came out in defence of Kitson by attacking the type of legal action Heenan had initiated. Petraeus did so in the foreword to a paper he wrote, 'Lawfare – the Judicialisation of War'. He argued that this development was 'as much of a threat to Britain's fighting capacity as would be a failure to meet NATO budgetary targets, and it risks putting the special relationship under increasing strain ... The extent to which those who served decades ago in Northern Ireland, including the highly distinguished soldier-scholar General Sir Frank Kitson, remain exposed to legal risk is striking and appalling'.[18]

The past would not go away. On 14 March 2021, Mr Justice McAlinden of the High Court in Belfast awarded the estate of Peggy Deery £270,000, the equivalent of €300,000. She had been shot on Bloody Sunday but managed to survive. She died in 1988, aged fifty-four, having suffered throughout her life with the physical and mental consequences of the shooting. A widow, she had become depressed and unable to care for her children. Her daughter Helen, who was only thirteen on Bloody Sunday, told the court that before the massacre her mother had sung songs to her children and told them bedtime stories. That had all stopped after the killings. The judge commented that the conduct of the soldiers had been 'imbued with a degree of malevolence and flagrancy which was truly exceptional'.

On 11 May 2021, the victims of the Ballymurphy massacre were exonerated at their inquests while the troops who had murdered them were heavily criticised. No one, however, has been – or is likely to be – prosecuted and convicted.

***

For some, Gen. Sir Frank Edward Kitson remains an aberration, the British bogeyman of the 'Troubles', but this view lets too many others slip off the hook. Throughout his time in Ireland Kitson acted with the full blessing and approval of Whitehall in general and the MoD in particular. Heath, Carrington, Maudling, Carver, Farrah-Hockley, Tuzo and Ford were admirers and co-conspirators in opening the counter-insurgency Pandora's box in Ireland. Kitson was, in many respects, 'following orders', their orders. Sadly, they all believed that the situation in Ireland justified an abrogation of ethical and legal constraints. Nonetheless, Kitson was the man on the ground who called the shots. Of this group, Kitson is the only one still alive and has many questions to answer:

* Is his conscience troubled by the multiple deaths, torture and the vilification of honourable people in Belfast and Derry that took place under his watch?
* What of Britain's role in sustaining the likes of Tommy Herron and Albert Baker, and what of the people they tortured and murdered in Belfast's romper rooms and elsewhere?
* What of the programmes of State-Loyalist collusion that continued for decades?[19]
* What of the corruption of elements of the RUC which were complicit in the Herron/UDA murders?
* What of the 'hooded men'?[20]
* What of the manipulation and corruption of elements of the press?
* What of the victims of the McGurk bar bombing?[21]
* The MRF may not have lasted for long but it was replaced by similar units such as the FRU which have engaged in murder together with Loyalist paramilitaries such as the UDA. One was the murder of the lawyer Patrick Finucane. What of all these murders?
* Does he still believe that Soldier F deserved to be 'mentioned in despatches'?

In July 2021, the charges against Soldier F were dropped for technical legal reasons. This was followed by an announcement that the British government would introduce legislation to halt the prosecution of all the British soldiers who had killed civilians during the 'Troubles'. It is undoubtedly the case that the grey-suited bureaucrats who now run Whitehall and MoD know perfectly well what took place in Ireland during the Dirty War. They would prefer to deny justice to the victims and their families than have Britain's name dragged through the mud. This may have been a factor in persuading Boris Johnson to propose a halt to all prosecutions against soldiers, even if it meant letting Republican and Loyalist killers walk free as well.

It is not inconceivable that Kitson, Wilford, Soldier F and others who are still alive have made threats behind the scenes that they will disclose their dark secrets to the public unless the hounds are called off.

The sad truth is that Kitson has probably given little or no thought to the trail of skeletons that litters his wake, those he shot by his own hand in Africa and South East Asia, let alone to those who perished on his orders after he became a desk killer in Lisburn.

There is little prospect that 'the highly distinguished soldier-scholar General Sir Frank Kitson' will apologise for what he did in Ireland. On the contrary, if he reflects at all, it will probably be with pride as he admires the decorations with which he has been festooned at Buckingham Palace for the service he rendered to his queen and country.

Chronology

August 1969: British troops arrive in Northern Ireland.

May 1970: Dublin Arms Crisis.

June 1970: Kitson appointed as Brigadier of 39 Brigade.

Battle of St Matthews.

July 1970: Falls Road Curfew.

September 1970: Kitson takes up his role as Brigadier of 39 Brigade.

July 1971 *Operation Hailstone.*

Lt Col Derek Wilford appointed commander of 1 Para.

Gen. Ford takes over as Commander of Land Forces NI.

August 1971: Internment introduced.

Ballymurphy massacre.

27 October 1971: Patrick MacLellan appointed Brigadier of 8 Brigade.

4 December 1971: UVF bomb McGurk's Bar.

7 January 1972: Ford dictates memo calling for use of live ammunition to defeat Derry Young Hooligans.

23 January 1972: Anti-internment protester attacked by paratroopers on Magilligan beach.

24 January 1972 (Monday): Wilford claims he was first told that 1 Para was to be deployed to Derry on this date.

MacLellan and Lagan meet to discuss how they will handle the forthcoming march.

Wilford is allegedly first told that 1 Para will be going to Derry for the NICRA march.

25 January 1972 (Tuesday): Observer B provides fabricated intelligence to his handlers.

26 January 1972 (Wednesday): MacLellan submits his plan to deal with the NICRA march to Gen. Ford.

27 January 1972 (Thursday): NICRA asked the IRA to stay away from their march.

Carver attends a cabinet meeting at 10 Downing Street at which the forthcoming march is discussed.

The joint security committee (JSC) meets in Belfast.

Peter McMullen bombs Palace Barracks.

28 January 1972 (Friday): Wilford flies over the Bogside and attends Ebrington conference and returns to Belfast.

The IRA agrees to stay away from the NICRA march.

Peter McMullen travels to Dublin either this Friday or the following day.

29 January 1972 (Saturday): Wilford briefs his commanders.

Other 1 Para briefings take place subsequent to this including that of Byron Lewis.

30 January 1972 (Sunday): Troops from 1 Para are transported to Derry.

31 January 1972: Maudling announced an inquiry into the massacre in the House of Commons.

Heath, Hailsham and Widgery meet in London to discuss the inquiry.

4 February 1972: Murray Sayle of *The Sunday Times* is shown a 'sand table' of the Bogside at Palace Barracks.

21 February 1972: Widgery commence hearings.

3 March: NICRA statements presented to Treasury solicitors.

4 March: NICRA statements are flown to Coleraine.

14 March 1972: Widgery finishes hearing evidence.

18 April: Officials from the MoD engage in a selective leaking of the Widgery Report to British journalists.

19 April 1972: Widgery report published.

1992–1998: Col Wilford gives a series of interviews to the BBC and Channel 4.

1995: Taoiseach John Bruton of Fine Gael designates civil servant to liaise with the families of the Bloody Sunday victims.

16 March 1997: *Sunday Business Post* publishes revelations about 'Soldier A' (Byron Lewis).

13 January 1998: Byron Lewis is attacked by a group acting on behalf of his former comrades in Support Company.

3 April 1998: Saville address at Guildhall to open the Inquiry.

15 June 2010: Saville Report is issued.

It was later confirmed that none of the victims of Bloody Sunday posed a threat to the paratroopers. British Prime Minister David Cameron subsequently apologised for the atrocity in the House of Commons.

Many years later the victims of the Ballymurphy atrocity were declared innocent.

ENDNOTES

1 He was 120% soldier'

1 Kitson, Frank, *Bunch of Five* (Faber and Faber London 1977) p.142
2 Kitson, *Gangs and Counter-Gangs* (Barrie & Rockliff, London, 1960), p. 1
3 Jackson, Gen. Sir Mike, *Soldier the Autobiography* (Bantam Press London 2007), p. 54.
4 Jackson became chief of the General Staff of the British army.
5 Jackson (2007), p. 54
6 *Ibid.*
7 Sean Boyne, 'The Fearless Brigadier', *This Week*, 8 January 1972, p. 9.
8 Private interview, 21 February 2021.
9 Statement of Colin Wallace to the Saville Inquiry dated 13 December 2000. Saville Exhibit KW0002 at para. 68.
10 Colin Wallace private interview, 22 July 2021.

2 Learning to Kill

1 Kitson (1960), p. 2.
2 *Ibid.*
3 *Ibid.*, p. 5.
4 *Ibid.*, p. 3.
5 Sean Boyne, 'The Fearless Brigadier', *This Week,* 8 January 1972, p. 9.
6 Kitson (1960), p. 8.
7 Cobain, Ian, *Cruel Britannia, A Secret History of Torture* (Portobello Books, London, 2012), p. 82.
8 *Ibid.*, p. 82.
9 *Ibid.*, p. 81.
10 *Ibid.*
11 Anderson, David, *Histories of the Hanged* (A Phoenix Paperback, London, 2005), p. 300.
12 Kitson (1960), p. 7.
13 *Ibid.*, p. 107.
14 *Ibid.*, p. 31.
15 *Ibid.*
16 *Ibid.*, p. xi.
17 *Ibid.*, p. 2.
18 *Ibid.*, p. 90.
19 *Ibid.*, pp. 13–14.

20 Anderson (2005), pp. 259.

21 Sean MacStíofáin, *Memoirs of a Revolutionary* (Gordon Cremonisi, London, 1975), p. 71.

22 *Ibid.*, p. 72.

23 Kitson (1960), p. 46.

24 *Ibid.*

25 Document in my possession.

3 GENOCIDE AND SLAVERY

1 'Counter-insurgency' symposium sponsored by the Rand Corporation at which Kitson spoke with the temporary rank of colonel, 16–20 April, 1962. Document in my possession.

2 The Kitson interview clip can be viewed at https://www.youtube.com/watch?v=FfyQiPTzgNI

3 Kitson, *Low Intensity Operations* (Faber and Faber, London, 1971), p. 49.

4 Kitson (1977), p. 144.

5 *Ibid.*, p. 74.

6 Dr Stephen Dorril, *MI6: Fifty Years of Special Operations* (Fourth Estate 2001).

7 Kitson (1977), p. 176.

8 John Newsinger, *British Counterinsurgency* (Palgrave Macmillan, Hampshire, 2015) p. 137.

9 Kitson (1977), p. 179.

10 David Smiley, *Arabia Assignment* (Leo Cooper, London, 1975), pp. 27–8.

11 *Ibid.*

12 Kitson (1977), pp. 246–7.

13 *Ibid*, p. 247.

14 Michael Carver, *Out of Step, The Memoirs of Field Marshal Lord Carver* (Hutchinson, London, 1989)

15 Kitson (1977), p. 253.

16 *Ibid.*

17 *Ibid.*, p. 277.

18 Interview with Colin Wallace, 25 July 2021.

19 Kitson also spent a year at the British Army Staff College at Camberley; a post in the Military Operations Branch of the War Office, responsible for the Middle East; a tour as army instructor at the Royal Navy College in Greenwich, England; and several months at the Armed Forces staff College at Norfolk, Virginia.

4 'Suppression of the Irish'

1 The CDC chairman, Tom Conaty, was asked by the first Secretary of State for Northern Ireland, William Whitelaw, to sit on a committee to advise him in 1972.

2 McCann, Eamonn, *War and an Irish Town* (Penguin Books Ltd, London, 1974), pp. 73–74.

3 Hudson was forty-seven when he left Northern Ireland after two years. He took up a post in Imperial Defence College in England.

4 39 Airportable Brigade was redesignated 39th infantry Brigade on 10 January 1972.

5 Private interview, 21 July 2021.

6 Robert Ramsey, *Ringside Seat* (Irish Academic Press, 2009, Dublin), p. 286.

7 *Ibid.*

8 Paddy Devlin, *Straight Left an Autobiography* (Blackstaff Press, Belfast, 1993), p. 126.

9 Kitson to PJ Woodfield 4 December 1971 para. 12; https://mcgurksbar.com/mrf-director-of-terrorism/

10 *Ibid.*, para. 9.

11 *Ibid.*, para. 12.

12 The MRF is sometimes referred to as the Mobile Reaction Force and Military Reconnaissance Force.

5 Drawing a Fist

1 Margaret Urwin, *Counter-Gangs, A History of Undercover Military units in Northern Ireland 1971–1976* (2012) available for download on Spinwatch: https://spinwatch.org/images/Countergangs1971-76.pdf

2 *Ibid.*

3 Roger Faligot, *Britain' Military Strategy in Ireland, The Kitson Experiment* (Brandon, Kerry, 1983), p. 19.

4 For a photograph of this and further comment: https://thebrokenelbow.com/2021/03/11/from-mau-mau-to-ira-some-things-didnt-change/

5 Edwards, Aaron, *Defending the Realm? The Politics of Britain's Small Wars Since 1945* (Manchester University Press, Manchester 2012), p. 195.

6 https://www.irishnews.com/news/2013/11/21/news/ministers-were-angry-at-not-being-warned-of-potential-stinkers-76329/

7 Private interview, 21 July 2021.

8 Ken Connor, *Ghost Force: The Secret History of the SAS* (Weidenfeld & Nicolson, London, 1998).

9 https://www.bbc.com/news/uk-24987465

6 Kɪᴛꜱᴏɴ'ꜱ Tᴏᴘ Bʀᴀꜱꜱ Fᴀɴ Cʟᴜʙ

1 Carver's statement to the Saville Inquiry 24 July 1999, para. 24.

2 *Ibid.*

3 Kitson (1971), p. xi.

4 In Borneo Tuzo's Gurkha battalions had taken part in operations to win the 'hearts and minds' of the local population, something that was deemed desirable in counter-insurgency operations. He was also involved in Operation Claret which had intercepted and repelled Indonesian troops who tried to cross the border into Borneo.

5 Carver statement to Saville Inquiry 24 July 1999, para. 3.

6 *Ibid.*, 29 July 1999, para 27.

7 Farrar-Hockley's interpretation of the problems in Northern Ireland was that 'the great majority of those taking part in active plotting and rioting are not doing so because they want to achieve an end, but because they enjoy violent behaviour on a tribal basis'; Jonathan Riley, *Oft in Danger, The Life and Campaigns of General Sir Anthony Farrar-Hockley* (Helion, & Company, West Midlands, 2015), p. 324.

8 Riley (2015), p. 325.

9 *Ibid.*, p. 326.

10 At the end of his tour as CLF NI, he became commandant of the Royal Military Academy Sandhurst.

11 Carver statement to the Saville Inquiry, 29 July 1999, para 26.

12 When Tuzo relinquished his post as GCO on 1 February 1973, he was replaced by Frank King.

13 Kitson to PJ Woodfield 4 December 1971 para. 12; https://mcgurksbar.com/mrf-director-of-terrorism/

14 Martin Dillon described how Carver 'let me into the secret of how he used to enter 10 Downing Street from a secret passageway linking the prime minister's residence with Whitehall. The passageway led to the garden of Number 10, and Carver normally used it to enter the residence. Once inside, he retrieved a key from a hook inside the door, and it granted him access to an upstairs room where a secret Committee, GEN 42, met to discuss Northern Ireland issues; Martin Dillon, *Crossing the Line, My Life on the Edge* (Merrion Press, Kildare 2017), p. 104.

15 Carver statement to the Saville Inquiry 29 July 1999, para 28.

16 *Ibid.*, para 29.

17 Readers interested in further details about them are directed to Martin Dillon's book, *The Dirty War.* See also Urwin (2012).

18 Carver (1989), p. 429.

19 Dillon (2014), p, 104.

20 Kitson's statement to the Saville Inquiry, 18 February 2000, para 3.

21 *Ibid.*, para 4.

22 Kitson interview with Jonathan Riley. See *Oft in Danger*, p. 326.

23 *Ibid.*

24 *Ibid.*

25 Ramsay (2009), p. 286.

26 Kitson's statement to the Saville Inquiry, 18 February 2000, para 6.

27 Riley (2015), p. 326.

28 Kitson's evidence to the Saville Inquiry, Tuesday, 24 September 2002. (Witnesses first provided the inquiry with statements and later testified in person.)

29 *Ibid.*

30 Overall, Kitson had eight battalions on four-month emergency tours at his disposal; another two on two-year tours with their families; and yet another stationed at Ballykinlar on a two-year tour. The latter was designated as a Province (sic.) Reserve.

7 COLLECTIVE PUNISHMENT

1 Kitson (1971), p. 90–1

2 Kitson (1977), p. 277.

3 Kitson (1971), p. 49.

4 *Ibid.*, p. 87.

5 Pringle, Peter and Jacobson, Philip, *Those Are Real Bullets, Aren't They?, Bloody Sunday, Derry, 30 January 1972* (Fourth Estate, London, 2000), p. 83.

6 Kitson statement to the Saville Inquiry, 18 October 2001, para 2 (h).

7 *Ibid.*, para 2 (e).

8 BBC Radio 4, 6 July 1999, interview with Col Derek Wilford; see also the chapter 'The Colonel's Clues' in this book.

9 Saville exhibit B1123; Ford undated PIN 154 68, p. 16.

10 Saville Document B1545, i.e. records of Byron Lewis (Soldier 027), p. 12 of 1975 account of life in 1 Para.

11 Asher, Michael, S*hoot to Kill: Journey Through Violence (*Cassell Military Paperbacks, London 2003), p.119.

12 *Ibid.*, pp. 119–20.

13 *Ibid.*, p. 120.

14 McCallion, Harry, *Killing Zone A Life in the Paras, the Recces, the SAS and the RUC* (Bloomsbury, London, 1995), pp. 28–9.

15 *Ibid.*, p. 32; McCallion describes how he subsequently joined the South African Defence Force and served in its Special Forces Reconnaissance Commando where his unit killed over 2,000 people in operations in Angola, Mozambique, Zambia and Rhodesia while only losing seventeen of their own number. This took place over a period of two years after which he returned to Britain and joined the SAS and went on to do a further tour of duty in Northern Ireland. For the full story, please see pp. 74–106 of his book.

16 Janizaries were members of the elite infantry units that formed the Ottoman Sultan's army.

17 Asher (2003), p. 120.

18 *Ibid.*, p. 116.

19 Kitson's statement to the Saville Inquiry, 18 October 2001, para 2 (f).

20 *Ibid.*

21 See Tribunal question 7.

22 Jackson (2007), p. 54.

23 Kitson statement to the Saville Inquiry, 18 October 2001, para 6 (a).

8 MILITARY INTELLIGENCE ASSET IN THE UDA

1 Carver (1989), p. 422.

2 Margaret Urwin, *A State in Denial* (Mercier Press, Cork, 2016) p. 41.

3 Faligot (1983), p. 19. This appeared in the section entitled, 'Counter-revolutionary Operations, 1st Part, Principles and General Aspects' at paragraph (f.).

4 This information was disclosed during a series of private interviews during 2020.

5 Ken Livingstone, *Livingstone's Labour* (Urwin Hyman, London, 1989), pp. 128-29.

6 Handwritten 1986 statement by Albert Baker, a copy in my possession, p. 3.

7 *Ibid.*, p. 1.

8 Tommy Lyttle of the Inner Council was another UDA leader who was in contact with British intelligence officers.

9 Livingstone (1989), pp. 128–9

10 *Ibid.*, p. 130.

11 For further details on Payne, see my article: https://villagemagazine.ie/the-official-ira-plot-to-murder-an-irish-times-journalist/

12 Livingstone (1989), p. 133.

13 *Ibid.*, p. 130.

14 Interview with Colin Wallace, 26 July 2021.

15   https://villagemagazine.ie/her-majestys-hatchetman-the-murder-of-pat-finucane/

16 Typically, an agent is under the control of his handlers and takes orders. A friendly contact or ally is a more independent figure.

17 Handwritten 1986 statement by Albert Baker, a copy in my possession, p. 2.

18 *Ibid*.

19 *Ibid*., p. 3.

20 *Ibid*., p. 4.

21 *Daily Mail,* 27 April 2015; see also: https://www.dailymail.co.uk/news/article-3057471/Retired-British-Army-General-80s-sued-death-Catholic-man-killed-loyalist-paramilitaries-Northern-Ireland-40-years-ago.html

9 PSYOPS

1 Kitson (1977), pp. 290–1.

2 Private interview with Colin Wallace 22 July 2021.

3 https://www.theguardian.com/uk/2001/may/22/bloodysunday.northern ireland

4 Liz Curtis, *Ireland the Propaganda War* (Pluto Press, London, 1984), pp. 119–120.

5 Wright and McKee were later 'disappeared' i.e., murdered and buried at a secret location.

6   https://villagemagazine.ie/mi5s-friend-in-the-media-passes-away-journalist-who-cast-doubt-on-the-truth-about-the-kincora-boys-home-scandal-has-died/

7 https://thebrokenelbow.com/2020/10/03/when-the-ira-plotted-to-kill-chris-ryder/ /

8 A detailed analysis of the McGurk's bar bomb deception which is written by me can be found at: https://villagemagazine.ie/a-pact-sworn-by-devils-how-a-british-prime-minister-sold-his-soul-to-acquire-votes-to-enable-the-uk-to-join-the-european-economic-community-the-forerunner-of-the-eu/

10 BEING LESS THAN FRANK

1 'Future Developments in Belfast: By Commander 39 Airportable Brigade', dated 4 December 1971.

2 *Ibid*., para. 1.

3 Carver (1989), p. 429.

4 Kitson's statement to the Saville Inquiry, 18 February 2000, para. 4.

5 Kitson's evidence to the Saville Inquiry, Tuesday, 24 September 2002.

11 THE FAILURE OF *OPERATION HAILSTONE*

1 A first hand account of this can be found in the memoirs of Paddy Doherty, *Paddy Bogside* (Mercier Press, Cork, 2001).

2 Jackson (2007), p.61.

3 *Ibid.*

4 *Ibid.*

5 Peter Taylor, *Brits: The War Against the IRA* (Bloomsbury, London, 2001)

6 The Province of Ulster is made up of nine counties of which three are in the Republic of Ireland. Hence the policy of which Kitson refers could not have applied to the entire province.

7 Saville Exhibit G3.24.

8 Military records indicate that 1RS were not in Northern Ireland at the time, having just completed a four-month tour in Belfast in December 1971. According to Kinchin-White, 'it often happens that a unit, or part of a unit, say company strength, could be deployed in an emergency situation.' Interview with Kinchin-White, 15 May 2021.

9 Parts of the order issued pursuant to the plan were put to Gen. Ford at Saville on 29 October 2002, Day 257. See p. 18 of the transcript of his evidence on the Saville Inquiry website.

10 Thomas Hennessy, *The Evolution of the Troubles* (Irish Academic Press Ltd, Dublin, 2007), pp. 263–4; see also Saville Exhibit CJ0001 i.e., documents relating to Gen. Michael Jackson.

11 Statement of Michael Jackson to the Saville Inquiry, 20 March 2000, paras 66 and 67.

12 Supplemental written question to Kitson, no. 5.

13 Pringle (2000), p. 69.

14 Statement of Wilford, 18 January 2001, para 26.

12 OPERATIONS *LINKLATER, DEMETRIUS*

1 2 Para began their Northern Ireland Emergency Tour on 22 April 1971 attached to 8 Brigade, Londonderry. They were redeployed to 39 Brigade in Belfast on 4 June where they were assigned to the South West Belfast area which included the Ballymurphy estate.

2 Riley, *Oft in Danger*, pp. 334–5.

3 *Ibid.*, p. 335.

4 Desmond Hamill, *Pig in the Middle, the Army in Northern Ireland, 1969–1985* (Methuen, London, 1985), p. 64.

5 Carver (1989), p. 409.

6 Lewis is mistaken about this. While an eleven-year-old boy was shot, he did not die. A nineteen-year-old youth, however, died. Elsewhere in Belfast, Desmond Healey, a fourteen-year-old was killed. On 10 August 1971 a seventeen-year-old John Beattie was killed in the Tiger Bay area of Belfast.

7 Saville Document B1545, i.e., documents relating to Byron Lewis (Soldier 027), p. 12 of 1975 account of life in 1 Para.

8 My account of the Ballymurphy massacre can be read at: https://villagemagazine.ie/war-criminals-kitson-and-wilford-the-brigadier-and-colonel-who-led-the-soldiers-who-perpetrated-the-ballymurphy-massacre/; see also: https://village magazine.ie /brigadier-kitsons-motive-for-murdering-unarmed-civilians-in-ballymurphy/

13 Kitson's 'Gallant' Killers

1 Boyne, 'The Fearless Brigadier', This Week, 8 January 1972, p. 12.

2 https://webarchive.nationalarchives.gov.uk/20101017062257/http://report.bloody-sunday-inquiry.org/transcripts/ Archive/Ts237.htm

14 The Music Box

1 Edward Heath, *The Course of My Life* (Dumpton Gap Group, London, 1998), pp. 427–8.

2 The Bowen Report by Roderic Bowen QC had set out guidelines about interrogation after complaints about torture in Aden in the 1960s.

3 Carver (1989), p. 411.

4 Cobain (2012), pp. 1–37.

5 Carver (1989), p. 411. The Compton inquiry was set up after allegations had been made of brutality by the security forces against those interned without trial. The Compton Report was published on 16 November 1971.

6 John McGuffin, *The Guineapigs* (Penguin, England, 1974)

7 Denis Faul and Raymond Murray, *The Hooded Men* (Wordwell Limited, Dublin, 2015; a republication of original July 1974 booklet).

15 'Your Fucking Minute's Ticking Away'

1 Carver (1989), p. 412.

2 *Ibid.*, p. 429.

3 Kevin Myers https://kevinmyers.ie/2021/05/21/ballymurphy-butchery -must-never-be-forgotten/

16 'Shoot Selected Ringleaders'

1 Carver statement to Saville Inquiry, para. 25.

2 Jackson (2007), p. 62.

3 Pringle (2000), p. 75.

4 Carver (1989), pp. 413–4.

5 *Ibid.*, p. 416.

6 Ford memorandum, para. 5, dated 7 January 1972. See archive of Ford documentation, p. 1129 archival documents and statements Saville Inquiry. https://webarchive.nationalarchives.gov.uk/20101017071251 /http://report.bloody-sunday-inquiry. org/evidence/B/B1123.pdf Ford memorandum, para. 6.

7 *Ibid.*, para. 7.

8 *Ibid.*

9 *Ibid.*

10 Kitson's evidence at Saville Inquiry, 24 September 2002..

11 *Ibid.*

12 *Ibid.*

13 Saville exhibit B1123; Ford undated PIN 154 68, p. 10.

17 KITSON'S POOR RECOLLECTION

1 Carver statement to Saville Inquiry, para. 13.

2 Evidence of John Hume, 21 January 2002.

3 Memo from Ford to Tuzo dated 7 January 1972. See Saville B1123, para. 6.

4 *Ibid.*, at para. 9.

5 Saville exhibit B1123; Gen. Ford statement to Saville Inquiry, 23 March 2000, para. 7.9, p. 17.

6 Gen. Ford statement to Saville Inquiry, para. 5.7, 23 March, p. 14.

7 Carver statement to Saville Inquiry, para. 12.

8 Pringle (2000), p. 79.

9 Jackson (2007), p. 62.

10 Kitson statement to the Saville Inquiry, 18 February 2000, para. 9.

11 *Ibid.*, para. 10.

18 MI5's SPY IN FREE DERRY

1 David Eastwood's statement to the Saville Inquiry, 11 April 2003.

2 These include the abuse of the residents of Kincora Boys' Home, Williamson House and elsewhere.

3 Paisley conducted the wedding services of two of McGrath's children.

4 In his statement to the Saville Inquiry dated 17 February 2000, at para. 2, under designation 'David', he informed Saville that he had held a meeting each morning with senior military officers and civilians

from the MoD. He also attended a daily meeting with the head of the Special Branch and the Military Intelligence Liaison Officer in the RUC. 'My role,' he stated, 'was to build an effective intelligence structure so there would be as free an exchange of intelligence between the Army and the RUC as possible'.

5 Eastwood Statement to Saville 11 April 2003, para. 21.

6 *Ibid.*, para. 23.

7 IRA auxiliaries were people who were prepared to help the IRA and were not members of the organisaton.

8 Statement of Observer B to the Saville Inquiry para. 8 p. 3. Undated. https://webarchive.nationalarchives. gov.uk/ 20101017060841/http:// report.bloody-sunday-inquiry.org/evidence-index/

9 *Ibid.*, para. 10, p. 3. Undated. https://webarchive.nationalarchives. gov.uk /20101017060841/http://report.bloody-sunday-inquiry.org/evidence -index/

10 Fianna Éireann, the youth wing of the IRA.

11 Statement of Observer B to the Saville Inquiry para. s 13 and 15, page 4. Undated. https://webarchive. nationalarchives.gov.uk/ 2010101 7060841/http://report.bloody-sunday-inquiry.org/evidence-index/

12 *Ibid.*, para. 16, p. 5, 6.

13 Statement of Martin McGuinness to Saville Inquiry, 19 December 2001, para. 72.

14 A number of IRA leaders fled Belfast as internment approached. Four IRA leaders gave a press conference afterwards to highlight the in-effectiveness of the swoops that had taken place: Seán MacStíofáin, Dáithí Ó Conaill, Seamus Twomey and Martin McGuinness. The latter was from Derry.

15 Statement of Wilford, 18 January 2001, para 50.3.

16 Eastwood statement, para. 8, 17 February 2000.

17 Transcript of the evidence of 'David' i.e. David Eastwood, 13 May 2003, pp. 28–9.

18 *Ibid.*, pp. 30–1.

19 Keeping the brigadier in the dark

1 Dannert wire is a military style of barbed or razor wire formed in large coils which can be expanded like a concertina.

2 Carver (1989), pp. 416–7.

3 Confirmed in the evidence of MacLellan on Tuesday, 19 November 2002, p. 38.

4 MacLellan, 19 November 2002, p. 65.

5 *Ibid.*, p. 66.
6 *Ibid.*
7 Carver statement to the Saville Inquiry, 24 July 1999, para. 14.
8 Pringle (2000), p. 85.

20 THE BOMBS AT PALACE BARRACKS

1 Most large military had Navy, Army and Air Force Institutes of 'naffis', facilities where food, clothing and other goods were sold.

2 Saville Document B1545, i.e. records of Byron Lewis (Soldier 027), p. 12 of 1975 account of life in 1 Para.

3 *Evening Echo*, 28 January 1972.

4 *Evening Herald,* 28 January 1972.

5 *Irish Press*, 28 January 1972.

6 Andrew Blake, 'Tales of a Terrorist in Northern Ireland', *The Boston Globe*, 2 September 1979 https://www.washingtonpost.com/archive/politics/1979/09/02/tales-of-a-terrorist-in-northern-ireland/1114a02d-5f3e-4863-9e66-56d6e83097f9/

7 Private interview, 9 February 2021.

8 *Boston Globe*, 2 September 1979

9 *Ibid.*

10 *Ibid.*

11 *Ibid.*

12 Kevin Kelly, *The Longest War* (Brandon Book Publishers Limited, Dingle, Co. Kerry, 1982), p. 162. .

13 *Boston Globe*, 2 September 1979.

14 *Ibid.*

15 *Ibid.*

16 MacStíofáin (1975), pp. 227–9.

17 *Ibid.*, p. 227.

18 This extract was introduced into evidence at the Saville Inquiry on 24 September 2002, see transcript pp. 41–42.

19 The transcript was read out to Kitson at the Saville Inquiry on Tuesday, 24 September 2002. See p. 41 for that day.

21 THE SAND TABLE

1 Evidence of Murray Sayle at the Saville Tribunal, 10 June 2002, pp. 75–8.

2 Analysis of model experts provided in April 2021.

3 *Ibid.*

4 Comments by second expert, May 2021.

5 Evidence of Wilford, Monday, 31 March 2003, pp. 69–70.

6 *Inside Story: Remembering Bloody Sunday*, BBC, 28 January 1992.

7 Evidence of Wilford, Tuesday, 25 March 2003, pp. 34–5.

22 THE BOGUS GUNMEN

1 Jackson (2007), p. 64.

2 Evidence of Major Edward Loden at the Widgery Tribunal; see transcript contained in Saville Exhibit 2212 at p. 2277, i.e. p. 35 of the transcript reproduced there.

3 *Inside Story: Remembering Bloody Sunday*, BBC, 28 January 1992.

4 *Ibid.*

5 Saville Inquiry, exhibit B944; statement made on 30 January 1972; see also the evidence tendered by Wilford on Monday, 31 March 2003, p. 84.

6 MacLellan in evidence on 19 November 2002, pp. 78–9.

7 Ferguson was the commander of 22 Light Air Defence Regiment Royal Artillery which had assumed the city battalion role in Derry in November 1971.

23 'WE WANT SOME KILLS TOMORROW'

1 Kitson Saville Inquiry, 24 September 2002, p. 136 of transcript of his evidence.

2 *Ibid.*, p. 138.

3 *Ibid.*

4 *Ibid.*

5 *Ibid.*

6 *Ibid.*, p.139.

7 Saville exhibit B5416, p.155.

8 Jackson (2007), p. 64.

9 'Lt 119' was the cypher provided at the Widgery inquiry to afford the lieutenant anonymity.

10 Saville exhibit B5416, statement of Soldier 027, 7 June 2000, pp. 156–68.

11 Para 60, p. 10 of statement to Saville, 7 June 2000.

12 Statement of Wilford, 18 January 2001, para 57.8.

13 *Ibid.*, para 58.

24 'LONDONDERRY'S SHARPEVILLE'

1 Evidence of Col Maurice Tugwell to the Saville Inquiry, 2 October 2002, p. 184.

2 Private interview with Colin Wallace, December 2020.

3 Interview of Col Derek Wilford conducted by Alex Thompson of

Channel 4 News, 17 January 1998. See also transcript contained in Saville Exhibit document B944, p. 1110.003.

4 On 21 March 1960, South African police opened fire on a gathering of anti-apartheid protesters in the township of Sharpeville. The crowd included women and children. 69 people were killed while over 180 were injured.

5 Saville Report chapter 9, paras 726–29.

6 *Hidden Truths: Bloody Sunday 1972* (Smart Art Press, 1998, edited by Trisha Ziff), p. 72.

7 Simon Winchester, *In Holy Terror* (Faber and Faber, London 1974) p. 194.

8 *Ibid.*, p. 195.

25 Straining at the Leash

1 Winchester, p. 195.

2 *Ibid.*

3 McCann, Eamon, *The Bloody Sunday Inquiry, The Families Speak Out* (Pluto Press, London and Dublin 2006), p. 128.

4 Douglas Murray, *Bloody Sunday, Truths, Lies and the Saville Inquiry* (Biteback Publishing, London, 2011), p. 119.

5 https://www.bbc.com/news/uk-northern-ireland-47559123. See also Murray (2011), p. 118.

6 Murray (2011), pp. 120–121.

7 https://www.bbc.com/news/uk-northern-ireland-47559123

8 Jackson (2007), p. 65.

26 'Rehearsed Blocking Positions'

1 Murray (2011), p. 32.

2 There are some typographical errors in the 1975 manuscript. None of them have been corrected here. This underlines the point that this was not a polished and edited manuscript ready for publication as a book or magazine article.

3 It is unlikely that the churchyard was under attack and that this was a mistake on the part of Lewis in the heat of the moment. He may have seen a stone thrown up by the wheels of one of the military vehicles.

4 The Großdeutschland Division was an elite combat unit of the Germany army that fought for Hitler on the Eastern Front against the Soviets.

5 Mullan (1997), p. 162

6 Saville Inquiry exhibit, B944. Statement of Col. Wilford, 30 January 1972.

7 Jackson (2007), p. 66.
8 Statement of Colin Wallace to the Saville Inquiry, 13 December 2000, paras 98 and 99. See Saville Exhibit KW0002.
9 Statement by INQ 2023 to Saville Inquiry, 1 October 2002, para. 16 which is to be found in Saville exhibit C2020.
10 Gerald Donaghy is sometimes referred to as Gerald Donaghey in publications.
11 https://www.lrb.co.uk/the-paper/v24/n13/murray-sayle/bloody-sunday -report

27 Disobeying the Major

1 Byron Lewis, Saville exhibit B1546, p. 1565.115.5.
2 *Ibid.*, p. 1565.014.4
3 https://www.youtube.com/watch?v=0izN111lXUg
4 Byron Lewis, Saville exhibit B1546, p. 1565.0145
5 *Ibid.*, p. 1565.007
6 Savill Exhibit B121, papers relating to Soldier F.
7 *Ibid.*

28 The Men in Civilian Clothes

1 Saville exhibit B1546 at page 1565.114.82
2 Evidence of Gen. Robert Ford at the Saville Inquiry, 12 November 2002, pp. 18–20 in reference to Video Number 8 at 8 minutes 53 seconds.
3 *Ibid.*
4 Lord Mitting's Inquiry was set up to inquire into the National Public Order Intelligence Unit (NPOIU) penetration of what were perceived as radical and left-wing groups by the British state. It was established in 2014 after media reports that undercover officers had entered into relationships with female activists some of whom had become pregnant. The officers disappeared and left the mothers without any support or assistance. The children did not know who their fathers were. NPOIU was a sinister organisation and infiltrated the campaign run by the family of Stephen Lawrence who was murdered by a gang of racist thugs in 1993. The Lawrence family was critical of the police inquiry into the murder.

29 Dum-Dum Bullets

1 Ziff (1998), p. 167.
2 Statement of Dr Raymond McClean, 15 July 1999, para. 50 (d). See Saville Exhibit AM105.

3 *Inside Story: Remembering Bloody Sunday,* BBC, 28 January 1992.

30 Soldier F's murderous platoon
1 Mullan (1997), p. 100.
2 Ziff (1998), p. 168.
3 McCann (2006), pp. 102–105.
4 *Ibid.*, pp. 88–9.
5 *Ibid.*, p. 90.
6 A copy of the photograph of the crumpled paramedic can be found in the selection of photographs in Don Mullan's book, *Eyewitness Bloody Sunday the Truth* (Wolfhound Press, Dublin 1997).

31 Killing 'Fenian Bastards'
1 Evidence of Antoinette Coyle at the Saville Inquiry on 21 March 2001.
2 Pringle and Jacobson (2000), p. 265.
3 *Ibid.*
4 Joanne O'Brien, *A Matter of Minutes, The Enduring Legacy of Bloody Sunday* (Wolfhound Press, Dublin 2002), p. 66.
5 Saville Exhibit B121, documents relating to Soldier F.
6 Conclusions of Saville Report, Vol. VII at 122.168.
7 *Ibid.*

32 Soldier F Beats and Tortures Prisoners
1 Statement of James Doherty; see Mullan (1997), pp. 248–49.
2 Jackson (2007), p. 67.
3 O'Keefe documents Saville exhibit H_0021.

33 Lying Like Troopers
1 https://youtube/3wbLNGOshLE?t=568
2 Ziff (1998), p. 76.
3 Carver (1989), pp. 418–19.
4 Carver statement to the Saville Inquiry, 29 July 1999, para 20.

34 A Powerful Reaction Against the Irish
1 Winchester (1974), p. 201.
2 McClean, Dr Raymond, *The Road to Bloody Sunday* (Ward River Press, Dublin, 1983), pp. 136–7.
3 Saville exhibit G104A.635.1, a transcript of a recording of a 15-minute telephone conversation between Taoiseach Jack Lynch and Ted Heath.
4 *Ibid.*
5 *Ibid.*

6 *Ibid.*

7 Carver (1989), p. 419.

8 According to his biographer John Young: 'Speeches strongly critical of the I.R.A. were not popular in some quarters and events such as the introduction of internment in the North in August 1971 and Bloody Sunday in January 1972, when thirteen people were shot dead in Derry, caused waves of revulsion to sweep the country. At Trinity College, Dublin, heckling and interruptions forced a premature end to at least one address [by Childers]. Taunts of 'Imperialist tool' greeted him elsewhere; see: John N. Young, Erskine H. Childers, President of Ireland (Colin Smythe, Buckinghamshire 1985), p. 155.

9 *Irish Independent*, Wednesday, 2 February 1972, p. 1.

10 *Ibid.*

11 Private interview, 24 March 2021.

12 Telegram 3 February 1972 Peck to FCO WLE/3/548/2 FROM FCO 87/26.

13 *Ibid.*

14 Taylor (2001), p. 107.

15 *Ibid.*, p. 109.

16 Asher (2003), p. 114.

17 *Ibid.*

18 Saville Document B1545, i.e. records of Byron Lewis (Soldier 027), p. 8 of 1975 account of life in 1 Para at 1565.014.8.

35 KITSON'S SECRET DEBRIEF

1 Evidence of Col Wilford, Wednesday, 2 April 2003, pp. 54–55.

2 *Ibid.*

3 Kitson evidence to the Saville Inquiry, Tuesday, 24 September 2002.

4 Statement of Kitson to the Saville Inquiry, 18 February 2000, para. 11.

5 https://villagemagazine.ie/war-criminals-kitson-and-wilford-the-brig-adier-and-colonel-who-led-the-soldiers-who-perpetrated-the-bally-murphy-massacre/

6 Jackson (2007), pp. 71–72.

7 Evidence of Kitson to Saville Inquiry, Tuesday, 24 September 2002, p. 41.

8 Kitson (1977), p 251.

36 HER MAJESTY'S CHARACTER ASSASSINS

1 Kitson (1971), p. 69.

2 A lengthy analysis by this author of the deceit and deception perpetrated by Widgery can be found at https://villagemagazine.ie/

the-guilt-of-an-unscrupulous-former-lord-chief-justice-in-the-sol-dier-f-cover-up- paratrooper-who-murdered-unarmed-civilians-on-bloody-sunday-has-been-protected-by-the-british-state-for-five-decades-an/

3 Widgery HL 101. HC220, published by HMSO, 18 April 1972.

4 Carver (1989), p. 418.

5 *Village* magazine https://villagemagazine.ie/licence-to-deceive/

6 See my book, *Deception and Lies* (Mercier Press, 2020), p. 294.

7 While FitzGerald went to great efforts to ingratiate himself with the British establishment, he was lampooned during at least one Foreign Office Christmas pantomime for what was portrayed as his sycophancy towards the Secretary of State for Northern Ireland. Later, when he became Taoiseach, he was treated with contempt on a number of occasions by Margaret Thatcher, most spectacularly during her infamous 'out, out, out' reaction to the New Ireland Forum report. Thatcher was also critical of him in her autobiography.

8 Institute for the Study of Conflict, *Ulster Debate: Report of a Study Group of the Institute for the Study of Conflict*, edited by Brian Crozier (Bodley Head, 17 Aug. 1972), p. 7.

9 The 'Mini-Manual of the Irish Guerrilla' was a forgery which can only have been produced by the IRD.

10 Crozier (1972), p. 62.

11 *Ibid.*, p. 73.

12 *Ibid.*

13 *This Week* magazine, 31 August 1972, pp. 19–27. The first paragraph explained that, 'This article is one contribution to "The Ulster Debate"', a report of a study group of the Institute for the Study of Conflict which is published by Bodley Head

14 See also my article Traduced at https://villagemagazine.ie/john-hume-never-received-an-apology-from-the-british-secret-ser-vice-for-the-character-assassination-campaign-they-conducted-against-him/

15 IRD-inspired newspaper reports also claimed that Arab groups, such as Black September, were arming the IRA. Meanwhile in Britain, the IRD forged documents linking senior British Labour Party figures to Sinn Féin.

16 *Village* magazine https://villagemagazine.ie/licence-to-deceive/

17 Peter Harclerode, *Para! Fifty Years of the Parachute Regiment* (London, Arms & Armour, 1992) p. 290.

18 *Ibid.*
19 Parker (2000), p. 251.
20 *Ibid.*, p. 349.

37 GETTING AWAY WITH MURDER

1 An article outlining my criticisms of the Saville Inquiry and Report can be found at: https://villagemagazine.ie/a-foul-unfinished-business-the-shortcomings-of-and-plots-against-savilles-bloody-sunday-inquiry/
2 McCann (2006), p. 50.
3 Evidence of Gen. Robert Ford at the Saville Inquiry, 6 November 2002, p. 102.
4 *Ibid.*, 29 October 2002, p. 26.
5 Evidence of Frank Kitson at the Saville Inquiry, 24 September 2002.
6 Preparation Training Arrangements for Units Going to Northern Ireland, WO 32/21954.
7 Statement of Frank Kitson to Saville 18 February 2000, para. 12.
8 Answer number 3 (a) of statement of Kitson dated 18 October 2001. Saville exhibit CK1.
9 Evidence of Lt-Col (later Gen.) Sir David Ramsbotham, to the Saville Inquiry, 30 October 2002, p. 91.
10 Answer number 8 of statement of Kitson dated 18 October 2003. Saville exhibit CK1.
11 Kitson, Frank, *Directing Operations* (Faber and Faber, London, 1989).
12 *Ibid.*, p. 56.
13 Evidence of Frank Kitson at the Saville Inquiry, 24 September 2002, p. 67.

38 MI5 TAKES AIM AT McGUINNESS

1 Interview with Des Long, 7 April 2021.
2 Shane O'Doherty in response to a blog by Ed Moloney on the Broken Elbow website.
3 David Shayler statement to Saville Inquiry, 22 January 2001.
4 Statement of William Carlin to the Saville Inquiry, 20 October 2003. See Saville Exhibit KC0005, para. 61.
5 Carlin, Willie, *Thatcher's Spy, My Life as an MI5 Agent Inside Sinn Féin*, Merrion Press, Kildare (2019).
6 *Ibid.*, pp. 158–9.

39 THE DECEIT AND AVARICE OF OBSERVER B

1 Statement of 'Julian' to the Saville Inquiry, 29 June 2001, para. 8.

2 Statement of David Eastwood to the Saville Inquiry, 11 April 203. Saville exhibit KD2.

3 Statement of 'Julian' 2 February 2002. Saville exhibit KJ4.

4 Penrose, ' MI5 "plotted" Ulster Strike', *The Sunday Times*, 22 March 1987.

5 Liam Clarke, ' Kincora: How three men alerted MI5 officers to home's dark secret … And still nothing was done to stop the child sex abuse; Belfast Telegraph, 6 August 2014; see also Belfast Telegraph, 16 July of 2014

6 Interview with Roy Garland May 2021.

7 Barry Penrose, 'The Enemy Within?: The case against MI5', T*he Sunday Times*, 3 May 1987.

8 Penrose, 'MI5 "plotted" Ulster Strike', *The Sunday Times*, 22 March 1987.

9 Paul Foot, *Who Framed Colin Wallace* (Pan Books, London 1989), p. 245.

10 Nelson was run by a military intelligence unit called the F o r c e Reconnaissance Unit (FRU). He was a proficient torturer who specialised in using electricity to extract confessions. He directed multiple murders in Belfast including the February 1989 murder of the Belfast solicitor Patrick Finucane. Ultimately, the Stevens Inquiry resulted in him being placed on trial. At his trial the head of the FRU, Gordon Kerr, spoke up in his favour.

11 Rees may have heard NIO and MI5 officers discuss the sexual activities of certain senior loyalist politicians and belatedly realised that the information emanated from MI5 spies with knowledge of the vice ring in Northern Ireland.

40 THE COLONEL'S CLUES

1 Taylor, Peter, *Provos: The IRA and Sinn Féin* (Bloomsbury, London, 1997), p. 125.

2 McCann (2006), p. 18.

3 Interview with Col Derek Wilford conducted by Alex Thompson of Channel 4 News, 17 January 1998; see also transcript contained in Saville Exhibit document B944 at p. 1110.003.

4 *Ibid.*, p. 1110.004.

5 Interview with Wilford on *Inside Story: Remembering Bloody Sunday,* BBC interview with Peter Taylor, 28 January 1992; see also transcript contained in Saville Exhibit document B944 at pp. 1034–5.

6 Interview with Col Derek Wilford conducted by Alex Thompson of Channel 4 News, 17 January 1998; see also transcript contained in Saville Exhibit document B944 at p. 1110.004.

7 *Ibid.*

8 Interview with Wilford on *Inside Story: Remembering Bloody Sunday*, BBC interview with Peter Taylor, 28 January 1992.

9 McCann (2006), p. 18.

10 Channel 4 News, 17 January 1988, and Saville Exhibit B944 at p. 1110.007.

11 *Ibid.*, p. 1110.003.

12 Evidence of Col Derek Wilford at the Saville Inquiry, 9 April 2003, pp. 78–9.

13 *Inside Story: Remembering Bloody Sunday*, BBC interview with Peter Taylor, 28 January 1992; see also transcript contained in Saville Exhibit document B944 at p. 1025.

14 Interview with Col Derek Wilford conducted by Alex Thompson of Channel 4 News, 17 January 1998. See also transcript contained in Saville Exhibit document B944 at p. 1110.004.

15 Evidence of Col Derek Wilford at the Saville Inquiry, , 26 March 2003, p. 66.

16 BBC Radio 4, 6 July 1999, interview with Col Derek Wilford.

41 KITSON, RECRUITMENT SERGEANT FOR THE IRA

1 Private interview with Des Long, 7 April 2021.

2 Kitson (1971), p. 24.

3 Paddy Devlin, *The Fall of the Northern Ireland Executive* (Self published, Belfast 1975), p.119.

4 https://villagemagazine.ie/dw/

5 Boyne, 'The Fearless Brigadier', *This Week*, 8 January 1972, p. 9.

6 Letter in my possession dated 20 December 1973 written by C. R. Huxtable of Room 5115 of the MoD.

7 Para. 30 of the End of Tour report of Col Robin Evelegh, Commanding Officer of the 3rd Royal Green Jackets. Document in my possession. Also available at National Archives WO305/5710.

8 Robin Evelegh, *Peace-Keeping in a Democratic Society – The Lessons of Northern Ireland* (C Hurst, London, 1978), p. 159.

9 Urwin (2012), p. 17.

10 Kevin Myers https://kevinmyers.ie/2021/05/21/ballymurphy-butchery -must-never-be-forgotten/

11 Glover later served as commander-in-chief, Land Forces, from 1985–87.

12 Copy of Glover's report in my possession.

13 Private interviews with a senior garda special branch officer and a former IRA intelligence officer who worked with McGuinness. The IRA officer disclosed an earlier plot against Mountbatten which was

abandoned in 1975.

14 Kitson, Frank, *Prince Rupert Portrait of a Soldier* (Constable, London, 1994).

15 Kitson, Frank, *Prince Rupert: Admiral and General-at-Sea* (Constable, London, 1997)

16 Kitson, Frank, *Old Ironsides: the Military Biography of Oliver Cromwell* (Weidenfeld and Nicolson, London, 2004)

17 Kitson, Frank, *When Britannia Ruled the Waves* (Halsgrove, Somerset, 2007).

18 Gen. David Petraeus, US Army (retired), Lawfare – the Judicialisation of War published by the Policy Exchange. https:// policyexchange.org.uk/publication/lawfare/

19 Two excellent books which examine the issue of Loyalist-State collusion are Anne Cadwallader's *Lethal Allies* (Mercier Press, Cork 2013) and Margaret Urwin, *A State in Denial* (Mercier Press, Cork, 2016).

20 A comprehensive account of their ordeal can be read in *The Hooded Men, British torture in Ireland August, October 1971* by Denis Faul and Raymond Murray (2015); see also Cobain's *Cruel Britannia*.

21 See also Ciarán MacAirt's, *The McGurk's Bar Bombing* (Frontline Noir, Glascow 2012) and *The McGurk's Bar Bombing Post-Script* (2020).

Bibliography

Allen, Charles, *The Savage Wars of Peace Soldiers' Voices, 1945–89* (Michael Joseph, 1990)

Anderson, David, *Histories of the Hanged* (A Phoenix Paperback, London, 2005)

Arrigonie, Harry, *British Colonialism: 30 Years Serving Democracy or Hypocrisy?* (Gaskell Publishers, 1998)

Asher, Michael, *Shoot to Kill: Journey Through Violence* (Cassell Military Paperbacks, London, 2003)

Bell, J. Boyer, *The Irish Troubles, A Generation of Violence, 1967–1992* (Gill and Macmillan, Dublin, 1993)

Bower, Tom, *The Perfect English Spy* (Heineman, London, 1990)

Burke, David, *Deception & Lies, the Hidden History of the Arms Crisis* (Mercier Press, Cork, 2020)

Burke Edward, *An Army of Tribes: British Army Cohesion, Deviancy and Murder in Northern Ireland* (Liverpool University Press, Liverpool, 2018)

Cadwallader, Anne, *Lethal Allies* (Mercier Press, Cork 2013)

Carlin, Willie, *Thatcher's Spy, My Life as an MI5 Agent Inside Sinn Féin* (Merrion Press, Kildare, 2019)

Carver, Michael, *Out of Step, The Memoirs of Field Marshal Lord Carver* (Hutchinson, London, 1989)

Cavendish, Anthony, *Inside Intelligence* (HarperCollins Publishers Ltd, London, 1990)

Cloake, John, *Templer: Tiger of Malaya: The Life of Field Marshal Sir Gerald Templer* (Harrap, London, 1985)

Cobain, Ian, *Cruel Britannia, A Secret History of Torture* (Portobello Books, London, 2012)

Connor, Ken, *Ghost Force: The Secret History Of The SAS* (Weidenfeld & Nicolson; London, 1998)

Curtis, Liz, *Ireland the Propaganda War* (Pluto Press, London, 1984)

De Baróid, Ciaran, *Ballymurphy in the Irish War* (Pluto Press, London, 1989)

Deacon, Richard, *'C' A Biography of Sir Maurice Oldfield, Head of MI6* (MacDonald, London, 1984)

Devlin Paddy, *The Fall of the Northern Ireland Executive* (Self Published, Belfast 1975)

— *Straight Left an Autobiography* (Blackstaff Press, Belfast, 1993)

Dillon, Martin, *The Dirty War* (Arrow; New edition, London, 1991)

— *Crossing the Line, My Life on the Edge* (Merrion Press, Kildare, 2017)

Dorril, Dr Stephen, *MI6: Fifty Years of Special Operations* (Fourth Estate 2001)

Edwards, Aaron, *Defending the Realm? The Politics of Britain's Small War Since 1945* (Manchester University Press, Manchester 2012)

—— *Mad Mitch's Tribal Law: Aden and the End of Empire* (Mainstream Publishing, Edinburgh and London, 2014)

Elkins, Caroline, *Imperial Reckoning, The Untold Story of Britain's Gulag in Kenyan* (Henry Holt and Co., New York 2005)

Evelegh, Robin, *Peace-Keeping in a Democratic Society – The Lessons of Northern Ireland* (C Hurst, London, 1978)

Faligot, Roger, *Britain' Military Strategy in Ireland, The Kitson Experiment* (Brandon, Kerry, 1983)

Faul, Denis and Murray, Raymond, *The Hooded Men* (Wordwell Limited, Dublin, 2015; a republication of original July 1974 booklet)

Faulkner, Brian, *Memoirs of a Statesman* (Weidenfeld and Nicolson, London, 1978)

Government of Ireland, *Bloody Sunday and the Report of the Widgery Tribunal, the Irish Government's Assessment of the New Material* (Irish Government publications, Dublin, 1997)

Hale, Christopher, *Massacre in Malaya: Exposing Britain's My Lai* (The History Press Ltd, 2013)

Hamill, Desmond, *Pig in the Middle: The Army in Northern Ireland 1969–84* (Methuen Publishing Ltd, 1986)

Harclerode, Peter, *Para! Fifty Years of the Parachute Regiment* (London, Arms & Armour, 1992)

Heath, Edward, T*he Course of My Life* (Dumpton Gap Group, London, 1998)

Hennessy, Thomas, *The Evolution of the Troubles 1970–72* (Irish Academic Press Ltd, Dublin, 25 October 2007)

Institute for the Study of Conflict, *Ulster Debate: Report of a Study Group of the Institute for the Study of Conflict* (Bodley Head, 17 Aug. 1972)

Jackson, Gen. Sir Mike, *Soldier the Autobiography* (Bantam Press, London 2007)

Kelley, Kevin, *The Longest War* (Brandon, Kerry, 1982)

Kitson, Frank, *Gangs and Countergangs* (Barrie and Rockliff, London 1960)

— *Low Intensity Operations* (Faber and Faber, London, 1971)

— *Bunch of Five (*Faber and Faber, London, 1977)

— *Directing Operations* (Faber and Faber, London, 1989)

Livingstone, Ken, *Livingstone's Labour* (Urwin Hyman, London, 1989)

MacAirt, Ciarán, *The McGurk's Bar Bombing* (Frontline Noir, Glasgow 2012)

___ *The McGurk's Bar Bombing Post-Script* (2020) which can be downloaded from https://mcgurksbar.com/wp-content/uploads/2020/10/McGurks-Bar-Post-Script-Final-Redux.pdf

McCann, Eamonn, *The Bloody Sunday Inquiry, The Families Speak Out* (Pluto Press, London and Dublin 2006)

— *War and an Irish Town* (Penguin Books Ltd, London, 1974)

McCann, Eamonn with Maureen Shiels and Bridie Hannigan, *Bloody Sunday in Derry: What Really Happened* (Brandon, Kerry, 1992)

McCallion, Harry, *Killing Zone: A Life in the Paras, the Recces, the SAS and the RUC* (Bloomsbury, London, 1995)

McClean, Dr Raymond, *The Road to Bloody Sunday* (Ward River Press, Dublin, 1983)

McGuffin, John, *The Guineapigs* (Penguin, England, 1974)

MacStíofáin, Seán, *Memoirs of a Revolutionary* (Gordon Cremonisi, London, 1975)

Mullan, Don, *Eyewitness Bloody Sunday the Truth* (Wolfhound Press, Dublin 1997)

Murray, Douglas, *Bloody Sunday, Truths, Lies and the Saville Inquiry* (Biteback Publishing, London, 2011)

Newsinger, John, *The Blood Never Dried* (Bookmarks Publications, London, 2006 and 2010)

— *British Counterinsurgency* (Palgrave Macmillan, Hampshire, 2015)

O'Brien, Conor Cruise, *Memoir My Life and Themes (*Poolbeg Press Ltd Dublin 1999)

O'Brien, Joanne O'Brien, *A Matter of Minutes, The Enduring Legacy of Bloody Sunday* (Wolfhound Press Dublin 2002)

Parker, John, *The Paras: The Inside Story of Britain's Toughest Regiment* (John Blake, 2012) Place

Pringle, Peter and Jacobson, Philip, *Those Are Real Bullets, Aren't They? Bloody Sunday, Derry, 30 January 1972* (Fourth Estate, London, 2000)

Ramsey Robert, *Ringside Seat* (Irish Academic Press, 2009, Dublin)

Riley, Jonathan, *Oft in Danger, The Life and Campaigns of General Sir Anthony Farrar-Hockley* (Helion & Company, West Midlands, 2015)

Smiley, David, *Arabian Assignment* (Leo Cooper, London, 1975)

— *Albanian Assignment* (Chatto & Windus, the Hogarth Press, London, 1984)

Taylor, Peter, *Provos: The IRA and Sinn Féin* (Bloomsbury, London, 1997)

— *Brits: The War Against the IRA* (Bloomsbury, London, 2001)

Urwin, Margaret, *A State in Denial* (Mercier Press, Cork, 2016)

— *Counter-Gangs, A History of Undercover Military units in Northern Ireland 1971–1976* (2012) available for download on Spinwatch: https://spinwatch.org/images/ Countergangs1971–76.pdf

Walsh, Prof. Dermot, *The Bloody Sunday Tribunal of Inquiry, a resounding defeat for truth, justice and the rule of law.* Available at https://cain.ulster.ac.uk/events/bsunday/walsh.htm

— *Bloody Sunday and the Rule of Law in Northern Ireland* (Gill and Macmillan, Dublin, 2000)

Winchester, Simon, *In Holy Terror* (Faber and Faber, London, 1974) p, 194.

Wright, Peter, *Spycatcher* (Viking Penguin Inc., New York. 1987)

Ziff, Trisha (editor), *Hidden Truths: Bloody Sunday 1972* (Smart Art Press 1998

INDEX